Portraits of Public Service

Portraits of Public Service

Untold Stories from the Front Lines

Edited by

STACI M. ZAVATTARO, JESSICA E. SOWA,
ALEXANDER C. HENDERSON, and
LAUREN HAMILTON EDWARDS

SUNY
PRESS

Published by State University of New York Press, Albany

For information, contact State University of New York Press, Albany, NY
www.sunypress.edu

Library of Congress Cataloging-in-Publication Data

Names: Zavattaro, Staci M., 1983– editor. | Sowa, Jessica E., 1975– editor. | Henderson, Alexander C., 1980– editor. | Hamilton Edwards, Lauren, 1982– editor.
Title: Portraits of public service : untold stories from the front lines / edited by Staci M. Zavattaro, Jessica E. Sowa, Alexander C. Henderson, and Lauren Hamilton Edwards.
Description: Albany : State University of New York Press, 2023. | Includes bibliographical references and index.
Identifiers: LCCN 2022046496 | ISBN 9781438493718 (hardcover : alk. paper) | ISBN 9781438493695 (ebook) | ISBN 9781438493701 (pbk. : alk. paper)
Subjects: LCSH: Civil service—United States—Case studies. | Bureaucracy—United States—Case studies. | Public service employment—United States—Case studies. | Civil service—Case studies. | Bureaucracy—Case studies. | Public service employment—Case studies.
Classification: LCC JK681 .P67 2023 | DDC 352.6/30973—dc23/eng/20221130
LC record available at https://lccn.loc.gov/2022046496

10 9 8 7 6 5 4 3 2 1

Contents

SECTION 1: BALANCING ACTS

Illustrations

Figures

Tables

Introduction

Stories as Knowledge Creation

STACI M. ZAVATTARO, JESSICA E. SOWA,
ALEXANDER C. HENDERSON, AND LAUREN HAMILTON EDWARDS

When we came up with the idea for this book during summer 2020, the world was gripped by some of the worst conditions of the still-ongoing (as of this writing) COVID-19 pandemic. In the United States, Dr. Anthony Fauci, director of the National Institute of Allergy and Infectious Diseases at the National Institutes of Health (NIH), suddenly became a household name. Before his name and face because synonymous with the U.S. crisis response, Dr. Fauci was a known expert in infectious diseases, leading the way for more than four decades on HIV/AIDS research (Science Friday, 2021). Like the HIV/AIDS virus, COVID-19 at its initial arrival in the United States and throughout the world held many mysteries—where did this come from? How does it spread? How does it mutate?

Dr. Fauci is a longtime public servant who has dedicated his life to understanding infectious diseases with a goal of keeping people healthy. Dr. Fauci easily could have left the public service at many times during his career and indeed had been asked to join the private sector when he reached retirement age (Rubenstein, 2020). But he continued to serve, and in that role, he was—and is—the subject of intense bullying from political leaders turning a public health crisis into one of politics and morals (Korecki & Owermohle, 2021). Seeing the immense pressure and bullying he experienced for his work, this led us to wonder why a public

1

servant who was largely serving behind the scenes before 2019 came to be the center of such intense scrutiny and attacks. We took that question and began reflecting on our own journeys into public service, knowing scholarship in our field also investigates the politicized nature of public service (Overeem, 2017; Spicer, 2010; Svara, 2001).

In our discussions, we went deeper into understanding what made us go into public service and what drives others to pursue these positions. We wanted others to understand the breadth and depth of what government is, does, and can be—thanks to the public employees serving in their roles, sometimes quietly behind the scenes. Research in public administration deftly details the functions of street-level bureaucrats interfacing with the public daily (Lipsky, 1980/2010; Maynard-Moody & Musheno, 2003), usually focusing on those with prominent and highly visible roles, such as police officers, teachers, firefighters, counselors, and so forth. Our aim with this book is to help broaden the understanding of public service and government by shining a light on those employees usually serving more behind-the-scenes roles but with great impact on people, policies, and public problems.

To do so, we wanted to share our own journeys into public service to situate the book within our field but also to showcase our belief in government's ability to be and do good even in the face of political, administrative, and social challenges.

Staci: *You might say my journey into public service began in fifth grade. When I was a kid, my elementary school had an essay contest where the winners would get to be elected officials for the day. Somehow, I won and was named kid mayor. We got to go to city hall and learn all about government. They also placed us into a small holding jail cell, and sadly that has stuck in my mind since! But something else must have stuck because when it came time to get a high school job, I went to work for my local government in Florida working on the teen website with my friend. We tried to write stories and cover topics that would engage teenagers with the city. That led to me serving on some of the city's volunteer boards as the teen representative.*

After college, I came home to South Florida and applied to graduate school. I wanted to earn my MPA because I wanted to bridge my two degrees in political science and journalism. Instead, I ended up getting a PhD in public administration while working for the same local government that hired me as a teenager. During my doctoral studies, I worked for the communications and marketing department helping write press releases, compiling scripts for the radio and TV stations, and working with department members on their various projects like the magazine and website. It was while working there I got my inspiration for my research into public branding, which I have been doing for more than a decade. I work for a public institution in Florida now training the next generation of public sector leaders who love government like I do.

Jessica: *Both of my parents served in the U.S. Navy, so I grew up with great admiration for those who choose to serve their country. My parents were always willing to step forward and fight for others, whether it was about busing for schoolchildren or running for school board. They taught me individuals could use their voice to make a difference. I grew up fascinated by government—but did not know exactly where I wanted to work (I definitely had a youthful dream to be the director of the Central Intelligence Agency). With a double-major in political science and English, when considering my next steps, one of my favorite (and toughest) professors, Dean Alfange, Jr., introduced me to the MPA. And the rest is history. I fell in love—public administration was the answer to a question haunting me but not yet fully formed in my mind. How do we take political and policy ideas and make them real, to actually make a difference in people's lives? Public administration was the answer.*

I was planning on working for local government, but I have always been academically inclined, and my professors encouraged me to go on for a PhD. I had my epiphany moment to continue on for my PhD while attending the Tennessee City Management Association Conference. I was listening to a panel on utility deregulation and the challenges for cities and realized I was thinking about how I would study the impact, in addition to the practice implications. A PhD in public administration was how I could wrestle with theory and practice—do exciting research, but research that can actually be relevant for public service. What I love about being a professor of public administration is I get to study public administration concepts and practices; interact with practitioners through consulting, training, and research; and train and guide future public servants in university classrooms—it is really the best of all worlds combined. Working in a public institution, training future public servants, I remain every day inspired by the stories and experiences of my students, and they are the best guides for whether I am asking important questions in my research.

Alex: *The stories of public servants have always fascinated me. My introduction to public service came during my high school years when I worked as a photographer for a local newspaper in suburban Philadelphia. I often found myself photographing fires, car accidents, and other emergencies, trying to document challenging incidents and the lifesaving work of first responders.*

When I approached my local fire department offering to be their official photographer, they indicated they already had one, but noted they were always looking for volunteer firefighters and emergency medical technicians. That somewhat offhand comment from a fire chief has shaped my entire professional and academic career for the last quarter century. The nearly 12 years that I served as a firefighter, emergency medical technician, fire officer, and administrator were profoundly impactful, and have given me an appreciation for the virtuous, demanding, and important work that front-line public and nonprofit servants do every day in emergency services and beyond.

The narratives that emerge from public and nonprofit service are a key mechanism for understanding culture, rules, behavior, and outcomes. The telling (and retelling) of stories are how public servants reflect on and make sense of recent incidents, how coworkers highlight and reinforce the appropriateness of behavior, how critical and inquisitive personnel identify and solve problems, how new members or employees learn about their colleagues, and how employees cope with the emotional challenges of work. Though my doctoral studies briefly took me away from the world of emergency services, I was drawn back into stories and the work of emergency services personnel as I began to write my dissertation, which focused on paramedics and their views of and reactions to difficult, complex, or challenging incidents. This thread of research, and my substantive interactions with in-service graduate students over the last decade as a professor, have reinforced how much I value the work government and nonprofit workers engage in every day and how much we can learn from their narratives of action. This edited volume, then, is both a collection of artifacts of public service and a testament to their work. Though research foci and methods ebb and flow in academic public administration, the need for and interest in narrative research is enduring and will always capture our attention.

Lauren: In my final year of undergraduate work in church ministry and theology, I thought I was destined to teach New Testament studies. Really. However, I kept getting drawn back to sociology and social work. I decided to turn my minor in sociology into a second major to be safe. I am so glad that I did. My urban sociology professor wisely suggested that I interview the city manager of Abilene, Texas, for a class assignment. I thought I would be bored. Instead, the city manager and I had to be interrupted two hours later so that he could get to his next meeting. I was far more interested in city infrastructure than I realized!

But this was not the first time I had learned about public administration, even though I did not remember it at the time. In my second year of my MPA, I found the test results for a career test I took in the eighth grade. Low and *behold, the first suggestion was public administration. It was a 94% match. I was destined for public service even before I knew what "public administration" meant! Like Staci, I started early.*

I admire public servants and all that they do. This love affair began as I worked in a mental health nonprofit during my first position and deepened when I worked for the city of Irving, Texas. My colleagues were committed to making the world around them better, whether through case management, water quality testing, or code enforcement. I also started my dissertation journey in the strategic planning department in Irving, seeing firsthand how thinking strategically can impact the inner workings of a city. I am currently a proud state employee in Maryland, as I am on faculty in a public institution. I am prouder to teach so many current and future public servants and to constantly learn from their stories.

Goal of the Book

We share our stories about journeying into public service to situate the book in a broader conversation about the citizen-state encounter (Guy, 2019; Nielsen et al., 2021). By citizen, we mean people receiving government services regardless of legal status. When public servants (whether in government or nonprofits, paid or volunteer) interact with citizens, that interaction creates meaning for both parties. That meaning is the state in action and contains multitudes in terms of understanding one's value in relation to the state, what it means to be a citizen and a public servant, and how individuals matter. While the field of public administration is expanding its methodological toolkit to include more advanced statistical modeling and experiments, if we ignore this inter-action and the sensemaking process that occurs in these encounters, we run the risk of losing the humanity at the center of our field (Ford, 2021; Weick, 1995). By no means are we advocating for decreasing quanti-tative rigor. Instead, what this volume shows is the breadth and depth of public service and why we need to understand lived experiences of public servants to illuminate for current and future generations of public administrators the complexities of good governance.

We do this through showing the power of stories and storytelling. Hummel (1991) reminds us that stories are critical ways managers develop and share knowledge about public service. Managers and scientists differ, Hummel (1991) argues, in the kinds of knowledge they need, when, and how. While scientists are constructed to be dispassionate rational actors, managers are driven by "the present community of those involved in a problem who must be brought along to constitute a solution" (Hummel, 1991, p. 33).

Stories allow people to translate what they see, live, hear, feel, and experience into something workable and manageable (Feldman et al., 2004). For example, Boje (1991, p. 106) argues that organizations themselves are storytelling systems whereby "storytelling is the preferred sense-making currency of human relationships among internal and external stakeholders." Stories are dynamic and living. Stone (1988) reminds us that stories can shape—for better or worse—policy and administrative outcomes because they are powerful ways of knowing. Therefore, the stories of public administrators are central to how we understand the field and public service in practice. and need to be captured.

Manoharan and Rangarajan (2022) introduce narrative competence into public administration, maintaining that public servants are themselves storytellers with important knowledge to share through their experiences. They argue that narrative moments and narrative capacities are how organizational change happens, and public servants need to be trained in storytelling similarly to any other competency. They identify some elements of a public administration storyteller, including drawing on experience, distinguishing between actors in the story, assessing story quality, and engaging in reflective practice (Manoharan & Rangarajan, 2022). Throughout our book, the authors have relied on public servants as storytellers, serving as the vehicle through which that lived experience is shared. Some authors use a first-person description to tell their own public service stories. Our book draws on this line of storytelling research to share lived experiences of public servants.

As researchers in public administration, we are not disconnected from the lives and processes we are studying. Reflexivity and interpretive research go hand in hand to deeply uncover the embedded knowledge practitioners have (Yanow, 2009). Our goal with this edited volume was to give researchers the space to tell their own stories, share their interpretive research, and derive lessons from both. We hope the volume benefits those wanting to learn more about the depth and breadth of public servants beyond highly visible frontline workers.

Our book builds on the work of other scholars who have taken a similar approach to shedding light on the lived experiences of public servants. *Public Administration Review*, one of the leading journals in the field, routinely publishes administrative profiles of distinguished public servants to distill the lessons of their service for the field; see for example Donna Shalala (Radin, 2007), Viola Baskerville (Hutchinson and Condit, 2009), Randi Weingarten (Kearney, 2011), and the administrators of Challenge.gov (Mergel and Desouza, 2013). In terms of books, Maynard-Moody and Musheno (2003) *Cops, Teachers and Counselors* is probably one of the most well-known volumes in public administration and management that uses stories to convey the complex decision-making process—and policy implementation powers—of street-level bureaucrats. Riccucci (1995) profiles people she calls "execucrats," the appointed officials working in the U.S. federal government carrying out important policy and programmatic functions. She notes how these professionals often are the target of blame and ridicule to score political points—a trend that continues in contemporary political and administrative spheres.

Likewise, Riccucci, Cooper and Wright (1992) profile public servants making a difference, focusing on their leadership skills and characters. Doig and Hargrove (1990) take another biographical approach through profiling well-known public servants, again with the goal of drawing lessons about leadership and decision-making. O'Leary (2020) captures the stories of public servants who have disagreements with the work of their organizations and challenge this work and their supervisors through creative dissent techniques. Our book carries this tradition not by focusing on profiles exclusively but by sharing research from various scholars globally about public servants in broad positions. Some, as you will read in this book, have high-level positions, while others are community service workers on the ground trying to improve community health and well-being. Our book is an extension of this street-level bureaucracy work rather than a competition. Authors in this book also showcase the power of stories and storytelling for generating knowledge.

Stories Throughout the Book

With this setting, the book presents stories in various formats. Some chapters are personal reflections from people in roles such as emergency management and tax assessment. Some chapters mirror what we have read in volumes such as *Cops, Teachers, and Counselors* (Maynard-Moody

& Musheno, 2003), with vignettes throughout sharing the lived experiences of public servants and considering the lessons of those vignettes for theory and practice. Others still reflect more academic writing, with findings from qualitative interviews presented. Another chapter reflects more of a profile of a public servant working for a U.S. federal agency.

We believe the chapters in the book do a nice job of presenting the various ways in which knowledge can be shared within our field. Stories from the first-person perspective shed light on what those people experience in their everyday jobs. The profile-style pieces can highlight this form of knowledge sharing in more descriptive work. More academic-style chapters present qualitative data analysis to find patterns that can apply to other fields. Readers ideally see a variety of methodological approaches where narratives and stories can be used as valid forms of knowledge (Hummel, 1991).

Stories are detailed and varied. They have plots. There is a beginning, middle, and end. There are characters in a place and space. Stories and narratives shape our realities—they socially construct our worlds (Jones, McBeth, & Shanahan, 2014). Stories from others—thinking about their lived experiences—are a powerful way of teaching and can help us practice empathy and understanding (Morgan & Dennehy, 2004). Our goal with each chapter is to have the public servants featured within share their stories and their lived experiences with readers.

The stories may take on different formats, yet each conveys lessons learned. Stories have themes such as fear, critical communication, heartbreak, empathy, understanding, struggle, and triumph. The stories, whether presented as first-person accounts or as part of a qualitative interview study, help convey the vastness of public service. A reader might not think about how a camera is a policy instrument, how a meteorologist is both a science communicator and community member, or how a vaccine volunteer is treated by those they are meant to serve. We hope each chapter is thought-provoking for all readers. We hope students can see themselves in some chapters. We hope some read these stories and spark a research agenda. Stories are crucial in bringing out lived experiences (Hummel, 1991). These lived experiences bring the public service to life for students, scholars, and all those interested in public administration and management. It did for us compiling this volume, and we are eager to share these stories with readers.

Plan of the Book

The volume is arranged into four parts, which evolved based on the themes in the narratives. In seeking chapters for this volume, we reached out to our colleagues in the United States and abroad—academics and practitioners—to solicit stories and examinations of public servants who may not regularly get attention in the literature. The resulting 15 chapters tell stories at different levels of governments, across different countries, and in many different settings. They illuminate that which makes public servants special in different contexts but also those characteristics and values that unite public servants across this multiplicity of settings.

Section 1 we have called Balancing Acts, reflecting the myriad roles public servants play—and how those roles sometimes affect their abilities to help stakeholders. For example, chapters shed light on the tension between oversight mechanisms versus using discretion to best help citizens. Sometimes this puts street-level bureaucrats into simultaneous roles of "good guys" versus "bad guys," as discretion and multiple roles can both be helpful and harmful (Sager et al., 2014).

The second section, titled Life and Death Pressure, reflects how some public servants—even beyond traditional first responders—face and make life-and-death decisions. Chapters in this section highlight various public servants providing communication, direction, and policy implementation that can help or harm individuals and communities. Rule abidance or rule deviation can have serious consequences, especially when talking about emergency services (Henderson, 2013). Some themes in this section overlap with section 1, whereby competing roles intersect with life-and-death decisions (see also Edlins & Larrison, 2020). For example, Overly details his firsthand experiences providing emergency services during the ongoing COVID-19 pandemic, the complexities of which forced him in many directions with myriad responsibilities.

Section 3 is called Possibly Misunderstood Roles and Responsibilities and brings to light parts of the public service that might not be clear to everyone. Chapters in this section reflect jobs and roles people *think* they know a lot about—public defenders, tax assessors—yet the realities of these jobs are more complex than meets the eye. Administrative systems are complex and dynamic (Klijn, 2008), and chapters in this section highlight that complexity through frontline workers' stories and experiences handling those ever-moving challenges.

The final section of our book we called Unexpected Realms of Democracy because stories there bring to light public servants influencing democratic norms and participation through their unique roles. For example, a wildlife photographer shares his story of how photographs influence public opinion and policy. Arts and culture representatives are also highlighted regarding how their programming affects community cohesion. The chapters showcase the varieties of street-level bureaucrats and their influence on public administration and policy (see Hupe & Hill, 2007).

Our hope is that this book has something for everyone. When we decided to write this book, we were thinking of several audiences, including students in our classes. Master of public administration students, particularly those who are brand-new to the field, will get to read about the full breadth of the world of public service—the highs and lows of what makes these careers worth the stressors. Or those students who are more experienced career public servants might open their eyes to additional roles and responsibilities they might not see in their silos. Our students can think about what they would do in the shoes of these public servants and carry those lessons forward thoughtfully in their careers. We also see this book speaking to those outside the classroom, including practitioners and researchers alike, with the hope that it spurs more research and storytelling like the following chapters.

We hope readers not only learn but also leave with additional questions to research or lessons to bring into their practice. The conclusion draws some lessons we have learned from reading each chapter and putting them together to tell the larger story of public service. We welcome ongoing dialogue about these lessons learned and hope public administration scholars pick up and continue these important themes and dialogues.

References

Boje, D. M. (1991). The storytelling organization: A study of story performance in an office supply firm. *Administrative Science Quarterly, 36*(1), 106–126. https://doi.org/10.2307/2393432

Cooper, T., & Wright, N. D. (1992). *Exemplary public administrators: Character and leadership in government.* University of Michigan Press.

Edlins, M., & Larrison, J. (2020). Street-level bureaucrats and the governance of unaccompanied minor children. *Public Policy and Administration, 35*(4), 402–423. https://doi.org/10.1177/0952076718811438

Feldman, M. S. et al. (2004). Making sense of stories: A rhetorical approach to narrative analysis. *Journal of Public Administration Research and Theory*, *14*(2), 147–170. https://doi.org/10.1093/jopart/muh010

Ford, M. R. (2021). Making people matter: Moving toward a humanity-based public administration. *Administration & Society*. doi: 10.1177/00953997211030213

Hargrove, E. C., & Doig, J. W. (1990). *Leadership and innovation: Entrepreneurs in government*. Johns Hopkins University Press.

Henderson, A. C. (2013). Examining policy implementation in health care: Rule abidance and deviation in emergency medical services. *Public Administration Review*, *73*(6), 799–809. https://www.jstor.org/stable/42003127

Hutchinson, J. R., & Condit, D. M. (2009). Being there matters—Redefining the model public servant: Viola O. Baskerville in profile. *Public Administration Review*, *69*(1), 29–38.

Hummel, R. (1991). Stories managers tell: Why they are valid as science. *Public Administration Review*, *51*(1), 31–41.

Hupe, P., & Hill, M. (2007). Street-level bureaucracy and public accountability. *Public Administration*, *85*(2), 279–299. https://doi.org/10.1111/j.1467-9299.2007.00650.x

Jones, M. D., McBeth, M. K., & Shanahan, E. A. (2014). Introducing the Narrative Policy

Framework. In: Jones, M. D., Shanahan, E. A., & McBeth, M. K. (eds). *The Science of Stories*. Palgrave Macmillan. https://doi.org/10.1057/9781137485861_1

Kearney, R. C. (2011). Randi Weingarten, the American Federation of Teachers, and the challenges of policy leadership in a hostile environment. *Public Administration Review*, *71*(5), 772–781.

Klijn, E. (2008). Complexity theory and public administration: what's new? *Public Management Review*, *10*(3), 299–317. https://doi.org/10.1080/14719030802002675

Korecki, N., & Owermhole, S. (2021). Attacks on Fauci grow more intense, personal, and conspiratorial. Retrieved from https://www.politico.com/news/2021/06/04/fauci-attacks-personal-conspiratorial-491896

Lipsky, M. (1980/2010). *Street-level bureaucracy: Dilemmas of the individual in public services*. Russell Sage Foundation.

Manoharan, A., & Rangarajan, N. (2022). Public administrators as storytellers: Nurturing narrative competence to enrich their professional identity. *Administrative Theory & Praxis*. https://doi.org/10.1080/10841806.2022.2086753

Maynard-Moody, S., & Musheno, M. (2003). *Cops, teachers, and counselors*. University of Michigan Press.

Mergel, I., & Desouza, K. C. (2013). Implementing open innovation in the public sector: The case of Challenge.gov. *Public Administration Review*, *73*(6), 882–890. https://doi.org/10.1111/puar.12141

Morgan, S., & Dennehy, R. F. (2004). Using stories to reframe the social construction of reality: A trio of activities. *Journal of Management Education*, *28*(3), 372–389. https://doi.org/10.1177/1052562904264380

Nielsen, V. L. et al. (2021). Citizen reactions to bureaucratic encounters: Different ways of coping with public authorities. *Journal of Public Administration Research and Theory, 31*(2), 381–398. https://doi.org/10.1093/jopart/muaa046

O'Leary, R. (2020). *The ethics of dissent: Managing guerrilla government* (3rd ed.). CQ Press.

Overeem, P. (2017). *The politic-administration dichotomy: Toward a constitutional perspective.* Taylor & Francis.

Radin, B. M. (2007). Qualified to learn the job: Donna Shalala. *Public Administration Review, 67*(3), 504–510. https://doi.org/10.1111/j.1540-6210.2007.00732.x

Riccucci, N. (1995). *Unsung heroes: Federal execucrats making a difference.* Georgetown University Press.

Rubenstein, David M. (2020). Coronavirus hero: Anthony Fauci is a great public servant in a time of great public need. *USA Today.* https://www.usatoday.com/story/opinion/2020/03/22/coronavirus-anthony-fauci-will-help-save-american-lives-column/2883981001/

Sager, F. et al. (2014). Street-level bureaucrats and new modes of governance: How conflicting roles affect the implementation of the Swiss Ordinance on Veterinary Medicinal Products. *Public Management Review, 16*(4), 481–502. https://doi.org/10.1080/14719037.2013.841979

Science Friday. (2021). Anthony Fauci reflects on 40 years of HIV/AIDS research. https://www.sciencefriday.com/segments/fauci-40th-aids-anniversary/

Spicer, M. (2010). *In defense of politics in public administration: A value pluralist perspective.* University of Alabama Press.

Stone, Deborah. 1988. *Policy paradox and political reason.* HarperCollins Publishers.

Svara, J. H. (2001). The myth of the dichotomy: Complementarity of politics and administration in the past and future of public administration. *Public Administration Review, 61*(2), 176–183. http://www.jstor.org/stable/977451

Weick, Karl E. (1995). *Sensemaking in Organizations.* Thousand Oaks, CA: SAGE Publications.

Yanow, D. (2009). Ways of knowing: Passionate humility and reflective practice in research and management. *American Review of Public Administration, 39*(6), 579–601. https://doi.org/10.1177/0275074009340049

Balancing Acts

While we had many options for how to arrange the book, we chose a thematic approach. Each section highlights the often-hidden roles street-level bureaucrats play in decision-making, policy design and implementation, and democratic responsibility. Readers will surely notice overlap between the outlined themes and chapters, meaning the work of public servants is cross-cutting and ever changing.

In this section we draw attention to how street-level bureaucrats and public servants balance multiple roles and purposes—even within jobs that might on paper seem clearly delineated. Lipsky (1980) noted in his work that street-level bureaucrats face dilemmas when carrying out their functions. Bureaucratic discretion can be both harmful and helpful, especially when people are seen as receiving special treatment (Lipsky, 1980).

Underlying the chapters is what we see as the complexity of public service. Complexity theory in public administration reflects interwoven governance processes with punctuations to the status quo (Teisman & Klijn, 2008). Context matters for understanding governance process, and if and how punctuations to existing bureaucratic structures can harm or improve the system (Teisman & Klijn, 2008).

As government complexity has grown, so too have the roles and responsibilities for street-level bureaucrats (Sager et al., 2014). For example, Sager et al. (2014) note that with increasing collaboration between the public and private sector, some private-sector actors also act as street-level bureaucrats when implementing government policy. New Public Management reforms have exacerbated this shift and role conflict (Tummers et al., 2012).

Tummers et al. (2012) identified three kinds of role conflicts: policy-professional, policy-client, and organizational-professional. The first refers to how policies or roles conflict with a person's professional identity and responsibilities. A policy-client conflict occurs when a street-level bureaucrat sees the client's role expectations as incongruent with policy expectations. Finally, an organization-policy conflict is when a person's roles and ethical responsibilities do not align with an organization's policy responsibilities.

We see some of these conflicts manifested in stories throughout this section. In chapter 1, Gabriela Lotta and Juliana Rocha Miranda detail how community health workers in Brazil face role conflicts when it comes to pleasing the state versus keeping communities safe. In chapter 2, Kelly Stevens interviews U.S. federal government meteorologists who share their stresses with providing lifesaving information to the community in a timely manner. We learn the political pressures meteorologists face when doing science.

Chapter 3 by Alicia Schatteman details the myriad roles librarians play at the local level. Indeed, some might think the librarian position is unidimensional, focusing on interactions with clientele, but the chapter sheds light on various political and community conflicts librarians face when delivering key services. Finally, in chapter 4, Moiz Abdul Majid and Sameen Mohsin Ali examine the tensions between teachers in Pakistan and those charged with monitoring their performance at the state level. While accountability for performance is important, the monitoring and disciplinary regimes result in teachers experiencing states of fear as pressure mounts to meet unreasonable performance targets.

Chapters in this section reflect the complex roles public servants working behind the scenes face when trying to execute government policies and practices. Sometimes those environments are complex, with competing rules, requirements, and regulations. As Robichau and Lynn Jr. note (2009), many existing policy implementation theories do not often take street-level bureaucrats into account, but the chapters in this section and throughout show the critical role they play not only in policy design but in implementation as well.

Our Experiences with Complexity and Changing Roles

In the introduction, we shared our stories about how we came to work in public service roles and why we value those positions and inherent challenges. To carry the story theme throughout, we want to share our own personal reflections regarding some of the themes presented in Section 1.

Staci: *What struck me most from the chapters in this section was how many of the public servants mentioned dual identities. The community health workers, for example, had to go back and forth between their expertise and desire to be active in the community. I never thought about librarians having a dual identity until reading about their complexities of navigating public yet contested spaces. As we write this in 2022, there are debates about banning books again from public libraries. Some commentators on social media are mad libraries are giving out books for free about these seemingly divisive topics. The exchanges are wild while also showcasing the point of our book that some people are not aware of the scope of public services and the critical role these organizations play in peoples' lives.*

As we noted in the introduction, the idea for the book came at the height of the COVID-19 pandemic in 2020. It was also a time of reckoning for America because police killings of unarmed Black Americans pushed social justice issues to the forefront of our collective conscious. In public adminis-tration, there became a call for teaching beyond the "classics" and to rethink our foundations. What we teach the next generation matters. How we think about current events matters. Our roles as professors became more complex and challenging when the pandemic conditions necessitated changing how we teach. Laws throughout the country also mandated what we can teach. As I write this story, I do not know if I can go into my classroom in Florida and talk confidently about slavery or Marxism. State law is not clear what exactly are divisive concepts and how someone might be punished for teaching such topics.

Dual identities are themselves complex. We have to be experts in the classroom yet are deeply affected by these new rules and laws. Somehow we are supposed to pretend that everything is fine and carry on as usual. There needs to be a moment of reckoning in higher education about who we are, what we want our students to achieve during their time in school and beyond, and how we navigate the world as people whose identities are constantly being challenged and erased. These complexities can lead to burnout and walkout. More stories need to be heard so we can properly reckon with this perfect storm. I really like the chapters here shedding light on these issues within various public service realms.

Jessica: *What these chapters brought home for me was the challenge of switching between roles as public servants and the various costs of that switching. Public service is a calling and responsibility, and all responsibilities bring an associated weight with them. These public servants are dedicated to their work—but they are also people, with real emotions, who are faced with* *having to consider those emotions in doing their jobs and living their lives, something that is becoming increasingly intertwined as the boundaries between work and life blend. When we put on "different hats" in our public service roles, do we fully account for the costs, on ourselves, on those with whom we interact, and for our organizations?*

When I lived in Baltimore City, I would often write in the public library in the afternoon. Looking at other citizens in the library, there would be people researching jobs with the help of the librarians, people reading books or watching movies. When school let out, the library would fill up (and I mean FILL UP) with schoolchildren, and the role of librarians would shift during this bridge period between school and home life. It always made me think about the complexity of being a librarian and their role as community brokers to many different groups of people—the patience and care it requires. I love how the chapter by Schatteman captures this.

Weather is something I grew up taking for granted, living in a region with the occasional snowstorm or hurricane but rarely anything devastating or life-changing weather events. As weather becomes more extreme and varied across the world, thinking about the public servants who are helping translate the science of weather for the everyday public and the weight they must feel in terms of the consequences of their predictive models was something I never considered before reading the chapter by Stevens in this section. Across the section, a continuing theme for me is how do we support these workers and help them navigate those dualities for the good of all those involved. This question is going to linger with me as I head back into the classroom to teach current and future public servants.

Alex: *The chapters in this section highlight the myriad roles that front-line workers occupy, and, though many of these are seem rather evident or obvious upon first look, it's important to pause and recognize the importance of these roles in thinking about core government and nonprofit services. It may be relatively easy to gloss over these street-level roles, but to do so would be to miss the fundamental complexity and value that they bring, and the effort and dedication it takes to enact those roles. This has been a theme of my research in the area of street-level bureaucracy, and in my instructional role working closely with in-service students who serve at the front lines of public, health care, and nonprofit service. Their everyday experiences are incredibly important to how we think about the effectiveness of government and nonprofit organizations. That these roles are constantly changing speaks to the resilience of street-level workers, and their need to deftly navigate various forms of complexity.*

Lauren: *The complexity of these positions, and the emotional toll, must be exhausting for public servants. I left this section more concerned than ever about the mental health of our public servants. Like Staci, I have also kept these chapters in mind as I keep up with current news stories. I would have never thought when I started teaching that I would be discussing emotional resilience and doing mental check-ins with my students. However, during the pandemic I realized that most of my students were struggling, as they were not only dealing with multiple roles at work but also at home. Often these multiple roles were more blurred than ever before.*

In Spark of Learning: Energizing the College Classroom with the Science of Emotion, *Sarah Rose Cavanaugh writes about how learning is essentially an emotional act. Serving is also an emotional act requiring empathy toward the public and each other (Guy 2020). Part of my journey as an educator in this field is to open up emotions in the classroom so that I model vulnerability and emotional resilience for my students. The pandemic taught me that this is not just a pedagogical choice but a necessity for my current and future students.*

References

Cavanaugh, Sarah Rose. (2016). *The spark of learning: Energizing the college classroom with the science of emotion.* West Virginia University Press.

Guy, M. E. (2020). To catch the sparrow that has flown. *Journal of Public Affairs Education, 26*(3), 264–275. https://doi.org/10.1080/15236803.2020.1759760

Lipsky, M. (1980/2010). *Street-level bureaucracy: Dilemmas of the individual in public services.* Russell Sage Foundation.

Robichau, R. W., & Lynn, L., Jr. (2009). The implementation of public policy: Still the missing link. *Policy Studies Journal, 37*(1), 21–36. https://doi.org/10.1111/j.1541-0072.2008.00293.x

Sager, F., Thomann, E., Zollinger, C., van der Heiden, N., & Mavrot, C. (2014). Street-level bureaucrats and new modes of governance: How conflicting roles affect the implementation of the Swiss Ordinance on Veterinary Medicinal Products. *Public Management Review, 16*(4), 481–502. https://doi.org/10.1080/14719037.2013.841979

Teisman, G. R., & Klijn, E. (2008). Complexity theory and public management. *Public Management Review, 10*(3), 287–297. https://doi.org/10.1080/14719030802002451

Tummers, L., Vermeeren, B., Steijn, B., & Bekkers, V. (2012). Public professionals and policy implementation. *Public Management Review, 14*(8), 1041–1059. https://doi.org/10.1080/14719037.2012.662443

1

Navigating Between the State and the Community

Stories from Community Health Workers

GABRIELA LOTTA AND JULIANA ROCHA MIRANDA

This work was supported by the Fundação de Amparo à Pesquisa do Estado de São Paulo [2019/13439-7, CEPID CEM].

Community health workers (CHWs) are frontline workers who work as a link between communities and health care providers. According to the World Health Organization (WHO), there are about 1.5 million Community Health Workers (CHWs) worldwide. They are deemed key actors in health quality improvement in many countries in Africa, Asia, and Latin America (Perry et al., 2014). However, despite their presence and relevance in many national health systems, CHWs remain mostly unseen by governments and policy analysts, and little is known about their trajectories, values, and motivations.

CHWs are usually recruited to act in public health services in the communities where they also live and have an integration role between health teams and the population, especially vulnerable groups such as the elderly, women, disabled, and others (Olaniran et al., 2017; Perry et al., 2014; van Ginneken, Lewin, & Berridge, 2010). Their everyday work involves a lot of preventive actions and health education, which encompasses identifying health needs, helping with epidemiological surveillance actions in the territories, keeping up with patients in long-term processing, promoting vaccination, and vector control actions (Hartzler et al., 2018). CHWs usually have no expertise in health issues. What makes their job indispensable is not professional knowledge but their community embeddedness and the linkages they build between the public and health teams (Olaniran et al., 2017).

This dual role—as a worker and as a community agent—differentiates them from usual street-level bureaucrats (Lotta & Marques, 2020) and potentializes some tensions already discussed in the literature, such as double embeddedness (Dubois, 1999) and the citizen-agent and state-agent narratives (Maynard-Moody & Musheno, 2003). These characteristics also increase the tensions between the pressures that operate on street-level bureaucrats: those derived from the state, such as the need to be productive and efficient, and those derived from citizens that require individualized and resolutive care (Lipsky, 2010).

The CHWs features described also unveil potential analytical elements to study these agents, such as the mentioned double embeddedness, the idea of policy translation, and bureaucratic representativeness. However, as mentioned before, despite the presence of CHWs in many countries and their importance in health systems, they are quite invisible in the literature. Despite their presence throughout the whole country and importance in policy implementation, they are usually also invisible for governments and decision makers.

In this chapter we shed light on those workers theoretically and empirically. We analyze CHWs as frontline workers who implement health policies by interacting with citizens daily. We address issues about what they do, how they work, their main challenges, and also what it means to be a frontline worker who also lives in the community where they work. We address questions raised by CHW's double embeddedness (to the state and to the community), such as where they come from, why they decide to become CHWs, their views about their role, and how they reconcile their values and beliefs with the needs of universal and integral delivery of public health.

The following discussion builds on a three-year data collection in which we have interviewed 120 Brazilian CHWs. We selected CHWs who work in the most vulnerable areas of the city of São Paulo. Interviews were organized in four parts: profile and trajectory, their daily work and interactions with citizens, how they see themselves and the policy, and stories of success and failure in the work. Regarding this last part, as we intended to hear their voices, the interviews were based on storytelling and tried to capture those concerns. In an adaptation of Maynard-Moody and Musheno's (2003) method, we have gathered and analyzed 136 stories told by them. All interviews were recorded and transcribed verbatim and later analyzed in NVivo software. For this chapter, we analyze the codes about their profile, the reasons to get into the job, the self-perception about work, the justifications of success and failure, and their interactions with citizens.

The chapter is organized in four sections that seek to answer all these questions. In the first one, we present CHWs in the Brazilian context. After that, each section relates to patterns that emerged from data analysis. In the second section, we discuss what it means to be a CHW. In the third section, we discuss their sense of self-importance based on their perceptions about success and failure. In the fourth section, we discuss how they navigate between the community and the state spheres. Finally, we present our concluding remarks.

CHWs in Brazil

Brazil, one of the largest countries in the world with one of the biggest public health systems (WHO, 2020), provides an interesting case to analyze CHWs, as these professionals are the main entrance door of the health system and take care of almost 70% of the population (Ministério da Saúde, 2020). The experience of CHWs in Brazil is the most institutionalized one, following WHO guidelines (WHO, 2018; Krieger et al., 2021).

There are 290,000 CHWs in Brazil who are central in the implementation of the National Health System—or Unified Health System (acronym in Portuguese: SUS). Founded in the wake of Brazil's constitutional principles of universal and free access to welfare services, SUS is now organized around three levels of health care: primary health care (PHC), which is focused on health prevention and promotion; and secondary and tertiary care, aimed at more specialized exams, treatments, and procedures.

The main policy that organizes the PHC services is the Family Health Strategy (FHS), which was conceived in 1997 and became central in PHC national policy in 2006. Even though it is attached to a street-level organization, the Basic Unit of Health (acronym in Portuguese: UBS), the FHS's main goal is to provide PHC on a local basis by addressing health issues and health risk factors in users' social contexts and directly in their residences. This implies an orientation toward users rather than a medical- or facility-centered service. FHS also aims to humanize health care, proposing solutions that are adapted to citizens' realities and needs (Silva & Dalmaso, 2002). Although the FHS is a universal policy, it is usually implemented in regions of greatest poverty and vulnerability, as the wealthiest citizens usually have private health insurance.

CHWs have existed in Brazil since the 1980s as part of embryonic local policy experiences and voluntary health promotion initiatives coming, for example, from the Catholic Church and popular health movements. Since 2006, the CHWs have been part of FHS teams, which are composed of one doctor, one nurse, one nursing assistant, and four to six CHWs. This is one of the main differences between the Brazilian CHWs and other experiences worldwide: they do not work alone and have a team with which to divide the responsibilities for care. Each team takes care of 1,000 families, and each CHW takes care of about 200 families that live in a specific geographic area. Their central roles are to visit patients at least once a month, track families and individuals' health profile, promote health education, and collect and organize data about the families (Silva & Dalmaso, 2002). As Brazilian CHWs work with teams, they provide guidance to families but also act as a bridge between them and the other health professionals.

Therefore, at the same time, CHWs channel information about citizens and communities to governments and they are gatekeepers of the health system, as they are citizens' main entrance to the service. In addition, as in other examples abroad, Brazilian CHWs live in the same social environment of people for whom they are responsible, which highlights how their social networks and values affect their everyday implementation of policies (Lotta & Marques, 2020; Nunes & Lotta, 2019). Also, it means CHWs are close and potentially affected by the same social inequalities they are supposed to handle in their everyday jobs.

Moreover, unlike many other experiences around the world (Bhatia, 2014; Maes et al., 2018), Brazilian CHWs are public servants. They are selected within the community, but they have formal contracts with the state, receive salaries, have labor rights, and have the duty to speak in the name of the state. This means that they can be seen as street-level bureaucrats even if, at the same time, they share an identity as a community agent (Lotta & Marques, 2020; Krieger et al., 2021). In the next section, we discuss what it means to be a CHW based on their profile and how they see themselves.

Being a CHW

As in the rest of the world (Najafizada, Bourgeault, & Labonté, 2019; Bathia, 2014), most Brazilian CHWs are women (78.1%), and more than half of them are Black women. Their main age group ranges from 31 to 40 years old (36.4%), followed by another that ranges from 41 to 50 years old (28.6%). Most CHWs have finished high school (71.8%), but some of them have dropped out after elementary school (16.5%). Those who went to college or did not finish elementary school are exceptions (Milanezi et al., 2020). CHWs' profiles reflect the Brazilian social structure and its vulnerabilities, where poor people are usually Black, live in vulnerable conditions, and are less educated.

The data from our research greatly reflect all these macro-sociological aspects. Our interviewees are mostly Black women living in the poor communities where they work. As we develop later, such embeddedness enables the construction of ties with the community. Moreover, these public servants face similar social conditions as those faced by people they are expected to approach in their everyday jobs. Most of them depend on the public health system to access health care and in general have no previous work experience within the health sector. Their professional trajectory is marked by precariousness in depreciated service jobs such as housecleaning, informal commerce, babysitting, and hairdressing, among others.

In this vulnerable context, becoming a CHW might be a way to diminish their vulnerability in comparison to their own neighbors. However, when compared with other health professionals in FHS, CHWs are the most fragile, considering their low salaries, their lowest positions in public administration, and their lack of training or specialization (Morosini, 2010; Nogueira, 2017; Morosini & Fonseca, 2018; Nunes, 2019). At the same time, having an institutional—even if subordinated—authority and a stable job can be socially valued as a social mobility (Siblot, 2006). This is one of the main reasons why they decide to join public service. When asked about why they have decided to become CHWs, most of them emphasize becoming a CHW as an *opportunity* to improve their families' lives, raising their children properly, or having a job even if they are elderly. Thus, their main motivation revolves around the attractiveness of income and employment offered by the CHW position.

To a lesser extent, they have also suggested that their motivation is due to work conditions specified by the FHS, such as avoiding long distances to work or personal preferences of working within the health sector. However, the second most mentioned reason was the idea of *helping* or *taking care* of people, which evokes a strong orientation toward citizens' needs by offering extra effort and attention aimed at their life enhancement as proposed by the concept of citizen agency (Maynard-Moody & Musheno, 2003).

This idea is reinforced by their definitions of what it means to be a CHW and what their jobs are meant to do. In both cases, the prevailing answer is helping and taking care of citizens. This answer also indicates that they develop a sense of vocation, idealism, and commitment to a cause, even if the first reason to become a CHW was the job opportunity.

Such motivation is reflected in a range of feelings and interpretations about themselves that they reveal when describing their daily work. On the one hand, they describe it as a *rewarding* job when they can do what they believe, such as when colleagues and patients recognize their value, when patients behave properly, and when procedure outcomes meet their expectations and solve patients' problems. Those elements engender their *gratitude* and self-realization for being CHW. On the other hand, they report *frustration* when the opposite happens—notably when patients are "resistant" to their recommendations (Lotta & Pires, 2020) and when the policy goals restrain their action to help people properly (Maynard-Moody & Musheno, 2003).

The meaning of what it is to help people comes from these frontline workers' self-regard of legitimacy to make definitions and judgments over users, supervisors, or policy makers (Maynard-Moody and Musheno, 2003). It also derives from the perception they have of being *essential* to policy implementation. They feel they are the core of FHS, as they are the bridge between community and health system. This perception makes them proud of their role. According to some narratives, even though physicians are admired for saving lives and being highly educated, CHW are the ones who make "*the beautiful work*" once "they *really know*" the people they follow up, and they "*know better*" than colleagues and managers what works well and what is necessary for patients. This interview excerpt exemplifies this argument: "without me he [the physician] would not save anyone, he would not actually know who is out there. An appointment is not enough to get to know a patient. He knows them because I go to a patient's home once or twice a month, I meet them in the market. So, the physician would not save his life if it was not for me."

The fundamentals of being able to make such connections lie in some abilities they claim they must have in their daily work. On the one hand, Brazilian CHWs face resource scarcity, low capacity of referral to specialized attention, and massive demand for appointments (Alonso et al., 2018). On the other hand, the job's nature of close contact makes CHWs a main target for citizens' complaints and demands even though their problem is not necessarily addressed in PHC or related to the CHWs' competence. As discussed in street-level bureaucracy literature, they deal both with the adverse structural conditions of work and with citizens' pressure for resolutive treatment (Lipsky, 1980; Brodkin, 2013; 2015).

Those elements altogether influence their perceptions of stress and pressure when executing their jobs. In extreme situations, the tension can create emotional difficulties and even lead to mental illness such as depression or anxiety. As a result, in CHWs' perception, their work is something that requires *flexibility*. By saying this, they mean they have to adapt themselves to everyday challenges such as meeting angry citizens, facing theirs' supervisors charging for results, and conquering citizens' trust.

In this way, CHWs are flexible because they handle conflicting and utterly difficult situations with their *ability to talk to people, kindness,* and *manners.* Such a characterization recalls gender studies and labor sociology discussions about the feminization of care professions (Biroli, 2018; Hirata, 2016) and, especially in the case of CHWs, the feminization of the frontline work (Durão & Menezes, 2016; Siblot, 2006). In general, the described abilities are taken as natural and intrinsic, which points to the naturalization of some features and attributes as female and socially depreciated (Siblot, 2006). An interesting illustration of such devaluation appears in a man's testimony that shows how it is advantageous to be a man and how he feels more respected than his female colleagues:

I'm a CHW, but I'm not gay. Everybody makes comments about this, that this service is meant for women or that men who work as CHW are kinda gays. And it is not true, ok? It's hard at the beginning, as you have to make questions about intimate issues for patients, such as gynecological exams, for example. But everyone gets used to it [. . .] Actually, in some moments it's easier because I'm a man. People aren't too aggressive towards me. It seems that when the CHW is a woman some patients are more aggressive. For example: a guy came to the clinic making a lot of noise, mistreating the receptionist—a girl. Then when I got there she came asking me to talk to him. And I said: "hey man, take it easy, it's not like that." That's when he calmed down.

The excerpt above illustrates how the practical knowledge of being a CHW is deeply grounded in "feminine" characteristics—to the point that a male CHW must defend his masculinity. Aside from the vulnerabilities accumulated by race and class issues, such devaluation is at the center of invisibility and disinterest in CHWs' voices. By listening to their trajectories, we have seen that this vulnerability is a core motivation for joining public service in that position. Over time, they develop a sense of idealism and vocational orientation toward citizens. Their narratives emphasize actions and efforts that sometimes go even beyond their legal designations to help citizens (Maynard-Moody & Musheno, 2003). These narratives also are evident in the next section, where we discuss the stories of success and failure.

Success and Failure: Motivations to Act

To understand how CHWs think about their work and make decisions about it, we analyzed the justifications they give to situations of success and failure. Adapting Maynard-Moody and Musheno's methodology, we asked them to tell us a success and a failure story they had experienced in their jobs. We have gathered 68 stories of each type (136 in total) as represented in the two examples below:

I have a patient, a man, who is 74 years old. He didn't accept anyone to get inside his house, he didn't want to take any medicines, he drinks a lot and was very resistant. I started talking to him, saying I am your worker, I can help you take care of yourself. Slowly, he started opening the gate of the house and later he started letting me in. And now he knows the day I will visit him and awaits me at the door. Now, he takes all regular exams, takes the medicine and is a great patient. He tells everyone how I helped him. It was an accomplishment for me!

I had a patient who was pregnant and a drug user. She was very aggressive with me. I tried hard to help her, but she didn't want to. When the baby was born, we tried to help her take care of the baby, but she complained all the time because she wanted to use drugs and didn't want us at her house. One day, I met her living on the street. She was very high and told me the baby died. I felt I could not help her, as she didn't accept our help. It was a really sad story for me.

The analysis of the 136 stories suggests that the meaning of success and failure is organized around three main elements: citizens' health conditions, CHWs' capacity to change citizens' behavior, and the acknowledgement CHWs receive for their efforts.

The first element describes how CHWs think they have success when the patient's illness can be treated and healed. On the other hand, they think they have a failure when the disease has no cure, and the patient ends up dead or is still sick. In this way, the idea of success is based on their capacity of helping to heal, while the idea of failure is attributed to something that is often beyond their control, such as an aggressive cancer or a lack of proper treatment in the specialized attention. The failure is, in this case, much more a matter of fate than a worker's fault.

The second element that organizes the justification for failure and success is the CHWs' capacities (or incapacities) to move users from a position of *resistant* to *adherent*—as they put it—to the service. This means when they can change a patient's behavior in the service. CHWs consider success when citizens become *adherent* and contribute to the CHW mission to help. This is the case of a pregnant woman who became adherent:

Well, there is this pregnant woman who used to be treated by another CHW and she used to give a lot of trouble. She ended up having a miscarriage and she wouldn't receive the CHW or the nurse. You know, she was hard to handle, she wouldn't comply. And then she changed to my territory. I don't know if it was my way of talking . . . but she started to receive me quite well. And now she's pregnant again and she does all the prenatal care. She wasn't like that before. (. . .)

She was a bit rebel, she wouldn't come to the appointments nor receive the nurse. Now she's no longer like that, she receives us very well, goes to appointments, doesn't give us trouble anymore.

On the other hand, they consider a failure when they are not able to change a patient's behavior and make him/her committed to the prescribed treatment. A typical resistant patient is Mrs. X, who stars in the failure story below:

Mrs. X was this lady who was terrified of injections (. . .). She was this widow lady who lived with her daughter. And everything I asked to this lady wasn't done. I took the doctor there and he asked some blood tests. I went there with the nurse to collect her blood, but she didn't accept it. Later, she was with a lot of pain in her eyes, and we referred her to the ophthalmologist. She had eight opportunities to go to an appointment and failed. She died and we found out she had cancer. It took us two years trying to make her adhere to the service and nothing happened. It was out of our control. We did our best.

Finally, the third element looks at whether CHWs are recognized for their efforts, meaning whether they receive acknowledgement for what they do. As we have shown, CHWs see their jobs as very important, and they identify success when they feel their efforts are recognized and failure when they are mistreated or disrespected by citizens. An example is the excerpt below:

I have this old lady [who] thanks me until now. She wanted to do a surgery in the eyes, but never managed to do it. From the moment I started treating her, I took the physician to her house and she got it. Now she hugs me, she cries thanking me for what I did for her. And I think it is a huge success. Because I obtained what she wanted for so long, and nowadays she says I am her guardian angel.

These three justifications about what is a failure or a success may coexist in the stories, and we show their incidence in Table 1.1:

Table 1.1. Dimensions of Success and Failures in Service Provision

	Stories of Success N=68	Stories of Failure N=68
Cure	"Available" 19 stories	"Unavailable" 33 stories
Changing behavior	"Possible" 42 stories	"Impossible" 51 stories
Effort's recognition	"Strong alliance with citizens" 13 stories	"Weak alliance with citizens" 7 stories

Source: Author-created.

The prevailing perception of success and failure has to do with the way CHWs regard citizens according to their behavior toward the service. Therefore, CHWs' motivation to act is strongly connected to their judgment about citizens' commitment to the service over time (Maynard-Moody & Musheno, 2003): If patients engage themselves and adhere to the service, it becomes a success story; if they refuse treatment and continue in a resistant position, it is a failure. CHWs describe their efforts of *persuading, guiding,* and *advising* as central to this possible change. If they get to make citizens fit into deservingness criteria they create, they feel their efforts have been awarded. In this situation, they are the ones responsible for such achievement. Otherwise, if they are not able to make a patient fit into the criteria, this means that citizens continue in a non-deserving condition, and they are the ones to blame. The failure is not a CHW's responsibility, as it is beyond their reach. As an example, one of them said: *"that's not my fault, as I insisted, but he did not want to change his behavior."*

Most success stories are related to CHWs' own efforts and merits in service. In only a few cases do they attribute the successful as an achievement of the public health service or their teams. This shows their motivation not as state agents but as citizen agents more inclined to cultural abidance (Maynard-Moody & Musheno, 2003). Failure otherwise is something usually narrated as beyond their control. It might be portrayed as a system problem, but most of the time, it is described as a citizen responsibility grounded in the social categories CHWs use to classify them as deserving or not (Harrits & Møller, 2011).

In conclusion, the stories suggest that CHWs justify their actions based both on state and citizen agents' narratives and navigate between them when they have success or failure. In the following section, we discuss how their double embeddedness also affects the way they work, how they experience their job, and how this transition between state and citizen agent narratives can be justified.

Navigating Between Spheres of Belongings

Since its origin in China in the 19th century, CHW is a profession designed to have territorial representativeness (Perry et al., 2014). The idea is that part of health prevention and promotion depends on developing services adapted to local needs and characteristics, considering the importance of social determinants of health. In this way, having a local resident as a health professional would be a cheap and easy solution to improve health services (Campbell & Scott, 2011; Perry et al., 2014).

In Brazil, this idea also sustains the design of CHW as a profession, with a particularity that, in the Brazilian experience, they are institutionalized as part of the state and are also part of a team. These characteristics make CHWs hybrid street-level bureaucrats. They represent the state, and, at the same time, they are part of the community. Therefore, they have double embeddedness that requires the ability to navigate between the different spheres of belonging. The point here is: How does this affect the way they work and implement policies?

Previous research has already suggested that this double embeddedness enables them to translate policies into patients' contexts (Lotta & Marques, 2020; Nunes & Lotta, 2019). Based on the knowledge they accumulate as being a bureaucrat and neighbor, they learn how to include the local language, local practices, references, and beliefs into policies. They do it by adapting practices and interaction styles that they use to communicate with citizens (Lotta & Marques, 2020). At the same time, they accumulate accurate knowledge about the community and patients' dynamics, which allows them to build improved diagnoses that are brought to the health teams. They work as a bridge transporting knowledge and adapting practices and interactions to both sides (Barros, Barbieri, Ivo, & da Silva, 2010; Das, Angeli, & van Schayck, 2020).

Their dual roles enable them to develop relational mechanisms and act as mediators between the state and the citizens in activities that go beyond health practices. As mediators, they act as gatekeepers who detain the information about how to get access to many services, such as education, social work, and others (Lotta & Marques, 2020; Lotta & Pavez, 2015). In this way, they may contribute to social inclusion and citizenship (Kock et al., 2017). And, at the same time, they may implement policies better attuned to local realities. In doing so, they manage to achieve greater adherence to the health services and promote social inclusion.

However, this double embeddedness may also have negative consequences for policy and for the CHWs themselves. For policy, as previous research also has suggested, CHWs' position as bureaucrats may transform them into powerful actors inside the communities (Nunes, 2019). As this power relies on privileged access to information and on the fact that they speak in the name of the state, they may use it in a negative way to select who receives what (Nunes & Lotta, 2019) and differentiate citizens based on their personal relations.

For CHWs, the fact that they live in the same place where they work exposes them to multiple difficult situations (Lotta et al., 2020). For example, often neighbors believe that they must be always available, even during non-work hours. Patients also ask for personal favors as if they were not professionals. Their private lives are exposed to the patients they treat, and if any problem happens at work, it is quickly transferred to their personal lives. Also, they must be able to differentiate their roles as professionals and as neighbors, for example, by not gossiping and by respecting the private information and lives of the people with whom they live. In this excerpt, a CHW describes some of these difficulties:

> There are many people who use drugs in my area. But they know I don't get involved and don't talk about it, so they trust me. Once there was a rumor that I (yes me!) had taken a baby from a woman and thrown it in the bin. So, the people were angry. I was doing my job that morning and didn't even know what was going on. When I got there, they showed me the photo on Facebook—"Look, see the photo of the baby." I replied that I didn't want to see it, that was not the right thing to do. Then the area's drug dealer wanted to talk to me; he looked right at my face and said: "In this place people can talk a lot of bullshit, and you have to be careful. Did you do anything that made anyone think that

you hurt that baby?" I said, "No, I vaccinate the dogs in the area and usually I have a syringe with me and a cooler for the vaccines. So, someone may have mistaken that. I would never do that." The drug dealer then said: "I can see it in your eyes that you did not do this."

As we have shown in this section, CHWs' social embeddedness exposes them to a close and ambiguous proximity to the citizens they take care of. In this context, they make their everyday discretionary decisions and thereafter adapt policy. Also, in this context, they navigate between state and citizen narratives to justify their decisions.

Conclusion

CHWs are present worldwide, especially in vulnerable and developing countries. Still, they remain less studied and largely unseen by governors and decision makers. In this chapter, we have shown how their silencing is related to their social and political positions: in general, CHWs are Black women with little education who live in vulnerable places. They mirror the social attributes of people they take care of, as they come from the same communities and share the same social realities and inequalities.

As we have seen, even though they primarily joined the public service to improve their life conditions and protect themselves from vulnerability, they develop a sense of vocation and idealism over time that make them feel essential to the health policy. What sustains that is, according to their answers, some abilities traditionally deemed female, such as instinct of care and communication. Given the work conditions and the feminization of frontline work, the CHW job both offers labor and income protections and exposes these women to multiple vulnerabilities.

The idea of vocation also appears in their perceptions about success and failure. Although health issues are important in how they justify success and failure, the acknowledgement they receive and their capacity to change patients' behavior are key elements in that justification. The stories reveal how much CHWs navigate between state-agent and citizen-agent narratives. In general, they assume the state-agent narrative to handle failure by blaming patients or incurable illnesses, and they assume the citizen-agent narrative when attributing success to their own efforts.

This navigation between state-agent and citizen-agent narratives also derives from their double embeddedness as citizens and street-level bureaucrats. On the one hand, it allows them to act as mediators and adapt policies to promote inclusion. On the other hand, it may have negative impacts on policy, for example when they use their discretion as state workers to differentiate between patients based on unofficial criteria, generating more vulnerability, or when embeddedness in the community exposes them to difficult situations in their work or private lives.

In conclusion, the case of CHWs has highlighted the importance of calling literature's attention to these invisible servers not only to give voice to what they have to say. It also reveals some particularities of their motivations and belonging that may contribute to the theory, as it addresses important issues to understand the impact of double embeddedness to policy implementation. It highlights how the brokerage works, how frontline workers act as gatekeepers, and the importance of thinking about mediation, which are questions that can be addressed in street-level bureaucracy theory. At the same time, the CHWs' case raises evidence to think about the impact of territorial representativity, an issue less studied in the theory about representative bureaucracy. Finally, it also has potential to contribute to the broader literature of policy implementation observing the particularities of Global South countries, where CHWs are spread.

References

Alonso, C. M. d. C., Béguin, P. D., & Duarte, F. J. d. C. M. (2018). Work of community health agents in the family health strategy: Meta-synthesis. *Revista de Saúde Pública, 52*(14), 1–13.

Barros, D. F. D., Barbieri, A. R., Ivo, M. L., & Silva, M. D. G. D. (2010). O contexto da formação dos agentes comunitários de saúde no Brasil. *Text & Contexto Enfermagem, 19*(1), 78–84.

Bhatia, K. (2014). Community health worker programs in India: A rights-based review. *Perspectives in Public Health, 134*(5), 276–282.

Biroli, F. (2018). *Gênero e desigualdades: limites da democracia no Brasil*. Boitempo.

Brodkin, E. Z. (2013). Commodification, inclusion or what? Workfare in everyday organizational life. In E. Z. Brodkin and G. Marston (Eds.), *Work and the Welfare State: Street-Level Organizations and Workfare Politics* (pp. 143–166). Georgetown University Press

Brodkin, E. Z. (2015). The inside story: Street-level research in the US and beyond. In P. Hupe, M. Hill, & A. Buffat (Eds.), *Understanding street-level bureaucracy* (pp. 25–42). Policy Press.

Campbell, C., & Scott, K. (2011). Retreat from Alma Ata? The WHO's report on Task Shifting to community health workers for AIDS care in poor countries. *Global Public Health, 6*(2), 125–138. https://doi.org/10.1080/17441690903334232

Das, M., Angeli, F., & van Schayck, O. C. (2020). Understanding self-construction of health among the slum dwellers of India: a culture-centred approach. *Sociology of Health & Illness, 42*(5), 1001–1023. https://doi.org/10.1111/1467-9566.13075

Dubois, V. (1999). *La vie au guichet. Relation administrative et traitement de la misère.* Economica.

Durão, A. V. R., & Menezes, C. A. F. D. (2016). Na esteira de EP Thompson: Relações sociais de gênero e o fazer-se agente comunitária de saúde no município do Rio de Janeiro. *Trabalho, Educação e Saúde, 14*(2), 355–376.

Harrits, G. S., & Møller, M. Ø. (2011). Categories and categorization: Towards a comprehensive sociological framework. *Distinktion: Scandinavian Journal of Social Theory, 12*(2), 229–247.

Hartzler, A. L., Tuzzio, L., Hsu, C., & Wagner, E. H. (2018). Roles and functions of community health workers in primary care. *The Annals of Family Medicine, 16*(3), 240–245. https://doi.org/10.1370/afm.2208

Hirata, H. (2016). O trabalho de cuidado. *Sur: revista internacional de direitos humanos, São Paulo, 13*(24), 53–64.

Krieger, M. G. M., Wenham, C., Nacif Pimenta, D., Nkya, T. E., Schall, B., Nunes, A. C., De Menezes, A., & Lotta, G. (2021). How do community health workers institutionalise: An analysis of Brazil's CHW programme. *Global Public Health.* https://doi.org/10.1080/17441692.2021.1940236

Lipsky, M. (2010). *Street-level bureaucracy: Dilemmas of the individual in public service.* Russell Sage Foundation.

Lotta, G., Wenham, C., Nunes, J., & Pimenta, D. N. (2020). Community health workers reveal COVID-19 disaster in Brazil. *The Lancet, 396*(10248), 365–366. https://doi.org/10.1016/S0140-6736(20)31521-X

Lotta, G. S., & Marques, E. C. (2020). How social networks affect policy implementation: An analysis of street-level bureaucrats' performance regarding a health policy. *Social Policy & Administration, 54*(3), 345–360. https://doi.org/10.1111/spol.12550

Lotta, G. S. L., & Pavez, T. R. (2010). Agentes de implementação: mediação, dinâmicas e estruturas relacionais. *Cadernos Gestão Pública e Cidadania, 15*(56), 109–125.

Lotta, G. S., & Pires, R. R. C. (2020). Categorizando usuários "fáceis" e "difíceis": Práticas cotidianas de implementação de políticas públicas e a produção de diferenças sociais. *Dados, 63*(4). https://doi.org/10.1590/dados.2020.63.4.219

Maes, K., Closser, S., Tesfaye, Y., Gilbert, Y., & Abesha, R. (2018). Volunteers in Ethiopia's women's development army are more deprived and distressed than their neighbors: Cross-sectional survey data from rural Ethiopia. *BMC Public Health*, 18(1), 1–11. https://doi.org/10.1186/s12889-018-5159-5

Maynard-Moody, S. W., Musheno, M., & Musheno, M. C. (2003). *Cops, teachers, counselors: Stories from the front lines of public service.* University of Michigan Press.

Milanezi, J., de Gusmão, H. N., Jardim Sousa, C., Bicalho Bertolozzi, T., Lotta, G., Fernandez, M., Corrêa, M., Vilela, E., & Ayer, C. (2020). Mulheres negras na pandemia: o caso de Agentes Comunitárias de Saúde (ACS). *Informativos Desigualdades Raciais e Covid-19*, AFRO CEBRAP, n. 5.

Ministério da Saúde (2020). Cadastro Nacional de Estabelecimentos de Saúde.

Morosini, M. V. (2010). *Educação e trabalho em disputa no SUS: a política de formação dos agentes comunitários de saúde.* EPSJV.

Morosini, M. V., & Fonseca, A. F. (2018). Community workers in primary health care in Brazil: An inventory of achievements and challenges. *Saúde Em Debate*, 42(Special Issue 1), 261–274. https://doi.org/10.1590/0103-11042018S117

Najafizada, S. A. M., Bourgeault, I. L., & Labonté, R. (2019). A gender analysis of a national community health workers program: A case study of Afghanistan. *Global Public Health*, 14(1), 23–36. https://doi.org/10.1080/174416 92.2018.1471515

Nogueira, M. L. (2017). *O processo histórico da Confederação Nacional dos Agentes Comunitários de Saúde: trabalho, educação e consciência política coletiva. Anais Seminário FNCPS: Saúde em Tempos de Retrocessos e Retirada de Direitos.* Biblioteca Digital de Teses e Dissertações.

Nunes, J. (2020). The everyday political economy of health: Community health workers and the response to the 2015 Zika outbreak in Brazil. *Review of International Political Economy*, 27(1), 146–166. https://doi.org/10.1080/09 692290.2019.1625800

Nunes, J., & Lotta, G. (2019). Discretion, power and the reproduction of inequality in health policy implementation: Practices, discursive styles and classifications of Brazil's community health workers. *Social Science & Medicine*, 242, 112551. https://doi.org/10.1016/j.socscimed.2019.112551

Olaniran, A., Smith, H., Unkels, R., Bar-Zeev, S., & van den Broek, N. (2017). Who is a community health worker?—a systematic review of definitions. *Global Health Action*, 10(1), 1272223. https://doi.org/10.1080/16549716.2 017.1272223

Perry, H. B., Zulliger, R., & Rogers, M. M. (2014). Community health workers in low-, middle-, and high-income countries: An overview of their history, recent evolution, and current effectiveness. *Annual Review of Public Health*, 35, 399–421. https://doi.org/10.1146/annurev-publhealth-032013-182354

Siblot, Y. (2006). Faire valoir ses droits au quotidien. Les services publics dans les quartiers populaires. *Lectures, les livres.* Le Press de Science Po, Paris.

Silva, J. A., & Dalmaso, A. S. W. (2002). *Agente comunitário de saúde: O ser, o saber, o fazer*. Editora FIOCRUZ.

van Ginneken, N., Lewin, S., & Berridge, V. (2010). The emergence of community health worker programmes in the late apartheid era in South Africa: An historical analysis. *Social Science & Medicine, 71*(6), 1110–1118. https://doi.org/10.1016/j.socscimed.2010.06.009

World Health Organization. (2018). *WHO guideline on health policy and system support to optimize community health worker programmes.* https://apps.who.int/iris/bitstream/handle/10665/275474/9789241550369-eng.pdf

2

Under the Radar

Stories from Government Meteorologists

KELLY A. STEVENS

The weather affects everyone, and sometimes lives and well-being depend on an accurate forecast. Meteorologists tend to bring a lot of passion to their work that helps fuel their motivation for continuously tracking and forecasting the weather to provide information to the public and decision makers alike. Yet most people do not fully understand the depth of the field and the profession. They think the field only consists of the broadcast meteorologists they see on TV or joke that meteorologists are always wrong. Meteorologists are sometimes even mistakenly blamed when the weather is not perfect for an outdoor event or when an anticipated snowstorm misses.

There are thousands of highly skilled meteorologists who work in the public sector, and yet they are one of the more poorly understood fields out there. To clear up these misconceptions, I interviewed seven government meteorologists to share their experiences working in the public sector. The meteorologists I spoke to are operational meteorologists, meaning they generate official forecasts for people to make decisions, which is a bit different from the other two career paths meteorologists may choose: broadcast meteorology or research. One meteorologist I spoke with started in broadcast, while everyone else went straight into operational meteorology from college, and most started their careers in the public sector as interns for the National Weather Service (NWS).

The National Weather Service employs more than 2,000 meteorologists, most of whom regularly analyze the weather to issue forecasts for their area or region (NWS, n.d.). The NWS falls under the National Oceanic and Atmospheric Administration (NOAA) in the US Federal Government and is part of the US Department of Commerce and thus an executive agency. Most of the meteorologists I interviewed are currently working for the NWS; however, I also spoke with meteorologists working in public agencies dedicated to emergency management, power marketing, and the armed forces.

These government meteorologists were attracted to this line of work because they consider the NWS and NOAA as the "ultimate weather authorities" and always held them in high regard. One meteorologist pointed out that "service" is even in the NWS title. Part of the NWS mission is to protect life and property, and everyone I spoke with mentioned this mission and the fact that they take it very seriously. NWS meteorologists are classified as essential public servants because their work contributes to the stability of critical functions and public safety. This chapter shares their stories of what makes their jobs essential, why they do what they do, and what they want the public and elected officials to know about their work.

What Is a Meteorologist, and What Do They Do?

According to the American Meteorological Society (AMS), a meteorologist is "an individual with specialized education who uses scientific principles to observe, understand, explain, or forecast phenomena in Earth's atmosphere and/or how the atmosphere affects Earth and life on the planet" (AMS, 2012). The AMS explains that specialized education typically includes a bachelor's or higher degree in meteorology or atmospheric science. Defining who qualifies as a meteorologist has become an interesting topic in recent times with the growth of social media and what the New York Times refers to as "armchair meteorologists" (Bogel-Burroughs & Mazzei, 2019). "Armchair meteorologists" participate in sharing their own personal weather forecasts on social media but are lacking that ever-so-important criterion: specialized education. Virtually anyone can create a website or Twitter account to share sensationalized forecasts of long-range model runs or worst-case scenarios that are unrealistic or inaccurate. These sources of false or hyped-up information add to the noise and confusion regarding what is an official forecast and who should be trusted to deliver accurate weather information. As a result, the work of a meteorologist in the public sector becomes even more difficult to do, as more time is being spent explaining to people what weather information is real and what is "clickbait" (Cappucci, 2020).

A true meteorologist has a meteorology degree that includes rigorous studies in atmospheric science, physics, mathematics, and computer science (Hill & Mulvey, 2012). Meteorologists need these supporting fields to understand dynamic and complex atmospheric processes more fully. While the field relies on sophisticated weather forecast models that use mathematical equations coupled with weather observations to generate estimates about what the weather will look like hours or days away, trained scientists are needed to interpret that information. Each model is a little different, using various combinations of equations, assumptions, and estimated observations in areas missing data (Durbin, 2018). Trained meteorologists know how to analyze and process all that information to generate a usable forecast for the public and decision makers.

One meteorologist I spoke with mentioned that the public can sometimes forget that it takes people to build and maintain these weather models, and added, "forecasts are more than just machines." She went on to explain the misconception that meteorological forecasts and even data, such as precipitation and temperature readings, are free and automatically generated by computers: "A lot of people just think that because things show up on the internet it's like they show up by magic. But there's a lot of people behind the forecast, satellites, radar maintenance, NOAA weather radio maintenance." The instruments and tools used to take these observations and generate forecasts are built, maintained, and quality controlled by meteorologists and agency scientists. Further, many of the meteorologists in the NWS provide and attend regular training opportunities to maintain and enhance their forecasting skills, as the state of the science and products is constantly changing.

This relates to another repeated theme in these interviews: Meteorologists do more than just provide forecasts for the public. The meteorologists I spoke with work for agencies, such as the NWS, that spend a lot of time cultivating key partnerships in the local and regional community so they can provide information for these communities to make informed decisions during weather events. For example, the NWS regularly provides forecast information to local airports, marinas, schools, local government, and emergency management agencies so they can plan operations accordingly. Katie Webster, the assistant director of planning for the North Carolina Division of Emergency Management, explained that one of the prominent aspects of her job is putting together a daily graphical package of forecast information from the seven NWS offices that cover North Carolina. This material is collected and packaged to create one "statewide picture" of weather information, which goes out to approximately 500 to 600 organizations daily, from daycare centers, corrections facilities, the Department of Transportation, and all the way up to the governor's office. She explained that it is important to provide an equitable understanding of risks and hazards for partners to make informed decisions on things such as closings, evacuations, and where to move resources in the event of an emergency.

Because of the importance of communicating risks and hazards to hundreds of partners with diverse needs and interests, some meteorologists spend a lot of time on education, training, and building relationships with their state and local community partners. Felecia Bowser, a warning coordination meteorologist for the NWS in Jackson, Mississippi, explained that about half of her job is spent educating partners, and the remaining half on engaging and building relationships with them. Another meteorologist explained that there are always people on social media second-guessing forecasts in a public setting, which becomes difficult to address during an active weather threat when forecasters are busier. He explained that they use clear weather days to build trust through social media outreach to be better able to move forward when bad weather strikes.

Several meteorologists explained that all the different agencies where meteorologists work are not well-known. For example, I interviewed Erik Pytlak, a meteorologist and manager of Weather and Streamflow Forecasting at the Bonneville Power Administration (BPA), which is part of the US Department of Energy. Pytlak's group helps inform the selling and distribution of electrical output from federally owned and operated hydroelectric dams in the Pacific Northwest (BPA, 2019). The group of meteorologists that he manages provides important weather and streamflow forecasts that help their agency function not only in terms of electricity sales, but also safety. The morning I spoke with him in February, they were preparing notices about a high avalanche threat in their territory due to weather conditions, which could affect BPA line workers that day. Despite the important role they play in the agency, they are often forgotten about as a "little group in a very big pond" in the power sector. However, recent events such as the Texas blackout in 2021 caused by a severe winter storm show that meteorologists and forecasting play a critical role in resiliency planning, especially as extreme weather events become more common because of global warming (Allen et al., 2016; Plumer, 2021).

Another meteorologist I spoke with currently works as a launch weather officer for the U.S. Air Force in the Space Force. She issues forecasts for rocket launches that can be scrubbed in the event of lightning, high winds, clouds, or rain, which can damage expensive equipment and affect the ability to successfully carry out a rocket launch. Not only is it important to accurately forecast the weather for launches, but they are also looking at ocean conditions and wave heights for ocean landings, which is a recent development in the field but also requires the right weather conditions to conduct.

These are just a few examples of different places meteorologists may work in the public sector. There are many NOAA agencies dedicated to weather and climate forecasting and research, such as the National Hurricane Center, Storm Prediction Center, and Climate Prediction Center. Additionally, meteorologists may work for the Department of Defense, National Aeronautics and Space Administration, and the Department of Agriculture (AMS, 2021). Their work duties may vary, but one thing they all share is an understanding that "the weather doesn't sleep."

The Weather Doesn't Sleep

Essential public servants are sometimes needed around the clock to provide the continuation of critical government functions. And, as was repeated to me multiple times throughout these interviews, "the weather doesn't sleep." For many operational meteorologists, this means shift work, including overnight hours on a rotating basis. For some, this entails coming into the office at 11:00 p.m. and leaving at 7:00 a.m. the next morning for one workweek each month. Shift work, even on a rotating basis, can place a significant toll on one's physical and mental health (Zhao et al., 2020), and most meteorologists I spoke with claimed that it becomes more difficult to do with age.

Rotating shift work can be particularly challenging for parents, requiring lots of coordination between family members and babysitters. Nonstandard work schedules can interfere with family routines and lead to "tag-team" parenting, which may affect family relationships and lead to more conflict (Zhao et al., 2020). Mothers in particular suffer even more from poor mental health due to shift work when compared with fathers (Zhao et al., 2020). Several meteorologists supported these research findings with personal reflections on working rotating shifts with young children at home. They explained that weather and emergencies do not always line up with family schedules. "Weather does not stop for school plays, or pick up times, or anything like that," stated one meteorologist. She went on to explain that the unpredictability of the weather and difficulty of not knowing when you will need to start working in the event of an emergency is one of the most challenging aspects of her job.

In addition to the challenges of shift work, extreme weather means working overtime. I spoke to meteorologists across the country who face all types of weather threats, including hurricanes, tornadoes, floods, wildfires, extreme heat or cold temperatures, ice storms, and blizzards, all of which can be deadly. "Ahead of a winter storm we're working 14- or 15-hour days," stated a meteorologist in emergency management in North Carolina.

I spoke with Danielle Manning, a lead forecaster for the NWS in New Orleans, Louisiana. The 2020 hurricane season was a record-breaking year for her office, which issued hurricane watches or warnings for eight storms. When an area is expecting significant impacts from extreme weather, such as tropical storm force winds, the local NWS forecasters begin working 12-hour shifts to provide more consistent coverage of weather developments. And overtime does not usually end until impacts subside, which could be at least 12 to 24 hours after the storm has moved on from the area. Manning explained that she worked more than 100 hours of overtime during the summer. Reflecting on the 2020 hurricane season, she said, "It gets taxing, it gets tiring, you know, the relentless onslaught." But that coverage is necessary to save life and property.

Melody Lovin, who worked for the NWS in Key West during Hurricane Irma in 2017, described her experience preparing for and riding out the storm while working. Irma made landfall as a Category 4 hurricane with 130 mph winds at Cudjoe Key, about 30 miles east of Key West (Cangialosi et al., 2018). The Federal Emergency Management Agency (FEMA) estimated that 90% of homes in the Middle and Lower Keys sustained some damage (Cangialosi et al., 2018), and 17 people in the Keys lost their lives because of the storm (Monroe County Florida, n.d.).

Lovin worked and rode out the storm from the NWS office in Key West with some of her colleagues for six days. Her family, along with 75% of residents in the Keys, evacuated beforehand. The NWS Key West Weather Forecast Office is a hurricane-resistant shelter that was completed in 2005 (NWS, n.d.b.). About 24 to 36 hours before the storm started, the office's meteorologist-in-charge, or head administrator, drove around to pick everybody up and head to the office to begin sheltering in place. Lovin continued working 8- to 12-hour shifts with her co-workers all while living at the office to take cover. Despite knowing that everyone would be sheltering in close quarters for the duration of the storm, there was an overwhelming response from her office of people willing to stay and work through Irma. As the storm approached, all of Florida watched and waited for the anticipated right turn Irma was forecasted to take, which would determine which part of the state would face the worst conditions of the storm. On September 9, Irma began its turn in the Florida Straits, strengthening slightly, and models locked in on a path that would bring Irma right through the vulnerable Keys (Cangialosi et al., 2018). Lovin describes the sickening sense of dread she felt while issuing watches and warnings for the storm: "Knowing that there were tens of thousands of people staying in the Florida Keys as Hurricane Irma was approaching was truly, like, sickening. To this day, I feel sick like looking back, waking up the morning of the storm knowing that within 24 to 48 hours people were going to die due to weather in my county-wide area, and there wasn't much I could do other than to keep screaming about how you need to get out."

Lovin and her colleagues who stayed had to sleep in offices with limited power and air conditioning. They collected rainwater for showers or to flush toilets. While reflecting on the intense physical and emotional demands of working severe and tropical weather events, Lovin and others explained that a lot of the work comes after the storm hits. There are storm damage surveys and after-the-storm reports that need to be written as soon as it is safe to do so. Meanwhile, there is little opportunity to attend to personal matters such as securing or restoring personal property before or after a storm. Lovin experienced mental burnout while continuing to work after Hurricane Irma and eventually took time off to reunite with her family who had fled to North Carolina. Lovin explains, "We're just exhausted. Public servants, especially meteorologists, we're just exhausted . . . Even if the weather continues, it's hard for us to unglue ourselves because it's always going to be someone asking for something and we have a hard time saying no." Like Lovin, the meteorologists I spoke with continue working overtime during stressful weather events because of commitments not only to their colleagues, but also the communities they live and work in.

Members of the Community

Despite the sacrifices it takes, these meteorologists, who have all had to work overtime at one point or another during an emergency event, willingly do it to protect the community they live in. Mark Fox, the meteorologist-in-charge at NWS Amarillo, TX, explains: "We're not just this faceless entity that interrupts your television programs . . . When we're putting out warnings, it's not just to put out warnings . . . We put out warnings because we want people to change their behavior in a way that may save their life."

With more than 100 NWS offices across the United States, many of the meteorologists I spoke with have moved three or more times to pursue promotion opportunities within the NWS. However, several grew up in the area they currently forecast for or have lived there for more than 10 years. No matter how long they have worked at their current office, everyone brought up the importance of the community in which they live. Several meteorologists mentioned that they feel like the public often forgets this. Manning reflected on the emotional toll of her work, saying: "After a severe weather event, especially if, you know, we got the warning out, let's say that there were injuries or fatalities with a tornado . . . even if I issued the warning, there was still a fatality, and so, I feel that. I take that home with me. I live in this community, I want to keep the people in this community safe, and it doesn't feel good when they're not."

Many government meteorologists give back to the local community in other ways by spending time in and outside the office educating others on weather and weather safety. Oftentimes, they spend time in local schools or provide tours of the office to students. While this was easier during pre-COVID-19 times, it was also one of their favorite aspects of the job. Felecia Bowser at NWS Jackson, MS, enjoys spending time with students and hopes to inspire young girls to pursue STEM fields by speaking with local schoolchildren. Like many others, she feels it is important that students see more diversity in the field.

In addition to educational visits, most operational forecasters take time working the social media desk at their office, which includes posting and responding to commenters on platforms such as Twitter and Facebook throughout the day. In a world with more information available through digital technologies that everyone has access to in a quick and continuous way, better communication strategies are constantly evolving. Strategies for more effective weather and risk communication target more interactive experiences with the public and decision makers, which might take place on social media (Morss et al., 2017).

One meteorologist explained that most of the feedback she receives at her office through social media is more positive than negative, and each meteorologist tries their best not to "feed the trolls" but to step in during teachable moments instead. They see this as a way to build trust with the public. Yet oftentimes negative comments derive from misunderstandings about who the NWS is, conflating them with private entities such as The Weather Channel, or on how to interpret uncertainty in a given forecast. And negative comments can be especially brutal when a forecast turns out to be wrong. Mark Fox explains:

> As meteorologists, we are the field goal kickers of disasters. You know, if we can make 85 field goals in a row but if we miss one at the end of the game, or when people are really needing you to make that perfect one, they forget about the 85 good ones and they remind you about the bad one. A good meteorologist, a good public servant, is going to ignore that as noise and know that for what it is.

While it is impossible to accurately predict the weather all the time, forecast accuracy using US-based weather models has been improving (Cappucci, 2021). Currently, 7-day forecasts can accurately predict the weather 80% of the time, which improves to 90% of the time for a 5-day forecast (NOAA, 2021). In addition, meteorologists are finding better ways to communicate risk and reach out to their communities. The passion and determination of meteorologists to carry out their mission to protect lives and property are driving the field forward.

The public and many government functions are affected by weather in numerous ways every day. Meteorologists in the public sector are working day and night to generate and disburse information for people and organizations to use to make decisions to protect life and safety. They regularly make sacrifices that affect their own lives and their family commitments to conduct their work. Like any other job, it can be really challenging to get 100% right all the time, but lives depend on their service. Their work is essential, but often poorly understood.

Despite being on the receiving end of many misconceptions about the field or public agencies, the meteorologists I spoke with love what they do and have few regrets about working in the public sector. They enjoy giving back to their community, even if it is not always visible to or appreciated by the public or elected officials. Every single person I spoke with is proud of the work they do to uphold the mission of the NWS to protect lives and property. Everyone also acknowledged that it is a difficult job, especially as global warming contributes to more extreme weather events. Even under this pressure, one meteorologist said one of the best aspects of his job is that there is always another turn "at bat" to do the job well and protect the local community.

References

Allen, M. R., Fernandez, S. J., Fu, J. S., & Olama, M. M. (2016). Impacts of climate change on sub-regional electricity demand and distribution in the southern United States. *Nature Energy, 1*, 16103. https://doi.org/10.1038/nenergy.2016.103

American Meteorological Society. (2012, September 20). *What is a meteorologist? A professional guideline.* https://www.ametsoc.org/index.cfm/ams/about-ams/ams-statements/professional-guideline-on-use-of-the-term-meteorologist/

American Meteorological Society. (2021). *Where do meteorologists work?* https://www.ametsoc.org/index.cfm/ams/education-careers/careers/career-guides-tools/where-do-meteorologists-work/#:~:text=U.S.%20Government&text=Other%20federal%20agencies%20such%20as,government%20agencies%20conduct%20atmospheric%20research

Bogel-Burroughs, N., & Mazzei, P. (2019, August 31). For forecasters, Hurricane Dorian has already been a handful. *New York Times.* https://www.nytimes.com/2019/08/31/us/hurricane-dorian-florida.html?

Bonneville Power Administration. (2020, October). *BPA facts.* https://www.bpa.gov/news/pubs/GeneralPublications/gi-BPA-Facts.pdf

Cangialosi, J. P., Latto, A. S., & Berg, R. (2018, June). Tropical cyclone report: Hurricane Irma. *National Hurricane Center.* https://www.nhc.noaa.gov/data/tcr/AL112017_Irma.pdf

Cappucci, M. (2021, March 22). NOAA launches major upgrade to flagship "American" weather prediction model. *The Washington Post.* https://www.washingtonpost.com/weather/2021/03/22/american-model-gfs-upgrade-noaa/

Cappucci, M. (2020, March 5). Meteorologists say they are sick of clickbait and misleading social media weather forecasts. *The Washington Post.* https://www.washingtonpost.com/weather/2020/03/05/clickbait-weather-forecasts-social-media/

Durbin, S. (2018, May 18). What are weather models, exactly, and how do they work? *The Washington Post.* https://www.washingtonpost.com/news/capital-weather-gang/wp/2018/05/18/what-exactly-are-weather-models-and-how-do-they-work/

Hill, J. D., & Mulvey, G. J. (2012) The ethics of defining a professional. *Bulletin of the American Meteorological Society, 93*(7), 1080–1082. https://doi.org/10.1175/BAMS-D-11-00205.1

Monroe County Florida. (n.d.). Hurricane Irma Recovery. https://www.monroe-county-fl.gov/726/Hurricane-Irma-Recovery

Morss, R. E., Demuth, J. L., Lazrus, H., Palen, L., Barton, C. M., Davis, C., . . . , Watts, J. (2017). Hazardous weather prediction and communication in the modern information environment. *Bulletin of the American Meteorological Society, 98*(12), 2653–2674. https://doi.org/10.1175/BAMS-D-16-0058.1

NOAA. (2021). How reliable are weather forecasts? *SciJinks: It's all about the weather!* https://scijinks.gov/forecast-reliability/#:~:text=The%20Short%20Answer%3A,90%20percent%20of%20the%20time

National Weather Service. (n.d.). Faces of the National Weather Service: Careers in meteorology. https://www.weather.gov/careers/meteorology

National Weather Service. (n.d.b.). History of the National Weather Service in Key West. https://www.weather.gov/key/history

Plumer, B. (2021, February 16). A glimpse of America's future: Climate change means trouble for power grids. *The New York Times.* https://www.nytimes.com/2021/02/16/climate/texas-power-grid-failures.html

3

Revisiting Librarians as Public Servants

ALICIA SCHATTEMAN

Librarians are not caretakers of artifacts. Librarians are not finders of things. Librarians are much more profoundly useful and powerful. Librarians are in the knowledge business. They—you—facilitate the creation of knowledge, and by doing so you improve society. Rather than building book museums, we—you and I—must build edifices of bricks and code to promote knowledge. Where once Carnegie built temples of books, we shall build workshops of the mind.

—Lankes, 2011, p. 63

Public libraries are one of this country's greatest achievements. The Library of Congress was created in 1800 when President John Adams approved a congressional act that moved the national capital from Philadelphia to Washington, DC. Then there are the state libraries, open to the public and used as archives of the state government and other official documents. The first local public library in the United States is generally accepted as being founded in 1731 by Benjamin Franklin in Philadelphia, but it was supported by paid members. Public libraries as we know them today began in 1833 in Peterborough, New Hampshire, funded by the municipality for the specific purpose of bringing a free library that was open to everyone in the community. The first free municipal library in a large community was founded in 1848 in Boston.

Columbia University opened the first American school of librarianship in 1887 under the leadership of Melvil Dewey, who had created the decimal classification in 1876 (Rockwood, 1968). The American Library Association was formed the same year on October 6, 1876, during the Centennial Exposition in Philadelphia with representatives from across the country. Today, there are more than 10,000 public libraries serving almost every community (Weigand, 2015). These institutions bring the community together and support a knowledgeable citizenry through public and open access to information.

Librarians are public servants in all ways. Public libraries are structurally units of government, either as a stand-alone government unit like a library district or a department of the government. Libraries function as public commons, an open public space that welcomes all with no barrier to entry and no paid membership requirement. Even without residency, anyone can access materials and programs. With residency, you have access to the world. Libraries gather us all together in the pursuit of learning and provide essential functions for a strong democracy and workforce, including job training, literacy, entrepreneurship, civic engagement, and much more. The purpose of this chapter is to examine the role of the librarian as a public servant, particularly how they view their work and their role in the community. The following section outlines the contribution of public librarians in service to communities historically and today.

Literature Review

Libraries were formed to bring knowledge and literacy to the entire population instead of remaining with the select few. In fact, libraries also inspired the creation of museums for the same reasons (Mattson, 2000). In 1876, Chicago Public Library Director William Frederick Poole defined public libraries as "free municipal libraries organized under state laws and supported by general taxation" (Green, 1913, p. 12). Poole also argued that if every taxpayer paid to support the public library, then every one of them should have access to those materials. But while materials were acquired and deemed acceptable, they were still judged severely by library trustees and their individual notions of social acceptability and norms.

The purpose of libraries, and subsequently museums, according to John Cotton Dana, was not to merely collect books or objects but to be of service to the community (Mattson, 2000). Dana wrote on these and other questions for the first time in 1889 as he planned for the new Denver Public Library. He was one of the preeminent thinkers during the progressive era in the United States (1896–1916), and it was argued that "Dana believed the library could facilitate and nurture the institutions of civil society" (Mattson, 2000, p. 522). Libraries functioned then and now as a great gathering place for people of all different backgrounds and incomes to quench their thirst for learning and all supported by public funds. Libraries were to support and advocate for self-improvement, to grow an informed citizenry. But libraries also provided a place to satisfy social and cultural interests, in that "public libraries encouraged self-improvement reading but acquiesced to cultural reading (popular fiction) in large part because patrons demanded it" (Wiegand, 2015, p. 38).

Beyond reading, research, and knowledge acquisition, libraries have always been used as community spaces, which means they also reflected the social norms of the day as they related to gender, class, and race. Libraries reflect, participate in, and create community. To meet growing urbanization, public libraries created branch libraries in neighborhoods and partnerships with public schools. In fact, libraries became de facto schools themselves for those who could not attend regular classes or needed extra support for their classes. Libraries may have been built for adults, but soon children came to the library with their parents, and libraries sought to first accommodate and then meet their needs as well. Libraries were also places where those traditionally left out of society could participate in community and the acquisition of knowledge, such as those who are unemployed or homeless. This level of community engagement, creating both welcoming spaces and support services, does create pressure on public library budgets and requires attention to what this means for the work of librarians.

Libraries, since their very earliest beginnings, have fought to continue their public service role and for their budgets. In these areas, not much has changed since the very beginning. In July 1893, the American Library Association adopted the motto "The best reading for the greatest number at the least cost." During the 1930s, many public libraries faced severe cuts because of the Great Depression. Chicago's Public Library had proposed to severely reduce its operating hours, but they were eventually restored because of a massive outpouring of support by Jane Addams and others (Herdman, 1943). These budget fights continued throughout the 20th into the 21st century, with library districts being created as separate government units to support the maintenance of these critical public services (Bauroth, 2015). There is also some research that suggests special districts also increase debt for local governments (Faulk & Killian, 2017). In addition, many public libraries today rely on affiliated nonprofit organizations such as library friends or foundations to supplement government funding (Schatteman & Bingle, 2015). These financial battles continue over how to resource public libraries and who has access to them. Librarians today are on the front line of these battles, advocating for the protection of these critical public spaces (Jaeger et al., 2017).

LIBRARIES AND LIBRARIANS' ROLES AND RESPONSIBILITIES

While business can solve some problems, "when it comes to the cultural, historical, political, and scientific record of a society, however, the public sector needs to play a leading role" (Palfrey, 2015, p. 231). Libraries form a "social compact" with their communities to have an open dialogue with and to serve the community, which take time and trust and require librarians to bring this compact to life in their interactions with the citizenry. Lankes (2016) argues that "the public library is the only civic organization tasked to provide direct service to citizens of all ages, all socio-economic groups, and all vocations" (p. 145). Libraries, and the librarians who work there, create a stronger, more cohesive community; a community of belonging, where everyone can improve themselves and their understanding of the world around them. Lankes (2016) suggests that libraries are the last truly civic institution. In fact, Lankes (2011) proposed that the "mission of librarians is to improve society through facilitating knowledge creation in their communities" (p. 15). Librarians share this unique and critical role, to not only serve but also strengthen communities.

LIBRARIANS AS PUBLIC SERVANTS

Libraries and the librarians who work within them uphold and defend some of our society's most sacred values such as privacy and are concerned with assaults on democratic ideals such as censorship. These public servants support digital literacy needs, defined as "the ability to use information and communication technologies to find, evaluate, create, and communicate information, requiring both cognitive and technical skills" (American Library Association, 2013, p. 2). Libraries provide necessary services year-round, and librarians react in a crisis as "second responders," a term first coined by Epstein (2017), such as during natural disasters, economic crises, and our current pandemic (Fallows, 2019), with the argument that "we are not triage, but recovery" (Epstein, 2017, September 28).

Libraries provide a safe and inviting space for people of all ages, backgrounds, and situation, including the homeless (Dowd, 2018). Just announced in March 2021, the Institute of Museum and Library Services awarded a grant for the "Libraries as Second Responders Project" to the Califa Group, a nonprofit membership group of all different types of libraries to help train library staff to work in communities impacted by COVID-19. That being said, when the list of essential workers was released across the country, many states did not define whether library workers were considered as front-line workers like other government employees such as public safety workers, teachers, and transit workers. In Illinois, librarians were not deemed essential government workers. Yet while people worked or studied from home, libraries were still being used, and staff needed to maintain or even increase services and outreach. Prior to COVID-19, many citizens recognized the importance of libraries to their lives, but during COVID, librarians stepped in to meet the digital needs of their communities. Librarians are on the front line of education, community, social capital development, and so many more aspects of public service. The purpose of this research is to examine the role of the librarian as a public servant, particularly how they view their work and their role in the community. The following sections outline the methodology and major findings.

Methodology

For this research, we interviewed library professionals from six Chicago, Illinois, suburban libraries about their roles and responsibilities (see Table 3.1 and Figure 3.1).[1] These communities represent a sample of suburban libraries, from small to larger populations. Two individuals from each library were interviewed for this research, the main or head librarian (director) and the librarian responsible for community programming and outreach. The interviews took place during February and March 2021 and lasted approximately 40 minutes each.

Table 3.1. Summary of Library Cases

Community	Library Type	Public Library Founded	County/ Counties	Population[1]
Aurora	Special District	1881	Kane, DuPage, Kendall, Will	199,927
Barrington	Special District	1926	Cook	77,000
Elgin	Special District	1894	Cook and Kane	110,849
Evanston	Municipal	1871	Cook	74,587
Oak Park	Municipal	1903	Cook	51,878
St. Charles	Special District	1906	DuPage and Kane	32,686

1. Most recent available (2019).

Source: Author-created.

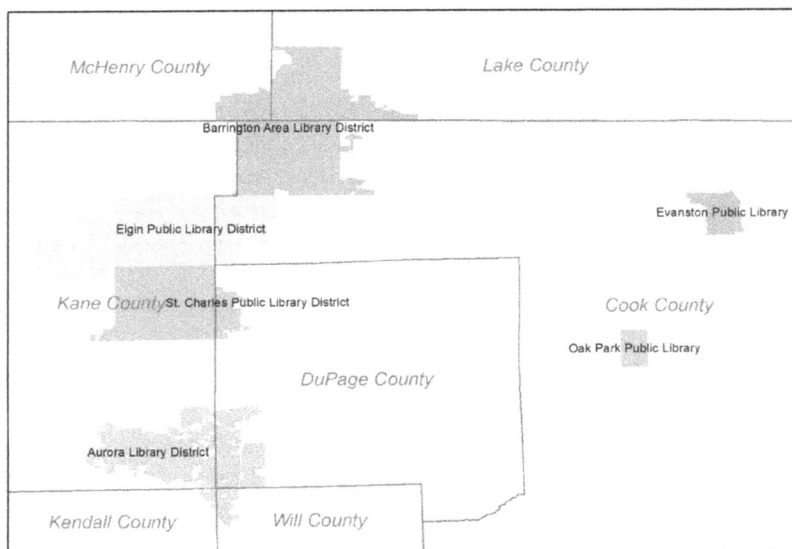

NORTHERN ILLINOIS UNIVERSITY
Center for
Governmental Studies
Outreach, Engagement, and Regional Development

Figure 3.1. Map of Library Cases. *Source*: This map was created by Sherrie Taylor, Senior Research Associate with the Center for Governmental Studies at Northern Illinois University for this project.

Results

During COVID-19, public libraries had to quickly adapt, which they have always done, to meet the needs of their community in new ways. The needs continued to grow despite libraries being physically closed. Summer programs continued. Schools moved to online, which meant some schoolchildren needed devices and internet to connect. In a time of national crisis, libraries remained critical to meeting our information needs. We interviewed local public librarians about their views on being a public servant and the challenges and opportunities in their work. We asked the librarians a set of questions about their roles and responsibilities and specifically if they used the term "public servant" to describe their work, and why or why not. We explore their responses to these questions and the themes that arose below.

AURORA

The Aurora library converted to a library district in July 2020 after a referendum. The City of Aurora levied the library rates based on property values, but as a district now, they levy a library tax directly based on what they need to operate rather than a percentage of city property valuation. The Aurora library district serves residents in four counties and is the largest library of the cases (Aurora Public Library District). We interviewed the executive director (ED) and communications manager (CM).

The ED has been with the library for 5 years and in her current position for 2 years. She does use the term "public servant" to describe what she does but "with some caveats." According to her, it is important to remember library services are paid for by taxpayers, and the term "public servant helps reinforce that." However, the library does not just wait to be "told what to do," but they "are stewards." The library has been a separate library district only since 2020. Because the transition was recent, she believes "their customers" do understand their governing structure.

The CM has been in her role for 3 years, responsible for all communications and marketing. She does not use the term "public servant" to describe what she does. She feels that the term would normally be used if they were city employees, but because they are a district, she does not feel it really applies to them. She thinks that maybe civil servant seems more familiar, but not public servant. She feels they now have more control over their budget since they converted to a district last year and are completely independent of municipal government. She believes residents probably have a better sense of how they operate because they became a district only recently. However, the library's "customers" probably do not understand their governance a great deal.

Like many units of local government, librarians seemed to agree that most residents do not understand their structure, for example, specifically how they are funded. While the Aurora librarians thought that their residents, whom they refer to as customers, might have some knowledge because of a recent referendum, the librarians did not think this was a deep understanding, but they were not really troubled by this. Instead, they agreed that as long as people were being served and had access to the resource they need, then understanding the governance structure was not as important. Aurora, along with some other libraries, has adopted a more business-like reference to customers, likely with the increasing pressures for government units to attract resources and tie many of those resources to a bottom-line, more in keeping with a business approach. Their view of public service is more about their understanding of their roles than how the residents or "customers" view them.

BARRINGTON

In 1969 and 1970, voters approved becoming a library district to serve portions of four counties across 72 square miles made up of 44,000 residents of seven communities and parts of six additional communities as well as some unincorporated areas. It is one of the geographically largest library districts in Illinois, crossing three counties (Barrington Area Public Library District 2021). We interviewed the ED and the community engagement librarian (CEL).

The ED has been with the library for 4 years but only as ED the last 2 months. She oversees all the staff and works directly with the board to manage the library. When asked if she uses the term "public servant," she agreed that she does use that term to describe her role. She admitted this comes mainly because she is paid by the public through taxes, and her first responsibility is to them. She sees one of her main responsibilities as helping her staff "be good stewards of public investment in the library." As a library district, they operate independently of the local government. She has worked in both municipal and library district public libraries and comments that the library district allows them more financial independence rather than the budget being given to the library by the municipality.

This library refers to its users as "customers," not patrons or residents. According to her, she believes her customers do understand their organizational structure. Because library district borders are not marked or always clear to those who live in the district, residents of a certain municipality may not know which library, if any, they are served by. The district is the second-largest in the state at 72 square miles. This creates confusion about who is in the district and who is not. This is not necessarily a negative or a positive. In other states, they have simplified where you can get and use a library card, such as in Ohio, where library cards can be used at any other public library in the state. This is not the case in Illinois. Each public library can join an interlibrary consortium, such as like Reaching Across Illinois Library System (RAILS) or System Wide Automated Network (SWAN), which offer interlibrary loans with participating libraries.

The CEL has been with the library for 8 years and in her current position for 4 years as the CEL. Part of her responsibilities is to support nonprofit organizations, so she also plans programs for them throughout the year. She does not use the term "public servant" to describe her profession, but she does agree that library employees are public servants. A librarian is more descriptive of what they do and easier to understand. Public servant, to her, is a broad but not incorrect term. This stems from their organizational structure and service area. There is sometimes confusion with their library district boundaries and who they serve. As a library district, they may not work as closely with municipal departments, such as the parks department or the police department, but they do have a good working relationship with the village in which they are located.

Similar to the previous case of Aurora, Barrington librarians seem to have a dual identity, first to their profession (librarians) and second as public servants, which they do not see in conflict with each other. Public servant appeared a slightly less desirable title for the work they do because they are not waiting to serve but rather are proactively trying to improve services based on professional librarian standards.

Elgin

We interviewed the community engagement manager (CEM) and chief executive officer (CEO)/ED. The ED has been in her position for 9 years. The board oversees their finances and adopt all policies for the library. They also advocate for the library. When asked if she had ever used the term public servant, she noted that "I have never heard that apply to the work of librarians." She believes it has a negative connotation because it implies that is their role, whereas she believes that libraries today align themselves more like a business, so they serve customers instead of being a "passive governmental entity." She also indicated this by referring to herself as the CEO of the library. While the library is a library district and operates independent of the municipal government, it works closely with the city government. Its structure is unique because it serves residents of five communities, not just the City of Elgin.

The CEM has been with the library for 27 years. She supervises a team of staff members who do outreach to seniors, schools, community engagement, community partnerships, special events to build awareness, and cultural events. She uses the term "public servant" in an informal sense but not in a professional sense. She finds it more of a philosophy, to serve the public, than a way to describe what she does. She considers herself a public servant in that she serves the community, but her professional identity comes from her profession as a librarian. The library in Elgin is a library district, a separate government unit from the municipality. It levies their own taxes, independent of the municipality. This district is large, 65 square miles in two counties, and encompass parts of five municipal governments. When asked if patrons understand their structure, "no one understands it." She thinks this is apparent every election season when residents from one county show up at the library to vote, because it is their library, but it is not where they vote because they live in a separate county. This challenge becomes more problematic when the library needs to go to referendum for an increase in the tax levy.

These librarians had similar reactions to the dual role of a librarian (as their profession) and a public servant (unit of government). Librarians often sit physically distant from the more common types of local government services (e.g., roads, police, parks), and residents receive their free services with only a residency requirement. Furthermore, while everyone may use roads in a community every day, not everyone uses library services. Payment for library services is also buried directly or indirectly in a property tax bill as well. Libraries in Illinois have their own elected boards, regardless of whether they are a stand-alone library district or a unit of the local government. This may also be confusing for residents to truly understand the governance and financial structure of librarians and the public services they provide.

Evanston

We interviewed the ED and engagement services manager (ESM). The ED has been with the library for 9 years. She uses the term "public servant" because it is at the core of what the library does. They are there to "respond to the needs and aspirations and curiosity of residents of all ages in ways that are helpful to them . . . it really is servant leadership that we are involved in." They operate as a municipal library, but they have a memorandum of understanding with the municipality to "reset their relationship to the city." They still cannot levy their own taxes like a district, but they operate independently from the city. The downside to their current arrangement is, in comparison with other communities of the same size, that they are "dramatically underfunded." This requires creative revenue ideas, particularly looking at earned revenue and philanthropy to grow their budget. She believes that patrons understand the library's mission, but probably not the nuances of their finances.

The ESM has been with the library 14 years and the past 2 in this position. She builds relationships across the community to further the goals of the library and meet its mission. She thinks of the term "public servant as tied to a government body," and she believes "it is our sole mission to serve the public." Evanston is responsible for levying the taxes for the library, but then they are directly deposited into the library's operating budget for its own purposes. Those funds are then overseen by the elected library board of trustees, and the ED does not report to the city manager.

These librarians expressed a stronger attachment to being public servants, possibly because they are not a stand-alone library district but a unit of local government. However, they operate under a memorandum of understanding (MOU) with the city rather than answering directly to the city manager, which makes them different from a standard local government department. As with all other libraries in Illinois, they have complete discretion with their budget once it is passed because those funds are transferred over to the library with oversight by a separately elected library board. In essence, these librarians work with two levels of elected boards and must be politically astute as well as adhere to the professional standards of their library profession.

OAK PARK

We interviewed the ED and the CEM of the library. The ED has been in his position for 8.5 years. He is responsible for all aspects of the library and works with the board of trustees to carry out those responsibilities. Their board is elected to a 4-year term. When asked if he uses the term "public servant," he noted that it is not an incorrect term, but it is "not one that I generally use." The Oak Park library is a village library, but it does not operate as a division of the municipal government. The ED does not report to the village manager, for example. He only reports to his Board of Trustees, even though it is technically a village library. Once a year the library board adopts a budget; it also must adopt a resolution so that the village will levy a tax to support the library. The library itself does not have the authority to levy the tax because it is a municipal library. Then the village includes that resolution in its levy ordinance for the village. This is governed by state law in Illinois, "for everything else that we do, we do as if we were our own unit of local government." When asked if he thought residents understood the governance structure of the library, he felt they likely did not think about it unless it impacts the services and programs.

The CEM has been with the library for 9 years but 2 years in her current role. She manages a team of individuals who focus their work on community engagement, "bringing the library outside of the library walls." They focus not only on bringing the library to residents but also on learning what the community needs and bringing that knowledge back to the library to improve their services, programs, and policies. They aim to be as responsive as possible to community needs. When asked if she used the term "public servant" to describe what she does at the library, she explained that she viewed the term as being more about one-way service delivery and she felt the library entered into partnerships with the community, that they do "not really work for but with the community." The library is part of the local government but a separate entity. It seeks alignment with the village's overall goals and meets with the village on the overall budget, "but otherwise we operate separately." This gives it a lot of autonomy to meet the needs of the community and be good stewards of the tax dollars it receives. The day-to-day management of the library is left to the library staff.

Similar to the other cases, librarians in Oak Park see themselves as professional librarians first. While public service may be what they do, it is not who they are. These librarians are stewards of the financial resources provided by the taxpayers but see their professional obligation as effectively managing those funds to support a strong community.

St. Charles

In 1978, the library went back to the voters to convert from a municipal library to a library district that would operate independently from the municipal government. The district could also expand the library boundaries to unserved neighboring communities and portions of the school district (St. Charles Public Library).

We interviewed the director and outreach services librarian (OSL). The director has been in her position for 4.5 years. She agreed that she would not use the word "public servant" to describe the library profession, but it does describe her role as a government official. So public servant describes her overall role, but librarian is more specific and is used regardless of the type of library or source of its funding. The library is a district and works closely with its municipal government partners. As a district, it receive direct support from residents through property taxes because it can separately levy taxes for the library. It has autonomy over its finances. A challenge is building strong relationships with other units of government, "to be included in conversations," which takes some extra advocacy by the library.

The OSL has been employed at this library for 6 years. He is responsible for coordinating outreach to the community, especially seniors' facilities. He agreed that he does use the term "public servant" to describe what he does, which is to provide a free service to all patrons as a public institution. The library is a library district, a separate taxing body. This structure allows the library its financial independence from the city, allowing library funding to remain more stable year after year. He noted that other municipal public libraries had to cut staffing and programming because of the large impact of COVID-19 on their municipal budgets due to reduced income from sales tax, for example.

Working within a separate library district not part of the local unit of government, these librarians felt a great deal of autonomy over their work and their library. They answered to one board and believed they had more stable funding than a municipal library. They also agreed with many other librarians in this study that their primary affiliation was to the library profession, and not specifically as a traditional public servant.

Librarians as Public Servants

There are several key themes that came up in the interviews that relate to the work of librarians as public servants.

VALUES

The librarians we interviewed certainly felt that they were public servants, because they were supported by public tax dollars and serviced the public. However, their identity as librarians was more powerful to most than their role as a public servant. Some took exception that public service was more of a one-way relationship that did not value their professional opinion about what residents need, where the librarians and the community are engaged in a partnership. Despite some differences about how the term was used, librarians had some different words for the people they serve, including patrons, residents, and customers. The public libraries in Illinois have a great deal of autonomy no matter what their legal structure is, municipal library or library district, especially when it comes to day-to-day management of the library. Because of this autonomy and the need to balance limited resources, it is possible that how they view the people they serve is also changing. Librarians do not see people as problems but as residents who need assistance with something "in need of services, support, and, yes, literacy. But ultimately in need of power. The power to support themselves and live dignified lives. The power to create and learn, not simply to survive" (Lankes, 2011, p. 80). The librarians in this study had a positive response to the word "public servant," but they did not feel it suited them well because they did so much more than wait to serve people, adhering to strong professional standards and values espoused by the library profession. The more removed they were from their local government, as a library district, for example, the weaker the connection to the term public servant.

GOVERNANCE

Public libraries in Illinois are governed by the Illinois Library System Act (75 ILCS 10/), the Illinois Local Library Act (75 ILCS 5/), the Library Incorporation Act (75 ILCS 60/), and the Public Library District Act of 1991 (75 ILCS 16/), among other statutes and administrative codes. All public libraries are subject to the Illinois Freedom of Information Act and the Open Meetings Act. The Illinois Library Association also produces materials to assist library trustees and staff with understanding relevant rules and regulations that govern Illinois public libraries. All library trustees in the state of Illinois are elected, and the board members operate under the same Freedom of Information Act and the Open Meetings Act. Regardless of whether libraries are municipal libraries or library districts, the library board is responsible for hiring and supervising the head librarian. However they see themselves, they are public servants in that they serve their communities and are supported by local tax dollars. Whether they are a district or a unit of local government, librarians must work within the confines of state rules and regulations that govern their profession.

PUBLIC COMMONS

The librarians we spoke with certainly talked about the physical spaces they occupy and how that space is used for all kinds of different purposes, from learning to entertainment to socialization to more community functions such as voting or cultural celebrations. Libraries are at the heart of communities, as "the Detroit Public Library director declared his institution a civic laboratory" (Wiegand, 2015, p. 125). With the pandemic, libraries shifted their face-to-face offerings to virtual spaces. This brought many challenges but also opportunities. Of course, the librarians are very aware of the use of publicly available, free Wi-Fi that libraries offer. Some libraries also promoted the use of outdoor Wi-Fi spots and use of the parking lot to access the library's internet. Public libraries are key community anchors contributing to an informed citizenry and offering a civic space for dialogue, debate, and learning. They are owned by the residents and exist for the residents. Public librarians bring their professional training and experience to design those physical spaces, which is always changing given the evolving technologies and physical disruptions of the pandemic to service delivery.

COVID-19

As part of the Stafford Act of 2010, the Federal Emergency Management Agency (FEMA) recognizes libraries as essential services with federal assistance and temporary relocation facilities in a disaster. Libraries can play numerous roles in disaster prevention, preparedness, response, and recovery (U.S. National Library of Medicine ND). However, during the current pandemic, librarians were forgotten or dismissed when it came to the classification as essential workers. During Phase 1B of the state of Illinois' vaccination campaign, people 65 and older; frontline workers, such as grocery store employees and teachers; and health care workers were eligible for the vaccines. The Centers for Disease Control and Prevention (CDC) did include librarians as essential workers in the July 2020 CDC report (CDC 2020). But by the December 2020 CDC Advisory Committee on Immunization Practices Interim Guidance, the CDC did not specifically include librarians in the definition of essential workers prioritized in either Phase 1b or Phase 1c of vaccine distribu-tion. Librarians and library workers provided essential services during the pandemic and worked in close contact with the general public yet were not regarded in this way for the vaccine rollout. Because they were not included in state classifications, they can be designated essential by County Health Departments, which some counties have done, but this is not universal. Without being included in priority vaccine rollout, library doors and any in-person services remained closed. This was especially problematic, as many schools closed during the pandemic. Therefore, assistance and internet access through the libraries also stopped. The Illinois Library Association advocated for the inclusion of library staff as essential workers in the vaccine rollout. Without being able to physi-cally open the doors, libraries turned to virtual engagement and outdoor offerings such as outdoor hotspots (Jones 2021).

The purpose of this chapter was to examine the role of librarians as public servants, particularly how they view their work and their role in the community. There are certain limitations that we must acknowl-edge. The responses represent the experiences of librarians in six public libraries in suburban Chicago, Illinois. They are illustrative of experi-ences of public libraries but are not representative of all public libraries in Illinois or elsewhere. They do, however, reinforce the importance of our public libraries to our lives and society.

Since the early 1800s, public libraries have served communities large and small across the country. They are one of the few places and spaces where community members can gather at no cost to access information on any topic they choose. Librarians are trained to not only acquire and organize collections but also to provide programs for residents of all ages in spaces that are conducive to connecting and learning. They also seek to uphold the highest ethical standards and have complex governing structures for maximum oversight by elected officials. This complexity, while it can increase transparency, may also be elusive to the average resident. As public libraries take on roles far beyond their historical mission of lending books, extending to all genres of information, literacy classes, information technology services, services to persons with all types of disabilities, community outreach, and even social service provision, librarians are at the forefront of our democracy. They provide the connectivity for individuals who enter their buildings or those who never enter a physical space. They do all of this in a quiet, unassuming way, strongly identifying with the library profession and accepting the role of public servant in a fitting way for librarians, humbly and with pride.

Note

1. I would like to acknowledge my undergraduate student, Riley McCabe, who conducted the interviews.

References

American Library Association. (2013). ALA Task Force releases digital literacy recommendations. http://www.ala.org/news/press-releases/2013/06/ala-task-force-releases-digital-literacy-recommendations

Aurora Public Library District. (2021). History. https://aurorapubliclibrary.org/history-3428.

Barrington Area Public Library District. (2021). About us. https://www.balibrary.org/about-us.

Bauroth, N. (2015). Hide in plain sight: The uneven proliferation of special districts across the United States by size and function. *Public Administration Quarterly*, 39(2): 295–324. https://www.jstor.org/stable/24772856

Centers for Disease Control and Prevention. (2020). AIPC interim guidance. https://www.cdc.gov/vaccines/covid-19/categories-essential-workers.html

Centers for Disease Control and Prevention. (2020). AIPC Work Group report. https://www.cdc.gov/vaccines/acip/meetings/downloads/slides-2020-07/COVID-07-Mbaeyi-508.pdf

Dowd, R. (2018). *The Librarian's guide to homelessness*. The American Library Association.

Epstein, S. (2017). We are the second responders. *Public Libraries Online*. News and Opinion. http://publiclibrariesonline.org/2017/09/we-are-the-second-responders/.

Fallows, D. (2019, May 23). When libraries are "second responders." *The Atlantic*. https://www.theatlantic.com/notes/2019/05/when-libraries-are-second-responders/590098/.

Faulk, D., and Killian, L. (2017). Special districts and local government debt: An analysis of "old northwest territory" states. *Public Budgeting & Finance*, 37(1): 112–134. https://doi.org/10.1111/pbaf.12122

Green, S. (1913). *The public library movement in the United States 1853–1893*. Boston Book Company.

Herdman, M. M. (1943). The public library in depression. *The Library Quarterly*, 13, 310–34. https://www.jstor.org/stable/4303148

Illinois Libraries. (1923). *Library anniversaries.* Illinois Library Extension Division, 5(4): 61–62.

Jaeger, P., Zerhusen, E., Gorham, U., Hill, R., & Taylor, N. (2017). Waking up to advocacy in a new political reality for libraries. *The Library Quarterly, 87*(4): 350–368. https://doi.org/10.1086/693492

Jones, A. (2021, February 27). Blount County Public Library installs first two outdoor Wi-Fi tables, plans for more. *The Daily Times.* https://www.the dailytimes.com/news/blount-county-public-library-installs-first-two-outdoor-wi-fi-tables-plans-for-more/article_5bcc4d43-0f44-5c8a-96a9-1dcd5f7a6914.html?fbclid=IwAR20vWQBJGj-Bj6T9I6TxRdjcOOkVOzcugcigqF0gmtq UGHEkAyEwvtSYGY#utm_campaign=blox&utm_source=facebook&utm_medium=social.

Lankes, R. D. (2016). *The new librarianship field guide.* The MIT Press.

Lankes, R. D. (2011). *The atlas of new librarianship.* The MIT Press.

Mattson, K. (2000). The librarian as secular minister to democracy: The life and ideas of John Cotton Dana. *Libraries and Culture, 35*(4): 514–534. https://www.jstor.org/stable/25548869

Palfrey, J. (2015). *Biblio Tech: Why libraries matter more than ever in the age of Google.* Basic Books.

Rockwood, R. (1968). Melvil Dewey and librarianship. *The Journal of Library History, 3*(4): 329–341. https://www.jstor.org/stable/25540127

Schatteman, A., and Bingle, B. (2015). Philanthropy supporting government: An analysis of local library funding. *Journal of Public and Nonprofit Affairs, 1*(2): 74–86. https://doi.org/10.20899/jpna.1.2.74-86

St. Charles Public Library. (2021). History of the library. https://www.scpld.org/history-library.

U.S. National Library of Medicine. (n.d.). The path to being recognized as essential services. https://www.nlm.nih.gov/dis_courses/seat_at_table/02-000.html

Wiegand, W. (2015). *Part of our lives: A people's history of the American public library.* Oxford University Press.

4

Teachers and Their Monitors

Negotiating Disciplinary Regimes in Pakistan

Moiz Abdul Majid and Sameen A. Mohsin Ali

The Punjab School Education Department (SED) is housed in a two-story, whitewashed building. Set back a little from the main road, the building is accessed through a wide alleyway between two other department buildings. To the right of this alley, there is a verandah stacked with broken chairs, uninstalled from some government office years ago and stored haphazardly until they might be needed again. At 8:30 a.m. on any given weekday morning, the broken, dusty, faded plastic seats are occupied by teachers. They have traveled from across the province in the hope of meeting with their department's administrative staff at the secretariat in Lahore to get their desired transfer or their problems and complaints resolved. By noon, the line of waiting teachers has not shifted much—the officer in charge of their posting has been in meetings all morning or is late getting into work. Many will need to make the trip again the next day or a few days later, bearing the costs of transport, an overnight stay, meals, and, of course, more time away from their duties.

Administrative officers inside the SED building are well aware of the teachers waiting outside, some of whom arrive as early as 6:30 a.m. However, there is little sympathy for teaching staff among the department's administrators. Teachers are regarded as "troublemakers," political actors relying on patronage and liable to take strike action when their demands are not met. In contrast, bureaucrats appointed to the secretariat in Lahore portray themselves as neutral arbiters of quality education, safeguarding the interests of students and maintaining an impersonal and clean operation by keeping teachers in line. This can make administrative staff cruel in their handling of teachers, even those with genuine concerns and complaints, driving a wedge between employees of the same department. For instance, a secretary's response to a widowed teacher seeking a transfer to be closer to her family was "There are a lot of widows."

Such cruelty is rooted, to some degree, in the New Public Management (NPM) approach. NPM seeks "to replace traditional rule-based, authority-driven processes with market-based, competition-driven tactics'" (Kettl, 2005, p. 3). It epitomizes the principles of decentralization, competition, discipline, performance monitoring, and incentivization in organizational governance (Dunleavy et al., 2005; Guerning, 2001; Hood, 1999; Lapsley, 2009; Manning, 2001; Pollitt, 1995; Soss et al., 2011). The idea is to set up standards of performance management that give employees regular goals; failure to meet these goals would result in penalization (Pires, 2011; Soss, Fording, & Schram, 2011). By devolving decision-making and sanctioning, NPM reformers argue for greater sensitivity and responsiveness to local needs. The aim is to institute an organizational structure that catalyzes service delivery by setting up channels of accountability based on employee performance evaluation, creating corrective mechanisms when and where needed (Marra, 2018). However, Soss, Fording, and Schram (2011) note that these reforms have simultaneously led to greater monitoring of "the *use* of discretion" and of performance. Though performance management is not usually considered through a disciplinary lens, Soss, Fording, and Schram (2011, p. 1205) use Foucault (1980) to argue that "the disciplinary power of the NPM shapes consciousness and behavior in ways that are deep and far reaching yet also fractured, inconsistent, and incomplete." As such, disciplinary performance management mechanisms are replicated not only in the relations frontline bureaucrats have with their colleagues, superiors, and juniors, but also with clients or citizens (Soss, Fording, & Schram 2011).

While Brodkin (2007; 2011), Moynihan (2008), and Radin (2006) outline the complexity of bureaucratic performance, Moynihan (2006; 2008) argues that, despite the pressure to perform, managerial staff on the frontline does not have the authority to bring about substantive change and is unable to challenge entrenched norms within which officials operate. Therefore, to meet performance targets, officials serve in silence while fudging the numbers and focusing on client groups that are easier to manage (Soss, Fording, & Schram 2011, p. 1209–10). In this chapter, we focus on experiences of this nature among frontline bureaucrats—teachers—in Punjab, Pakistan, with monitoring and disciplinary regimes put into place through NPM-influenced reform policies.

Drawing on semi-structured interviews with embedded street-level bureaucrats and their monitors and superiors, we show that monitoring and disciplinary regimes result in teachers experiencing states of fear as pressure mounts to meet unreasonable performance targets. These states of fear are experienced particularly by women—in addition to being constantly monitored and disciplined at work and by a patriarchal society, they are also subjected to harassment in the workplace. Serving in silence in the absence of secure avenues for formal complaint, teachers develop discretionary strategies to adapt to disciplinary regimes. As embedded bureaucrats, they use their knowledge of their communities to ensure targets are met while also engaging in extralegal or illegal behavior to avoid penalties under the monitoring regime. However, such discretion serves not as a means of including teachers in policy making but a way for teachers to protect themselves from the punitive action and administrative overreach enabled by monitoring regimes. The narrative evidence we present in this chapter shows that monitoring and disciplinary regimes sideline the needs, experiences, and insights of frontline or street-level bureaucrats and offer few incentives for teachers to perform. Consequently, imbalance results between the administrative staff and street-level bureaucrats in the department, increasing levels of stress among departmental employees and, arguably, resulting in civil servants "entering a new and disquieting phase of vulnerability" (Hays & Sowa, 2006).

This chapter proceeds as follows: After detailing our method, we briefly provide context for this chapter's discussion of the impact of monitoring and disciplinary regimes on frontline workers. We note the importance of public service employment in Pakistan, introduce the department that is the focus of this chapter, the Punjab School Education Department (SED), and the reform initiative that led to the adoption of an NPM model in the department, the Punjab Education Sector Reform Program and Roadmap. Drawing on narrative accounts of the implementation of the monitoring and disciplinary regime put in place by the reform program to improve educational outcomes, we center the frontline bureaucrat—the teacher—in this account of education reform. We recount the processes by which monitoring took place and detail teachers' accounts of their struggles and discretionary strategies to meet performance targets and handle the demands of monitoring staff. We discuss, in particular, reports of harassment of women teachers at the hands of monitoring staff and the strategies they developed to ward off unwelcome advances in the absence of robust reporting mechanisms. We conclude by reflecting on the nature of discretionary power that street-level bureaucrats hold and the impact of their exclusion from policy-making processes.

Methods

The data for this chapter were collected in two parts. The first set of interviews were conducted in 2014–2015 and the second set in 2019. Both phases included in-depth, semi-structured interviews and semi-participant observation in the offices of the Punjab School Education Department in Lahore and in other surrounding districts, and in schools in Lahore.

In the first round of interviews, the focus was on respondents who were serving in administrative posts in the department, most of whom had started out as teachers and risen through the ranks. The questions were phrased to elicit respondents' personal experiences on a set of analytic themes, including politicization of appointments, the implementation of reform, the exercise of political pressure, prior experiences with seeking transfers, and accounts of serving in the field. Responses from each interview were manually transcribed and entered into a standard coding matrix developed based on a thorough review of the literature to identify recurrent themes, and observations from each interview were recorded alongside as memos.

In the second round of interviews, the focus was on frontline bureaucrats—teachers and monitoring and evaluation assistants (MEAs)—to give voice to experiences rarely centered in policy conversations in low- and middle-income countries. Interview questions revolved around the themes of working in schools and experiences with the new monitoring regime: a) history of service, b) nature and process of work, c) issues faced during work, d) how issues at work were dealt with and resolved, and e) feelings associated with work. Respondents were encouraged to discuss their daily routine and the emotional/psychological states brought about by challenges in the workplace. As such, the conversation evolved organically through narration of respondents' experiences with little need for prompts. However, most respondents were hesitant or uncomfortable with their interviews being recorded because of the fear of being reprimanded for speaking about the education system. As a result, notes were taken during the interviews and later manually coded based on the categories above to develop memos. At times, when the head teacher was not available, it was possible to interview teachers separately. But in some cases, interviews took place in a group setting—the head teacher would invite a group of teachers to participate in the interview in their office and would be present throughout the conversation. Though this presented obvious constraints in terms of what the teachers could say, the narrative nature of the interview allowed more open expression, particularly regarding experiences with monitoring staff.

Our interviews range across Punjab education bureaucracy's hierarchy: from generalist additional and deputy secretaries serving in Lahore to frontline staff such as teachers and monitors. While we approached administrative staff in the secretariat and in nearby districts, and teachers serving in schools in Lahore directly, monitors were approached through the District Monitoring Office (DMO) because they were only accessible if the superior officer granted permission. Interviews were carried out in offices or schools. In approaching teachers, schools were selected in the suburbs of Lahore and identified using the database provided by the Punjab School Census. The rationale behind this was that while the status of Lahore as the provincial capital means stronger monitoring and enforcement, the peripheries of the city are sometimes overlooked and have weaker mechanisms at work.

Public Service in Pakistan

Public service is the most stable form of employment available to citizens in Pakistan and, according to Mosharraf Zaidi of *Alif Ailaan*, a DFID/FCDO funded campaign to improve education provision in Pakistan,[1] "one of the biggest instruments of social mobility in the country." A government job, even at the lowest rung of the administrative ladder, brings with it job security and a guaranteed pension. Dismissals from service are rare; bureaucrats who fail to perform are asked to retire early. When cases of corruption or other forms of wrongdoing are filed, the investigation process takes years, and more years are added on by taking the matter to court. The result is that public service is guaranteed and much coveted employment in a country with a population of more than 207 million, according to the 2017 census, and where the unemployment rate in 2020, according to the World Bank (2020), is 4.65% (Pakistan Bureau of Statistics, n.d).

Unsurprisingly, Pakistan's bureaucracy is prone to politicization (Ali, 2020) and rife with petty corruption. Competition for public sector jobs is intense, particularly as the government's wage bill grows and hiring declines; and bribes, falsified documents, and political pressure to appoint specific people to available posts are all rampant (Bari et al., 2013, pp. 93, 99). In the offices of politicians holding public office—for example, speaker of the assembly—every constituency visit results in a stack of small paper slips with names and posts handwritten on them being brought into the office to be typed up and collated by the politician's staff. The list is then sent to a contact in the relevant department so that the names can be added to the recruitment list. Departmental staff, such as clerks, are complicit in these practices, helping to distribute jobs to those favored by influential politicians or bureaucrats by approving "*jaali*" (fake) documents and merit lists, and aiding these politicized appointees in absenteeism.

Politicized illegal appointments make the inequalities within the public sector starkly visible. A former teacher who had been promoted to an administrative role said, "Those who have access to files, those who can give money to get the jobs that they want—they get the [good] postings. Officials want to oblige these people." In a number of cases, senior district bureaucrats recount that politicians demand to see teacher transfer lists so they can be checked and approved (Ali, 2018). Of course, administrative staff in the department are aware of these practices—the former teacher admitted that the "department does acknowledge services, acknowledges honesty . . . admits that *ziadti* (injustice) was done, even at the Secretary level." But the department is unable to provide the support to reverse the injustice, even when there are serious consequences in delaying promotions and refusing transfer requests, especially for women teachers.

Teachers in the Pakistani Public Imagination

Teaching is typically disregarded as a serious profession in Pakistan. Administrative staff serving in the Punjab School Education Department, for example, often have a low opinion of teaching staff. Teaching is regarded as part-time work and as inferior to medicine or engineering, for example. It is also a profession often associated with women. A posting as a teacher is regarded as a means of giving young women something to do until they are married off. As one retired teacher put it, "[People] say, this girl is roaming free, have her appointed as a teacher." As a result, teaching staff are not regarded as being necessarily interested in, or committed to, teaching and learning.

At the same time, teachers are regarded as being political representatives because of their embeddedness in their local communities (Pepinsky, Pierskalla, & Sacks 2017). Most teaching staff prefer to be appointed to schools in or near their home district, and disputes, court cases, and disciplinary procedures over transfers to schools closer to their homes are commonplace. The consequence is that they are subjected to persistent pressure from local communities to grant favors. These could range from appointing a relative as a security guard at the school to giving them the contract for building the school boundary wall or establishing a school canteen. These practices are sufficiently common for the impression to take hold that teachers in the public school system lack incentives for improving the quality of education available to students because they are benefiting from corrupt practices. Teachers themselves see their position as inherently unstable, caught between their department's administrative staff and community influencers. As such, they seek to cement their position and gain as much advantage (financial or otherwise) as they can from their position.

The Punjab Education Sector Reform Program

The Punjab Education Sector Reform Program (PESRP) started in 2004. Its objectives were to improve "(a) participation and completion; (b) quality; and (c) leadership, management, and accountability" in the education sector, with a particular focus on assessment and data collection (Project Appraisal Document, 2016, pp. 8–9). These goals were in line with the emphasis on improving service provision by the provincial ruling party between 2008 and 2018, the Pakistan Muslim League–Nawaz (PML-N) with the chief minister of Punjab at the time, Shahbaz Sharif, taking a personal interest in the reform program. As a result, the program received a considerable amount of dedicated attention from senior officials in the province. The result was an improvement in teacher and student attendance rates even in districts that had historically performed inadequately on these indicators (Barber, 2013).

One of the key drivers of this reform program was reducing large-scale political appointments of teachers. In Punjab's School Education Department, the volume of postings and transfers is immense. A 2015 estimate by Mosharraf Zaidi of *Alif Ailaan* was that the Punjab School Education Department had 350,000 employees, while the deputy secretary of elementary education in 2015 quoted a figure of 450,000 employees. The Punjab School Education Department hires, manages, and monitors all these teachers and head teachers across Punjab's 36 districts. Though curriculum development has remained centralized at the provincial and federal levels, devolution under the 18th Amendment to the 1973 Constitution led to the setting up of District Education Authorities. Each of Punjab's 36 authorities was headed by an executive district officer (EDO), a department employee promoted through the teaching ranks, and a team of officers and monitors to collect data and report on student and teacher attendance and performance, upkeep of infrastructure, and manage district transfers.

The PESRP began by targeting the recruitment, transfer, and performance monitoring of teaching staff at the district level. On recruitment, the public display of applicant merit lists was a small transparency innovation to allow for any fudging of scores to be caught by the applicants themselves. Transfers were blocked for the duration of the academic year, with requests being entertained only during the summer vacation, barring exceptional cases. But by far the most elaborate reforms were to the monitoring and enforcement mechanisms of the department with the setting up of an entire hierarchy to check the attendance and performance of teachers in schools across the province. As the School Education Department rolled out this new monitoring system, the divide between the department's administrative staff and its frontline workers—that is, teaching staff—became starkly visible. Administrative staff firmly believed (or behaved as if they did) that their reforms were justified and would produce lasting results, even though they had not at any point considered teachers' experiences or opinions in the design of the new monitoring regime. As a result, teachers found themselves having to conform to new practices and expectations that placed them in high-pressure situations with the expectation to perform or face penalties.

The Process of Monitoring

In a school in Jallo, a village now subsumed as a suburb of the city of Lahore, the office of the head teacher was a small, chilly, and dimly lit room with whitewashed walls and a cement floor. The head teacher sat behind a large wooden desk with a few documents scattered across the surface. A middle-aged man with graying hair, dressed in a crisp shalwar kameez (a traditional dress combining pants and flowing shirt or tunic), the head teacher was answering questions when his mobile phone rang. At first, he ignored it, trying to focus on the questions he was being asked. But the phone kept ringing, again and again, as someone was clearly desperate to reach him. Finally he answered the phone. It was a head teacher from another school, a woman, asking for help. She had been away from the school to handle some personal issues when the monitoring and evaluation assistant (MEA) decided to make a surprise visit. Therefore, she was marked as absent by the MEA in their report to the department. She would now have to pay a fine, and the only way to avoid doing so would be to have the MEA change their recorded observation of her absence. Her panicked calls to the Jallo head teacher revealed her fear and stress, her search for any way out of having a black mark on her record and having to pay the fine.

The system of monitoring has a simple structure. Each school is visited by an MEA once a month. The MEAs are recruited from a pool of retired armed forces employees and are given a motorbike and petrol allowance by the government. The former is a significant detail: The military is a widely respected institution in Pakistan, perceived as being the only disciplined, meritorious, and fair organization in the country. An MEA justified the hiring of retired military personnel as monitors by saying, "Military people are not corrupt but extremely disciplined, they take intense care in the monitoring process and hence produce good results." This perception of efficiency and incorruptibility was corroborated by a head teacher who defended MEAs by saying, "They are very good people and are just doing their duty."

An MEA is randomly assigned two union councils (the smallest administrative unit in Pakistan with a population of between 25,000 and 35,000 people) and can choose to visit the schools in them in any order and at any time in the month, including surprise visits. Schools must meet certain targets that the SED has set, targets for which the MEA collects data. During the visit, the MEA fills out a form on a government-provided tablet, and the data about a particular school are synced with the department database and updated in real time. Failure to meet these targets, as a teacher explained, leads to "disciplinary hearings at the district education officer (DEO) office, which always leads to fines and, some cases, even the blocking of our pay increments."

Schools are also visited by an assistant education officer (AEO) two to three times a month. AEOs are typically teachers who are elevated to a monitoring post in a particular district. Their main responsibility is to not only monitor schools' progress on the indicators that the MEA checks, but also help teachers in terms of pedagogy and any other complaints that they might have with the system. Last, the schools also self-report data through the School Information System (SIS). These self-reported data form the base of the annual school census that is published online by the Policy Management and Implementation Unit (PMIU). All data are collected on dedicated Android applications that were developed specifically for these purposes. For monitoring staff, the introduction of technology means that the "system is foolproof," as per one district monitoring officer—there is little critical reflection on data collection processes.

There are two broad issues with the new monitoring system that this chapter addresses. The first is the pressure on teaching staff to meet targets set arbitrarily with little consideration for context or circumstance. The second is an exploration of the new distribution of power engendered by the monitoring regime and, consequently, a teacher's place in the department under monitoring and disciplinary regimes commonly adopted by those following NPM policies.

Meeting Targets

On a cold, gloomy winter morning in December, students were sitting for their exams, spread out inside their classrooms and outside in the hallways of their school, located in the suburbs of Lahore. The school was a large, whitewashed compound surrounded by uncarpeted, muddy roads in a predominantly working-class neighborhood. Seated in a bare and cold staffroom, a member of the Punjab Teachers' Union explained: "The targets for schools are not set after consulting teachers within schools. They are not representative of ground realities and contexts and that is why teachers, no matter how much they work, cannot meet them."

Other public-school teachers had also pointed out that they were constantly working on meeting targets that the department had set without consulting them. Two types of targets were set: one for student enrolment and teacher attendance at 90%, and the other financial in terms of school expenditures.

School finances can be divided into two broad types. The first are contractual agreements for the provision of school equipment or services (e.g., furniture or canteens). These are the responsibility of the head teacher and an area where there is immense interference by local officials, particularly politicians seeking to distribute contracts to their supporters, including via bribery, intimidation, and threats of violence. The second are funds made available to schools by the department. Here, teachers find themselves caught in a vicious cycle because money is always tight because of the irregular release of funds by the department. As a result, funds for investments in school infrastructure (e.g., furniture, boundary walls, paint, repairs) and salaries for a guard or a caretaker for the premises are hard to come by. But when monitoring teams visit the school, they are required to check and report on the condition of school buildings. As a result of the lack or irregularity of available funds, teachers find themselves facing penalties under the disciplinary regime for circumstances beyond their control.

Enrollment and attendance targets set at 90% are a key area of concern for teachers because of how unrealistic these targets are. This is especially true because student attendance in Punjab is, according to the Multiple Indicator Cluster Survey (MICS) 2017–2018, only 65% for primary school, with just 66% completing primary school (Punjab Bureau of Statistics Punjab, 2018). At times, these unreasonable targets have prevented district executive education officers from being able to recruit teachers for administrative posts such as that of an AEO (Ali, 2018, p. 200).

Ensuring Attendance

The emphasis on student attendance numbers has meant that enrolling children in school and ensuring their attendance has become part of the teaching staff's job. This means that they must contend with the dynamics of parental responsibility and family structure in their community. In the winter, children skip school because it is too cold for them to attend, and at other times, a teacher explained: "We try getting children from their homes but the rural context plays a part in keeping children away. The *biradari* system is used [as an excuse by parents] to explain many absences. Children have to skip school if anyone in the *biraderi* [kin group] is going through things like marriage or death, etc." Whatever the reason, teachers are not typically able to change parents' minds on sending their children to school; parents may not think the quality of education or facilities (particularly toilets and boundary walls in schools for girls) is sufficient to pull the child away from household tasks or a paying job.

Teachers argue that it should not be their responsibility to get students to school; it is the parents who must be the ones to ensure that the child attends. A representative from the Punjab Teachers' Union reiterated this point: "The job description of a teacher inside the school and classroom boundary is that of a person who helps groom you, finish the syllabus, and helps you think." Nonetheless, the new monitoring system led to a significant shift in expectations of teachers with no concomitant change in compensation.

Teacher attendance is itself a source of great anxiety and stress for teachers. The fear of a surprise visit from a monitor makes teachers afraid to take leave in cases of emergency. As one teacher said, "If you want to get married, you must ask the MEA first." As a result, the concept of "*dabao*" or pressure came up repeatedly. By using this term, teachers emphasize the extreme stress they are under as they try to meet set targets against various odds. One teacher said: "There is a lot of *dabao* (pressure) on primary school [staff] from the government. Because of this, teachers aren't focusing on teaching but are focusing on things like attendance which are not under their control."

As teachers felt their work boiling down to dealing with administrative hurdles alone, the work became increasingly draining and demoralizing. A primary school teacher commented, "Being the head teacher of a primary school is a headache, they have turned the head teacher into a clerk." Not only do teachers feel disempowered and undervalued, but a poor rating for a school or a complaint about a teacher by an MEA can have serious consequences. Teachers can have their yearly increments blocked, they can be transferred to a different district, or might have a show cause notice on their record and be called in to explain to their superiors why they failed to meet set targets. Officials higher up in the bureaucracy believed that these punishments were justified as action taken against teachers who were not meeting targets—an SED official said, "Teachers get punishments according to the crime. You can take away increments and maybe even remove them [from their post]."

The punitive process begins with a letter from the DEO asking the head teacher to present themselves to explain their failure to meet a target. A head teacher said that these hearings are such that "We aren't allowed to speak or defend ourselves and are sent away with a punishment." The punishment, in the case of this particular head teacher, was fines that she had to pay. In other cases, teachers' yearly increments have been blocked because their students failed to meet a certain percentage score on their final exams. A teacher lamented, "They block our increments for things that are totally out of our control."

Though there were consequences for not meeting attendance and financial targets, there was little incentive offered to meet them. Therefore, for teachers, there is much to lose and little to gain from the monitoring regime. A teacher's union representative, seated in a classroom with bare walls and uncomfortable wooden chairs while his students sat unsupervised in the next room, said, "The teacher has the lowest incentive to perform in the whole system, and you have the greatest level of restrictions and punishments leveled at the teachers."

This was corroborated by a high-ranking official at the SED; clad in a crisp ivory shalwar kameez and gray waistcoat, his desk covered with a green baize cloth and stacks of files, he said, "Why should we give the teacher an incentive for doing their duty? We [already] do give them a best teacher award."

The only incentive teachers have, therefore, is that they get to maintain the normal trajectory of their career in financial terms if they meet targets. In fact, the PESRP focused little on teacher motivation or support and did little to recognize that teachers' dealings with their department's administrative hierarchy and the pressures and indignities of the job will often result in a loss of whatever motivation they may have entered public service with.

The Exercise of Discretion

The fear of punitive action meant that even when teachers fundamentally disagreed with set targets, they nonetheless did everything they could to meet them, using what discretion was available to them (see Henderson & Pandey, 2013; Lipsky, 1980; Riccucci, 2005). In this instance at least, discretion is less an exercise of power and autonomy and more a means of self-preservation and protection from punitive measures.

The key decision-making space available to teachers as street-level bureaucrats was that, though the SED had set student attendance targets, it had not specified strategies for bringing students to school. This meant that teachers had considerable discretion in what methods they used to ensure attendance. The simplest and most often used tactic was the phone call. Teachers would call parents constantly until they brought their children to school or "got annoyed and turned off their phones," a teacher explained. The next step in enforcing student attendance was to send the school watchman or caretaker to the neighborhood to get the children. In a school in Jallo, Lahore, a teacher would go door to door to get the children to come to school, typically on their own route to work in the morning. The final step used to meet attendance targets was to hire a pick and drop service for the students. This was done by only one school surveyed for this study, and they funded it with school funds. All in all, teachers innovated in an area where policy was silent to meet set targets.

In some circumstances, teachers also opted for illegal means to meet targets. One teacher revealed that they used their connections with people appointed to examination centers to be allowed in to help their students cheat. By helping students on their examinations, the teacher could ensure that enough students passed to meet departmental targets, and they would get their increments. Teachers would also bribe MEAs, often with food. A few teachers mentioned that food was "the path to an MEA's heart." If teachers treated the MEA right, they might be lenient and allow teachers to game the system by not recording absences or lapses. Such bribery was particularly evident during the Literacy and Numeracy Drive (LND) tests that MEAs carried out in schools. MEAs were supposed to pick three children at random at a school for this test. If a teacher had been nice to the MEA and had offered them food, the MEA would allow the teacher to choose these students. Teachers would choose the highest-achieving students in the class for this test, thus skewing their scores and allowing the teacher to safeguard their increments and meet targets.

However, corrupt behavior was not the exclusive domain of the teachers—MEAs too had considerable discretion as frontline monitors. Some MEAs sold life insurance policies on the side, and if teachers agreed to buy them, the MEA would be more lenient with them. Teachers were aware that such behavior was a breach of codes of conduct, but with few options to safely report such practices, they were forced into playing along.

Harassment

Aside from punitive repercussions, the monitoring process itself can be traumatizing for teachers. The most consistent reason for this is harassment by MEAs. Women make up a significant number of teaching staff in Pakistan (Bari et al., 2013, p. 46); teaching is regarded as a suitable profession for young girls because it does not require a 9-to-5 office commitment, and the department makes various accommodations for women teachers (e.g., a wedlock policy that allows a husband and wife to be transferred together and posted nearby, maternity leave, special consideration for women seeking a transfer, and so on).

However, women teachers are often in a precarious position in male-dominated environments, particularly in the context of monitoring and evaluation. Bari et al. (2013, p. 132) note that "teachers have raised concerns about the monitoring staff being badgering and intrusive." Among our respondents, female teachers spoke with resignation about the behavior of MEAs, saying that "MEAs can be overly familiar" and "[MEAs] look at us as if they have never seen a woman before." Well aware that complaints about such harassment would result in MEAs exacting revenge, teachers must bear with an uncomfortable and potentially unsafe work environment. One teacher explained, "The MEA comes to school at a time when there is no one else on the premises [but me]. He is extremely strict, criticizing us over the smallest things."

The power dynamic created by the monitoring regime is particularly pertinent when it comes to cases of harassment or other complaints. The new monitoring hierarchy makes teachers subordinate to less-qualified monitors. The MEA is a functionary or even an enforcer, with no teaching qualifications and little knowledge of the field in which they are conducting checks. As the teacher's union representative put it, "The MEA knows nothing about education. The teacher has a master's or PhD while the MEA is a high school graduate."

In addition to the MEA's higher rank and considerable power over teachers, it is particularly important to understand the imbalance of power between retired armed forces MEAs and civilian teachers. As retired military men, MEAs have significant influence through armed forces' networks and can exert pressure on teaching staff not only in their role as monitors but also through their connections among retired and serving officers in other places. Therefore, teachers are always at a disadvantage in dealings with their monitors.

Reporting harassment is also difficult in a male-dominated environment. The PMIU noted that complaints could be registered anonymously or through a male superior so as to maintain the teacher's anonymity. Teachers noted that they did sometimes complain to AEOs, who were sympathetic and took the case forward. However, teachers themselves did not feel that they could approach the administrative staff in the department with these complaints because "They will not do anything [to help] and [all that will happen is that] the MEAs will then make our lives difficult." This is not surprising—male staff, particularly monitors, can be dismissive of women's work in teaching positions and regard complainants as troublemakers. In one instance, the DMO office was full of men discussing a specific woman teacher. One MEA there commented, "She doesn't work at school, but she does work on herself." Effectively, then, the MEA is a position of power, and abuse of that power is easily exercised on junior staff, particularly women, damaging their reputation and creating an unwelcoming work environment.

Conclusion

On October 30, 2019, the secretary of education of Punjab approved a new School Improvement Framework (SIF) through an official notification. It stated that the current system of imposing fines on teaching staff to discipline them would be abolished immediately and would be replaced by a new system that would emphasize cooperation and incentivizing teachers to improve performance. The recognition of the importance of incentivizing performance among street-level bureaucrats is heartening and signals a shift away from punitive and harsh monitoring and disciplinary regimes. Nonetheless, this change in policy does not alter the exclusion of frontline bureaucrats from decision-making processes, nor does it counter the contempt many in senior posts have for bureaucrats they consider to be too embedded in their local communities, or the power managerial and monitoring staff have over their careers. Policies continue to be adopted and targets set without consultation with frontline staff, and reform of program deliverables are achieved on the backs of teachers living in a constant state of fear and anxiety.

Certainly, the disconnect between street-level bureaucrats and departmental managers opens the door for the exercise of considerable discretion—legal, extra-legal, and illegal—by the former, as Lipsky (1980) described. While this discretion can be empowering for some embedded bureaucrats—emerging from an in-depth understanding of communities and the lived reality of reform programs and policies—it is important to acknowledge that many frontline workers' exercise of discretion is a means of clawing back decision-making space and protection for themselves from the vagaries of transfers, unreasonable targets, withholding of increments, and harassment. In many cases, because no assured avenues for complaint or redressal exist, and teachers fear reprisals, they will continue to serve and suffer in silence.

Note

1. More information on the campaign, which ran from 2013 to 2018, is available here: https://www.dai.com/our-work/projects/pakistan-transforming-education-pakistan-tep

References

Ali, S. A. M. (2018). Staffing the state: The politicisation of bureaucratic appointments in Pakistan. Unpublished PhD dissertation, SOAS University of London. https://doi.org/10.25501/SOAS.00026180

Ali, S. A. M. (2020). Party patronage and merit-based bureaucratic reform in Pakistan. *Commonwealth and Comparative Politics*, 58(2), 184–201. https://doi.org/10.1080/14662043.2020.1743161

Barber, M. (2013, March). The good news from Pakistan. Reform Research Trust. https://www.google.com/url?sa=t&rct=j&q=&esrc=s&source=web&cd=&ved=2ahUKEwjCroKqy9_0AhWeoXIEHWmsCnUQFnoECAMQAQ&url=https%3A%2F%2Fkatelyndonnelly.com%2Fs%2FThe-good-news-from-Pakistan.pdf&usg=AOvVaw1n59mIHWJNNWI7rKSPZ7ex

Bari, F., Raza, R., Aslam, M., Khan, B., & Maqsood, N. (2013). *An investigation into teacher recruitment and retention in Punjab*. IDEAS–Institute of Development and Economic Alternatives. https://ideaspak.org/wp-content/files_mf/1538462005TeacherRecruitmentandRetention.pdf

Brodkin, E. Z. (2007). Bureaucracy redux: Management reformism and the welfare state. *Journal of Public Administration Research and Theory, 17*, 1–17. https://doi.org/10.1093/jopart/muj019

Brodkin, E. Z. (2011). Policy work: Street-level organizations under new managerialism. *Journal of Public Administration Research and Theory, 21*(Suppl 2), i253–i277. https://doi.org/10.1093/jopart/muq093

Dodge, J., Ospina, S. M., & Foldy, E. G. (2005). Integrating rigor and relevance in public administration scholarship: The contribution of narrative inquiry. *Public Administration Review, 65*(3), 286–300. https://doi.org/10.1111/j.1540-6210.2005.00454.x

Dunleavy, P. (2005). New public management is dead—Long live digital-era governance. *Journal of Public Administration Research and Theory, 16*(3), 467–494. https://doi.org/10.1093/jopart/mui057

Foucault, M. (1980). Power and strategies. In C. Gordon (Ed.), *Power/Knowledge—Selected interviews and other writings, 1972–1977* (pp. 134–145). Harvester Press.

Gruening, G. (2001). Origin and theoretical basis of new public management. *International Public Management Journal, 4*(1), 1–25. https://doi.org/10.1016/S1096-7494(01)00041-1

Habib, M. 2010. The contract reform policy's impact on teacher absenteeism: Perceptions of teachers and principles in Lahore, Pakistan. PhD dissertation, George Washington University.

Hays, S. W., and Sowa, J. E. (2006). A broader look at the "accountability" movement: Some grim realities in state civil service systems. *Review of Public Personnel Administration, 26*(2), 102–117. https://doi.org/10.1177/0734371X06287462

Henderson, A. C., & Pandey, S. K. (2013). Leadership in street-level bureaucracy: An exploratory study of supervisor-worker interactions in emergency medical services. *International Review of Public Administration, 18*(1), 7–23. https://doi.org/10.1080/12294659.2013.10805237

Hood, C. (1995). The "new public management" in the 1980s: Variations on a theme. *Accounting, Organizations and Society, 20* (2–3), 93–109. https://doi.org/10.1016/0361-3682(93)E0001-W

Kettl, D. F. (2005). The global public management revolution: A report on the transformation of governance. Brookings Institution.

Lapsley, I. (2009). New public management: The cruelest invention of the human spirit? *Abacus, 45*(1), 1–21. https://doi.org/10.1111/j.1467-6281.2009.00275.x

Lipsky, M. 1980. Street-level bureaucracy: Dilemmas of the individual in public services. Russell Sage Foundation.

Manning, N. (2001). The legacy of the new public management in developing countries. *International Review of Administrative Sciences, 67*(2), 297–312. https://doi.org/10.1177/0020852301672009

Marra, M. (2018). The ambiguities of performance-based governance reforms in Italy: Reviving the fortunes of evaluation and performance measurement. *Evaluation and Program Planning, 69*, 173–182. https://doi.org/10.1016/j.evalprogplan.2017.02.006

Moynihan, D. P. (2006). Managing for results in state government: Evaluating a decade of reform. *Public Administration Review, 66*(1), 77–89. https://doi.org/10.1111/j.1540-6210.2006.00557.x

Moynihan, D. P. (2008). The dynamics of performance management: Constructing information and reform. Georgetown University Press.

Pakistan Bureau of Statistics. (n.d.). Population census. https://www.pbs.gov.pk/content/population-census

Pepinsky, T. B., Pierskalla, J. H., & Sacks, A. (2017) Bureaucracy and service delivery. *Annual Review of Political Science, 20*(1), 249–268. https://doi.org/10.1146/annurev-polisci-051215-022705

Pollitt, C. (1995). Justification by works or by faith? *Evaluation, 1*(2), 133–154. https://doi.org/10.1177/13563890950010020

Punjab Bureau of Statistics, Planning & Development Board, Government of the Punjab. (2018, November). Punjab survey findings report—Multiple indicator cluster survey 2017–2018. https://microdata.worldbank.org/index.php/catalog/3559/related-materials

Pires, R. R. (2010). Beyond the fear of discretion: Flexibility, performance, and accountability in the management of regulatory bureaucracies. *Regulation & Governance, 5*(1), 43–69. https://doi.org/10.1111/j.1748-5991.2010.01083.x

Radin, B. A. (2006). *Challenging the performance movement: Accountability, complexity, and democratic values.* Georgetown University Press.

Riccucci, N. M. (2005). *How management matters: Street-level bureaucrats and welfare reform.* Georgetown University Press.

Scott, J. C. (1998). *Seeing like a state: How certain schemes to improve the human condition have failed.* Yale University Press.

Soss, J., Fording, R., & Schram, S. F. (2011). The organization of discipline: From performance management to perversity and punishment. *Journal of Public Administration Research and Theory, 21*(Suppl 2), I203–I232. https://doi.org/10.1093/jopart/muq095

World Bank. (2016). *Project appraisal document.* World Bank Group.

World Bank. (2020). *Unemployment, total (% of total labor force) (modeled ILO estimate) Pakistan | Data.* World Bank Data. https://data.worldbank.org/indicator/SL.UEM.TOTL.ZS?locations=PK

Section 2

Life and Death Pressure

The importance of public servants' street-level roles is apparent from the preceding chapters. Examining the work of health care workers, educators, librarians, and meteorologists, the chapters illuminated how public servants balance multiple roles and how those roles are often overlooked despite their presence in the everyday life of the public. The second section of this volume extends this conversation of important and often unrecognized frontline roles to examine roles that are equally common but also characterized by outcomes that have potentially significant life-or-death consequences for service recipients or the public (Maynard-Moody & Musheno, 2003).

Public and nonprofit services rely on the decision-making capabilities of frontline workers, which may take place in challenging, uncertain, and time-bound contexts (Lipsky, 1980). The everyday tasks of those in public safety, emergency management, and related public functions are profoundly consequential, and this work necessarily requires significant knowledge of rules, procedures, unique characteristics of situations, and the myriad outcomes that may result from specific types of action or inaction (Henderson, 2013). Though the public may view the work as extraordinary or heroic, street-level bureaucrats in these professions may view these as somewhat routine because of their experience.

The chapters in this section touch on several types of professions or interactions in which the role of street-level bureaucrats is especially critical, potentially with life-or-death results emerging from individual decision-making and action. In chapter 5, Stephanie Dolamore and Geoffrey Whitebread examine American Sign Language (ASL) interpreters as frontline personnel in emergency situations. As visible and public-facing figures, these individuals become a critical bridge between public institutions and the deaf community. This chapter sheds light on interpreters' choices to assume these roles, their work during crises, and prosocial rule-breaking behaviors intended to protect the deaf community in challenging circumstances. Sean McCandless, in chapter 6, examines the critical and often overlooked job of air traffic controllers. The public relies on these personnel to maintain order in a complex and pressure-filled environment, often without spending a significant amount of time actively considering the work itself. This chapter contributes to our understanding of these positions by discussing cases in which air traffic controllers' actions contributed to a life-or-death outcome, their core tasks, the physical spaces they inhabit, the stressors that characterize the job, and future challenges for these positions and public service generally. Finally, in chapter 7, Kyle Overly details the roles and responsibilities of emergency managers, key officials who ensure that frameworks for disaster and crises response are in place and manage complex interorganizational responses to these incidents, often outside the public eye.

Together, these chapters highlight the complex and high-stakes nature of street-level work, where the interaction of situations, rule enactment, culture, and discretionary decisions may mean the difference between life and death for service recipients and may shape quality of life in significant ways.

Our Reflections on Life-and-Death Pressures in Public Service

Staci: *I have always loved old cemeteries. I am not sure why. There is something interesting to me about the history, the landscape, the stories. During a conference, I dragged all my fellow co-editors into the cemetery across the street from our meeting building. Okay, I admit I made them come with me several times. We learned so much by reading headstones, Googling people buried beneath. The slave section of the cemetery really stood out for what was missing—any explanation of the people buried there. Social equity issues emerge even in death.*

One day, I decided to take this interest and turn it into a research project. I began studying public servants directly involved with death management. I learned so much about cemetery operations, the complexity of running these public spaces. I then transitioned into studying medical examiners and coroners, finding out how and why they do what they do. Why do some people choose to surround themselves with death each day? These are questions we do not often think about when it comes to understanding the breadth and depth of public service.

While I have not directly been in a life-and-death position as a public servant, it is easy to recognize the importance of these roles in our daily lives. We usually notice when something goes wrong—a building collapse, another mass shooting, a plane crash, a weather event, a fire, a car crash, a workplace accident. The list of risk is nearly endless. Indeed, the chapter later in this book about wildlife photography might not seem to draw on risk, but they are dealing with wild animals, with predators. I really love the chapter here about American Sign Language interpreters, as people might ignore or even make fun of these critical public servants because they are not thinking about their neighbors who need this language to get lifesaving information. What I hope the chapters in this section do is show readers how much risk public servants take when carrying out their everyday jobs, with the goal of keeping us all safe.

Alex: Frontline public service roles are, without a doubt, consequential, and the chapters in this section illustrate this nicely. The work that street-level personnel engage in on a day-to-day basis has a profound and lasting impact on direct service recipients, their families, on communities, and on the public servants themselves. Much of my professional and volunteer work prior to my academic career was in fire and emergency medical services, and my research, teaching, and service activities are still firmly situated in these areas. Life-and-death situations and decision-making are very much a part of those functions, which made these several chapters even more engaging for me.

An important takeaway here comes via the same mechanisms outlined elsewhere in this volume—generating a more robust understanding of and appreciation for specific street-level functions though specific and focused attention. We may see and acknowledge the presence of an American Sign Language interpreter at an emergency press conference, but we may not fully grasp the importance of those individuals in communicating life-and-death information for a person who is part of the D/deaf community. That information and resulting decision-making may literally save a life or may significantly impact quality of life decisions that come in response to a disaster or crisis. We rely on the work of air traffic controllers and emergency managers to create conditions that allow us to move through our local communities and around the world safely, often without giving significant attention to their roles. Their work may be physically or temporally removed from the everyday experiences of the public, but it's tremendously important work.

While many may not be attentive to these jobs or make take them for granted (unless there is a focal emergency or incident that draws our attention back to their work), the work is always there. The situations, the people, the decisions, and the pressures exist every day whether or not we appreciate or witness them—and street-level workers experience those stresses and burdens of the work on a day-to-day basis. Much has been written about coping mechanisms in street-level work, and more recently about emotional labor in different types of frontline professions. There's more work to be done here focusing on how organizations support employees as they engage in these challenging roles, including employee assistance programs, peer support mechanisms, and job design that can ameliorate some of these issues. These several chapters help us to humanize those roles a bit, to appreciate their work more deeply as a step forward in this process.

References

Henderson, A. C. (2013). Examining policy implementation in health care: Rule abidance and deviation in emergency medical services. *Public Administration Review*, 73(6), 799–809. https://doi.org/10.1111/puar.12146

Lipsky, M. (1980). *Street-level bureaucracy: Dilemmas of the individual in public services*. Russell Sage Foundation.

Maynard-Moody, S., & Musheno, M. (2003). *Cops, teachers, counselors: Stories from the front-lines of public service*. The University of Michigan Press.

5

(In)visible and (Mis)understood

The Public Service Work of American Sign Language (ASL) Interpreters during Emergencies

Stephanie Dolamore and Geoffrey Whitebread

For as long as humans have desired to communicate, we have used our bodies and signed languages to exchange ideas. There is a long and rich history of people using signs to communicate, including hunter-gatherers using hand signals, and, in the geographic region of North America, there are Native American communities that have used signs to communicate for centuries (Armstrong, 2011). More recently, American Sign Language (ASL) was studied in the 1960s by linguist Dr. William Stokoe and validated as a language by documenting its origins, phonology, and parameters (Maher, 1996; Stokoe, 2005). Sadly, the United States does not have any accurate estimates for the number of people who use ASL because the US Census focuses on spoken languages and does not collect data on ASL or those who consider themselves culturally Deaf.

Defining or describing people with disabilities overall, or a specific subpopulation within the community, requires unpacking the different models used for disabilities (Racino, 2014). The dominant narrative is the medical model in which disability(ies) is derived from "disease, trauma, or health condition that impairs or disrupts physiological or cognitive functioning" (Drum et al., 2009, p. 28). As a testament to the dominance of this pathological perspective of disability, there are estimates of the number of individuals who experience hearing loss in the United States.[1] Nearly one in eight individuals over the age of 12 has hearing loss in both ears, and nearly one in five individuals over the age of 12 has hearing loss in one ear (Hearing Health Foundation, 2018). However, these official numbers do not reveal the whole story. Many people who are D/deaf break away from a pathological model of hearing loss and embrace a culturally centered model of Deafness. Unlike the medical model, the social model of disability emphasizes the deficits in society, or inaccessible barriers created by social environments, rather than conceptualizing the problem as a deficit with the individual (Drum et al., 2009; Racino, 2014). For some people who are Deaf,[2] ASL is their native and primary language learned through signing parents. For others, ASL is learned later in life either through socialization or instruction (Mitchell et al., 2006).

While the United States does not have a positive reputation for promoting ASL for the D/deaf community (Glickman & Hall, 2018; Hall, 2017), there are laws that protect the civil rights of people who are D/deaf. These laws include the Rehabilitation Act of 1973, the Americans with Disabilities Act of 1990, and the Individuals with Disabilities Education Act of 1990 (previously the Education for All Handicapped Children Act of 1975). These laws protect the rights of D/deaf people to have effective communication access in government, public, or private commercial settings, which can include ASL interpreters but also Communication Access Realtime Translation (CART), assistive listening devices, or other auxiliary aids or services (National Association of the Deaf, 2021b, 2021a). For this chapter, we limit our exploration to the role of ASL interpreters for the D/deaf community.

For a person who is D/deaf and an ASL user to have effective, real-time access to communication with a hearing individual who does not know ASL, communication is supported by an ASL interpreter. These professionals can be either hearing or Deaf, certified or not certified, and licensed or not licensed depending on the geographic location of the work and the content of the interpretation job. Hearing interpreters operate much like a telephone; they can intake spoken language and interpret the communicated ideas into ASL for the D/deaf person and vice versa. The interpreter also relays subtleties of the communication including speaker tone, inflection, and other contextual information that helps people more fully understand the meaning of the conversation. Deaf interpreters operate with a team of hearing interpreters but enhance the interpretation using their native understanding and fluency of ASL. Deaf interpreters reduce the English-centered nature of many hearing interpreters, thereby reducing the cognitive strain on D/deaf individuals, as well as making the content more accessible to those not fluent in English. In this sense, using Deaf interpreters is comparable to viewing photos in high resolution. The clarity and depth provided by Deaf interpreters is exceptional.

The profession of ASL interpreting has evolved and closely follows the documentation of ASL linguistics (Roy & Napier, 2015). Interpretation work occurs in two broad categories: community interpreting and platform interpreting. Community interpreting involves doctor appointments, court hearings, job interviews, school meetings, and other interactions people encounter outside the home. Platform interpreting involves individuals interpreting for a group such as concerts or press conferences. While the Americans with Disabilities Act defines the requirements of and for ASL interpreters, ensuring access to qualified ASL interpreters remains elusive. For example, in 2020, the National Association for the Deaf litigated and won a lawsuit to ensure ASL interpreters were provided at White House Press Briefings related to COVID-19 (National Association of the Deaf, 2020). In 2021, the General Assembly in the state of Maryland is considering legislation to regulate the licensure and quality of ASL interpreters in their state (Maryland General Assembly, 2021a, 2021b).

We assert that ASL interpreters, especially those who operate in highly visible roles supporting government operations, are unrecognized public servants. In many respects, ASL interpreters occupy a frontline role, which research identifies as occupying "a fundamental role" in emergency responses (Henderson, 2012, p. 217). During 2020 and continuing into 2021, at the time of writing this chapter, ASL interpreters supporting COVID-19 press conferences are very literally the visual representation of the government-citizen encounter. In their role, dually providing service and connecting people to information, ASL interpreters also influence the affective experiences of government in the Deaf community consistent with the work of all public servants as asserted by Guy (2019). ASL interpreters advance the public interest and are actively involved in the challenges of public administration such as "social equity concerns, intersectionality of public problems . . . and quandaries about how to ensure representativeness" (Guy & Ely, 2018, p. 493). In this chapter, we explore the stories provided to us by ASL interpreters who serve in public-facing roles. We learned about their origin stories, or how they came to be public servants, and how they adapt to the public nature of their work. Using narration, we recount their stories to illuminate their work as crucial public servants working among us.

Interview Methodology

As highly visible but also largely misunderstood public servants, our investigation into public-facing ASL interpreters was qualitative and exploratory to understand how they came to provide public interpreting and how they perceive the public service value associated with their work. We sought to answer the following research questions: (1) How do ASL interpreters join the public service? (2) How do ASL interpreters adapt to their public-facing role when perceived as an agent of the state?

To answer these questions, we designed a purposeful sample across three categories: (1) ASL interpreters who support a public official in highly visible and publicly facing roles (such as during press conferences for a state governor); (2) diverse geographic representation from all 50 states and the District of Columbia; (3) intentional inclusion of Deaf, Hard of Hearing, hearing, and Child of Deaf Adult(s) (CODA) interpreters. Our research process first began by developing and submitting our research protocol to the Gallaudet University Institutional Review Board, which ruled our project as approved under expedited review on November 13, 2020. We then made a list of all possible interpreters using the most comparable set of experiences possible; this included interpreters who provided support to the 50 state governors and the mayor of Washington, DC, for the first messages about COVID-19 in the early months of 2020. To identify participants, we used internet searches of state websites, YouTube channels, and official state or local government Facebook pages. When direct contact information was available, we reached out to the ASL interpreter directly. When that information was not publicly available, we contacted the chief communications officer or used webform submissions to request the contact information for ASL interpretation teams.

Efforts to contact interpreters in all 50 states generated positive leads from 20 states. All non-responsive states were contacted one additional time to request participation. From the 20 positive leads, we conducted 19 interviews with ASL interpreters who lived in 15 different states. To ensure a diverse geographic representation in our findings, we completed two interviews for each of the eight regions of the United States using the classifications outlined by the US Bureau of Economic Analysis (BEA, 2019).[3] Interviews were conducted in ASL or English, depending on the communication preference of the research participant. Interviews were coded manually using an inductive coding process, and each interview was coded by both members of the research team. This purposeful sampling method is an appropriate technique to use when a ready sample is not available or would be impossible to achieve (Creswell & Poth, 2017; Miles et al., 2013; Yin, 2015), but there are limitations to our findings specifically in the generalizability due to both the sampling procedure and exploratory nature of our work. Nonetheless, the diversity and breadth of the information shared by participants, as well as observations that resonate across our interviews and our lived experiences working with the Deaf community, sufficiently validate our methodology. Further, we analyzed our observations for convergence and found saturation in our interviews with recurring themes appearing regularly in our conversations. We acknowledge the limitations of our work, but also the unique con-tributions these stories bring to an inclusive conceptualization of public servants and the communities they serve. As pointed out by Zavattaro, "there is a beauty in asking someone why and how" they do their work in public service (2020, p. 96).

In the following section, we present three illustrative examples of ASL interpreters from our study. These stories provide qualitative descrip-tions of our central observations from the interviews using narration to present the findings. Each story was crafted intentionally, drawing on quotes and trends across all 19 interviews. These examples are provided as first-person narratives to allow the reader to "meet" these interpreters and learn their stories in a way that is similar to how we as researchers met these individuals. We also have written these examples in the first person to allow the reader to try to see different situations through the perspective of three public-facing interpreters and to help the reader understand how these different individuals interact with the world.

The structure of the narratives is also intentionally comparable. Recall that we set out to address two research questions: (1) How do ASL interpreters join the public service? (2) How do ASL interpreters adapt to their public-facing role when perceived as an agent of the state? Our interview protocol asked each participant about their background, how they define public service, and how they engage with the community. We structured these narratives to purposefully address these three areas, and in the same order, for coherence and comparison. However, because we also used a semi-structured approach to the interviews, the organization of these stories does not mean this is the order the information was conveyed in the interviews. In presenting our illustrative examples, we assigned titles to each story to highlight how the ASL interpreters adapted to their public roles.

Illustrative Narrative 1: Valuing Public Needs

Hi! Thank you for the question about my background. So, I am a Deaf Child of Deaf Adults (CODA). Also, I grew up as a visible figure in the Deaf community. I was a star athlete in my Deaf school and went on to participate in the international Deaf Olympics. My parents were very active members of the Deaf community. Like many of my Deaf friends, my family was more liberal. I'm still very active in the community. I cherish this community. They're my friends, my family, my colleagues, and even my clients.

Growing up, my family valued education and had the resources and knowledge to get me into good programs. As a result, I'm what you might call a "true bilingual." I have native proficiency in both written English and American Sign Language. In my job, I am a Deaf interpreter. This means that I provide native-level fluency in my ASL interpretation. This is important to help many who are not bilingual in my community have full access to the "hearing world." I frequently work with Deaf people who have less knowledge about English or low language access. I'm frequently called into jobs where I can provide more accessibility than a hearing interpreter, although these jobs are rarely in front of large public audiences.

When COVID hit, my job changed dramatically. Suddenly I was getting calls from public officials in my state—mayors and the governor—to interpret their press conferences. Remember, early on these press conferences were happening daily. It was tiring, but I'm thankful I had a lot of support. My governor—a Republican—made it known to his team early on that I was a FULL member of the press conference team. He would come out and address me by name for each press conference and thank me for being there. This relationship with him made it easier to advocate for the changes that needed to be made to increase accessibility: I needed to be standing next to the governor; I needed to share the screen with the governor, and not be relegated to a small box in the corner of the television screen that is hard to see; I needed people to understand why captions aren't accessible to everyone. The governor's team made it happen. Deaf people across my state had full access to life-or-death information.

I'm the ASL interpreter on the TV for nearly every press conference. I'm doing my best to interpret for an invisible audience that I can't see. I choose a register that I think fits most people in my community, although I get lots of feedback on social media to help me improve. Sometimes I can follow the governor's speaking fairly closely. Other times, the English just isn't compatible with ASL. So I summarize his comments in a logical way for a visual language. The key is to communicate the central message. Over time, I also notice that my relationship with the community has changed. People started coming to me for information as a "trusted source." How bad is it? How do I get a mask? Is it safe to get groceries? Sometimes they thought I worked for the governor!

Six months into the pandemic the situation changed. The governor quarantined as a result of exposure to COVID. But in general, the urgency of the situation was diminishing. The press conferences went from daily to weekly. Eventually, the governor's office farmed out the responsibility of planning press conferences to the Department of Public Health. And that is when they stopped booking interpreters.

Illustrative Narrative 2:
Balancing Public Needs with Established Norms

Oh, hello! Nice to meet you. I am happy to share my background with you. I grew up on the coast but now I live in the mountains. Funny how that happened, huh? When I took ASL in college I selected it because I thought it would be an easy class. I never went and, surprise, I failed it. I had to take it again and since I was actually going to class, I found out that I really liked ASL. I think I fell in love with ASL and I just decided I wanted to be an ASL interpreter after that. There were no Deaf culture or interpreting classes where I went to college. That wasn't even a thing until later. So when I finished my ASL classes one to four, I was talking with a friend of mine who is a teacher and she said, "You should think about becoming an interpreter!" I didn't even know that was a thing. I looked into it, and there were only six programs in the whole country for it. So, I moved here to attend college and never left.

I have only ever worked here, and I really enjoy it. I have at times traveled for conferences and things like that, but this is my primary market. I did get my master's degree out of state, but that was all done online, and now I teach at the interpreting program at the community college. Most of my work is teaching at the community college right now, but I still do interpreting work on the side. The reason I got connected with you is because of my involvement doing interpreting for public emergencies. I work with the state agency to support access during emergencies such as hurricanes, chemical spills, or wildfires. Anything that is an emergency, this state agency supports the statewide response, and they like to have ASL interpreters at press conferences. I have done a lot of those public press conferences. It is totally different than private interpreting. You have to think about the community that is getting this information all the time. When I am interpreting in these settings, it is a life-or-death situation. I am serving the public because I provide immediate access to important information in an equitable way. The Deaf community does not have to worry about reading the captions or trying to figure out where the transcript for the event is, they can just watch the news and get the information they need.

The work I have done with the state has changed since COVID-19 became a real issue. Before 2020, there may be a handful of emergencies a year. But with COVID-19, we were having weekly press briefings. I am proud to be supporting the community, but I also have a lot of fear. I am constantly worried about backlash from the community if I sign something wrong or if I make a mistake. Social media can be really cruel, so I just stay off of it right now. So, for me, this work has equal parts of pride and fear. I am responsible to the community and I want them to be satisfied with my work. It has also been a struggle for the hearing community to understand why we need ASL interpreters and since I am on the TV, I now have friends and family asking me about the Deaf community. Like, why can't they just read the captions? I have to explain how that process works and how it is not equal access as required under the ADA.

But the most interesting part for me has been how I navigate running into Deaf people, like at the store or something. If they missed the press conference but they know I interpreted for the governor, they might ask me what happened today at the press conference? Oh, that is tricky. I know in other situations I would not be able to say anything. You know, if I was at a doctor's office for an interpreting job and someone saw me leaving, I would not be allowed to say what I was doing or what happened. But these press briefings are so important. I feel like I am walking around with golden information about safety and public health. If someone asked me in the store what happened, I tell them. I feel like I would be remiss to not continue giving that information to someone. Of course, I also tell them where to go to get more information, but I will definitely share with them what happened.

Illustrative Narrative 3: Adhering to Established Norms

Hi! That is a good question about my background. So, I've worked as an ASL interpreter for 20 years. It is interesting to think about how I got started doing this work because I don't think I ever thought about becoming an ASL interpreter until I went back to college as an adult. I was a single mom and trying to figure out a job that would give me the flexibility to take my kids to school while also being able to pay the bills. I took two ASL classes and then one of my teachers said I should think about interpreting. I didn't know a thing about it, but the community college had a program, so I enrolled.

I could take classes part-time and still take care of my kids. When I graduated, I was able to get a contract job, which allowed me to make my own hours. I guess, twenty years later, it has worked out! Haha.

I have done nearly every kind of interpreting there is to do. I started out actually as a special education teacher at a school for Deaf children and I did interpreting part-time on the side. Eventually, when I finished my degree, I switched to doing interpreting full-time. I have done community-based interpreting for almost twenty years, including medical and mental health interpreting. I also really enjoy doing interpreting for Deaf artists such as plays or other performance arts. I don't enjoy interpreting in the court so I have not done a lot of that work. I have worked on cruise ships, before COVID of course, and for shows in Las Vegas. That is fun work!

I am certified through Registry of Interpreters for the Deaf and the state licensure board. I do regular training every year to maintain my certification and licensure. I am very familiar with the Code of Professional Conduct. I think the CPC is one of the most important documents we have as interpreters. We need to always be aware of the rules that govern our work and our actions as interpreters. Historically, the role of interpreters has been tenuous. For a time, interpreters were oppressive and told people where to sit, for example. Later, interpreters were like robots who just repeated everything and never really looked Deaf people in the eyes. I think now it is about being professional. I fundamentally see my role during an interpreting job to be a telephone between a hearing person and a Deaf person. I am not there to add anything, like to mediate or to explain. If the Deaf person does not understand, they need to ask questions and I will communicate that. If the hearing person does not understand a response, they need to ask for clarification. My job is to provide the connection and allow them to have a relationship. I guess I am kind of like a tool, I am just there to make it happen. How I feel or what I think does not really matter. If I observe something, like a doctor berating a Deaf person, I am not ethically allowed to say anything. I will report that to my supervisor later, but I cannot do anything about that in the moment.

Our role in the community is important. We provide access to communication that allows Deaf people to have interactions with doctors, churches, theaters, or community services. That's just a few examples. We support births and funerals. We support positive things and sad things that happen, so we are seen as important in the Deaf community. But I can't cry in a situation just because I am empathizing with someone. I might know their history and I might know all about them, but I need to be professional. I must be a professional because they need to trust me as a neutral person in those situations. You don't think about a telephone when you get bad news, right? You just talk on the phone. That's how I need to be. There, but don't look at me, I'm not really there. It is interesting though since we have started doing more work with press conferences for COVID how many more people in the Deaf community ask questions in public. Like, do I understand this correctly? I find that tricky because I am technically bound to confidentiality even though it was a public event. Once I leave a press conference, I need to forget all about it. If I run into a Deaf person at the store later, I always direct them to the website where the information is. Maybe that is not what they are looking for but I can't break the rules.

Making Sense of the Stories

The illustrative examples are rich with details about who the interpreters are and how they completed their work during 2020. In the following section, we analyze findings from our interviews by comparing and contrasting the illustrative examples. First, we explore similarities and differences in the origin stories for the ASL interpreters. Following this, we examine the different ways that ASL interpreters adapt to the public nature of their roles, especially in 2020.

Origins for Entering Public Service

The illustrative narratives present three different origin stories for ASL interpreters. We have one story about a Deaf interpreter who grew up in a Deaf family and two stories about hearing individuals who learned about the profession while attending ASL classes in college. Each individual chose interpreting for different reasons such as work flexibility, interest and passion for the language, or commitment to the Deaf community. This variation reflects the observations across all of our interviews. Based on these observations, we are curious about the impact of these motivations on other aspects of the interpreter's work. For example, if the intention for choosing interpretation is to have workplace flexibility, is that ASL interpreter more or less likely to see themselves as a public servant? Does this impact, implicitly or explicitly, the decisions they make as an ASL interpreter, such as integrating cultural awareness or making register adjustments for Deaf clients? At this time, we do not feel that our current data collection has addressed these questions, and additional research is needed.

Despite the apparent differences in these stories, we do see similarities about the origins of these public servants as well. In these illustrative examples, the ASL interpreters indicate that ASL interpretation was often not a profession that they either knew about or wanted to do growing up. These stories are reflective of the observations from all but one of our interviews. Across all but one interview, the vast majority of ASL interpreters revealed that they did not intentionally choose interpreting as a profession, with many indicating that either they were unaware of the profession or, in the case of Deaf interpreters or hearing CODA interpreters, they were aware of the profession but did not want to be an ASL interpreter when they grew up. Despite reluctance or unawareness of the profession, the vast majority of ASL interpreters we interviewed were passionate about their work and deeply committed to providing access to the Deaf community.

Adapting to the Public Role of Emergency ASL Interpreting

The illustrative examples incorporate several different situations faced by public servants in the highly emergent and evolving context of platform interpreting. In the multiple crises that defined 2020, interpreters found themselves attempting to operate with the traditional ASL interpreter code of professional conduct while simultaneously carrying the burden of public service delivery. The ASL interpreter code of professional conduct was developed before interpreters became frontline responders to public emergencies. This context is important because it results in the ethical dilemmas interpreters faced in 2020. The tensions between the public service role and the ASL interpreter role sometimes worked to bend the rules of ASL interpreting, but in other cases, interpreters were wholly compliant with existing rules. Stemming from a deep commitment to the Deaf community and wanting to protect the Deaf community during a global crisis, many interpreters encountered unique circumstances that questioned a strict interpretation of ethical rules. In this sense, we observed how interpreters implemented, or did not, prosocial rule-breaking (see Borry & Henderson, 2020; Fleming, 2020) as a means of adapting to the public nature of their work. Put another way, there were times when ASL interpreters were faced with challenging ethical dilemmas unique to the evolving nature of their role as public servants in 2020. This evolution highlights the unique role of a public servant supporting interactions between the state and the community: They face difficult decisions that require skillful discretion and decision-making. We unpack some examples of this decision-making below.

The first observation of adapting to their public role involves how interpreters interacted with the community following platform interpretation. Traditionally, the need to protect the privacy of interpreting sessions is essential to earning and maintaining the trust of clients. However, faced with an ongoing life-or-death situations being addressed through public press conferences, interpreters would sometimes share information about a crisis or correct misinformation about a situation in public. In this way, interpreters operated in a gray area between traditional interpreting values of privacy and the public service values of transparency and public interest. In the first illustrative example, this individual became a trusted source for information, suggesting they freely provided information to the community, emphasizing a deep commitment to public needs. On the other end of the spectrum, in the third illustrative example, the individual felt it would be unethical to break these rules, showing a commitment to established norms for ASL interpreters. In the middle of the spectrum, as observed in the second illustrative example, the individual felt conflicted about the decision to be made but ultimately felt that the moral obligation to protecting the public was of greater importance than technically following the code of professional conduct for interpreters. These illustrative examples mirror our observations in the interviews where many interpreters felt comfortable bending the rules to serve the public needs of the community, though some did not.

Regarding the second observation of adapting to the public nature of their work, interpreters faced decisions about how to follow rules related to communication and interpretation choices. Traditionally, interpreters rely on a combination of strategies to match the language need of a single or defined group of client(s) in a given situation, such as checking in with a client during interpretation and clarifying sign choices. When conducting interpretation on the televised platform with no D/deaf audience members present, interpreters were now operating without this feedback and left to decide the style and register with which they convey information to a general audience. In some instances, interpreters took significant liberties in their interpretation with the conscious awareness they wanted the information to be as accessible as possible, if not technically following the order of information given. For example, in the first two illustrative examples, we observe how interpreters understood their goal was to provide interpretation to reach the widest audience possible. In the third illustrative example, the ASL interpreter saw themselves as a tool and rejected the notion of adjusting their register. These choices reflect the incorporation of prosocial rule breaking for some, but not all, ASL interpreters as a means to adapt to the public nature of their work.

The public service dilemmas faced by ASL interpreters in 2020, particularly those related to prosocial rule breaking, were likely encountered while alone and without direct supervisor or technical guidance relevant to the social context of the situation. The awareness needed to navigate those decisions was complex, including understanding the technical obligations of the code of professional conduct, moral obligation as a public servant, and public service commitment to the Deaf community. But, like those faced by many public servants, these dilemmas did not garner public attention. Instead, as many of the participants explained in the interviews, media attention was more likely to focus on the facial expressions of ASL interpreters at press conferences rather than on issues of access or the needs of the Deaf community. In this way, the ASL interpreters were visible to many outside the Deaf community and therefore misunderstood by most. Regardless, ASL interpreters faced numerous situations and had to muddle their way through the changing circumstances of their job in real time.

Conclusion

This chapter set out to establish the role of ASL interpreters as public servants who play a valuable role in the community, especially during emergencies. We presented three illustrative examples, summarized from 19 interviews with ASL interpreters who provided platform interpreting for public officials in 2020. Our findings provide insights into the different origins for these public servants as well as examples of how ASL interpreters adapt to the public nature of their role when perceived as agents of the state. The instances of prosocial rule breaking we explore in our findings appear to be impacted by both the discretion faced by ASL interpreters in 2020 and their orientation to public service, though more work is needed to tease this out.

All good research leads to more questions than answers, and we feel this is the case for our work as well. ASL interpreters play a pivotal role in the delivery of emergency information in communities, especially during 2020. However, our work has only explored two dimensions of their work, and we are left with additional questions about the role of other prosocial public service values in ASL interpreting. For example, what role does empathy play in the sign choices made by ASL interpreters on the platform? Is this influenced by community engagement, such as connections with the Deaf community? We also remain curious about further explorations of ethical choices made by ASL interpreters and mediating effects on their ethical decision-making. With all these questions in mind, we look forward to future work on ASL interpreters as public servants.

Dedication

We dedicate this chapter to all of the Deaf and hearing sign language interpreters supporting the Deaf, Hard of Hearing, and DeafBlind community around the world. In particular, we dedicate this chapter to Patty Sakal, a Child of Deaf Adults and a skilled American Sign Language and Hawaiian Sign Language interpreter, who passed away from complications due to COVID-19 on January 15, 2021. May her memory be a blessing to her family and the Deaf community.

Notes

1. In this chapter we use the term "hearing loss" to denote the physiological limitations on the brain to access sound information using the biological

functions of the ear. We recognize that hearing loss has negative connotations grounded in audism, ableism, and hearing epistemologies. It is used here as a more accessible term for a general audience without a background in the Deaf Community. We wish to acknowledge our full support and understanding about the conceptualization of Deaf Gain (Bauman & Murray, 2014) as an important contribution to understanding the social construction of Deafness.

2. We use the term D/deaf to include all deaf people, including culturally Deaf, disabled deaf, hard of hearing, late deafened, and DeafBlind individuals. We recognize this a broad and diverse group of individuals who experience a range of physiological experiences and cultural identities connected to their D/deafness.

3. The eight BES regions include New England (Massachusetts, Connecticut, New Hampshire, Maine, Rhode Island, and Vermont), Great Lakes (Illinois, Ohio, Michigan, Indiana, Wisconsin), Mideast (New York, Pennsylvania, New Jersey, Maryland, Delaware, District of Columbia), Far West (California, Washington, Oregon, Nevada, Hawaii, Alaska), Plains (Missouri, Minnesota, Iowa, Kansas, Nebraska, South Dakota, North Dakota), Rocky Mountains (Colorado, Utah, Idaho, Montana, Wyoming), Southeast (Florida, Georgia, North Carolina, Virginia, Tennessee, South Carolina, Alabama, Louisiana, Kentucky, Arkansas, Mississippi, West Virginia), and Southwest (Texas, Arizona, Oklahoma, New Mexico). See BEA, 2019.

References

Armstrong, D. F. (2011). *Show of hands: A natural history of sign language*. University Press.

Bauman, H.-D. L., & Murray, J. J. (Eds.). (2014). *Deaf gain: Raising the stakes for human diversity* (1st ed.). University of Minnesota Press.

Bureau of Economic Analysis. (2019). BEA Regions. https://apps.bea.gov/regional/docs/regions.cfm

Borry, E. L., & Henderson, A. C. (2020). Patients, protocols, and prosocial behavior: Rule breaking in frontline health care. *The American Review of Public Administration, 50*(1), 45–61. https://doi.org/10.1177/0275074019862680

Creswell, J. W., & Poth, C. N. (2017). *Qualitative inquiry and research design: Choosing among five approaches* (4th ed.). SAGE Publications, Inc.

Drum, C. E., Krahn, G. L., & Besani, H., Jr. (2009). *Disability and public health*. American Public Health Association.

Fleming, C. J. (2020). Prosocial rule breaking at the street level: The roles of leaders, peers, and bureaucracy. *Public Management Review, 22*(8), 1191–1216. https://doi.org/10.1080/14719037.2019.1619817

Glickman, N. S., & Hall, W. C. (2018). *Language deprivation and deaf mental health*. Routledge.

Guy, M. E. (2019). Expanding the toolbox: Why the citizen-state encounter demands it. *Public Performance & Management Review, 44*(5), 1100–1117. https://doi.org/10.1080/15309576.2019.1677255

Guy, M. E., & Ely, T. L. (2018). *Essentials of public service* (1st ed.). Melvin & Leigh, Publishers.

Hall, W. C. (2017). What you don't know can hurt you: The risk of language deprivation by impairing sign language development in deaf children. *Maternal and Child Health Journal, 21*(5), 961–965. https://doi.org/10.1007/s10995-017-2287-y

Hearing Health Foundation. (2018). *Hearing loss & tinnitus statistics.* https://hearinghealthfoundation.org/hearing-loss-tinnitus-statistics

Henderson, A. (2012). The critical role of street-level bureaucrats in disaster and crisis response. In *Handbook of Critical Incident Analysis.* Routledge.

Maher, J. (1996). *Seeing language in sign: The work of William C. Stokoe.* Gallaudet University Press.

Maryland General Assembly. (2021a). *Legislation—HB0535.* http://mgaleg.maryland.gov/mgawebsite/Legislation/Details/HB0535?ys=2021rs

Maryland General Assembly. (2021b). *Legislation—SB0431.* http://mgaleg.maryland.gov/mgawebsite/Legislation/Details/SB0431?ys=2021RS

Miles, M. B., Huberman, A. M., & Saldaña, J. (2013). *Qualitative data analysis: A methods sourcebook* (3rd ed.). Sage Publications, Inc.

Mitchell, R. E., Young, T. A., Bachleda, B., & Karchmer, M. A. (2006). How many people use ASL in the United States? Why estimates need updating. *Sign Language Studies, 6*(3), 306–335. https://doi.org/10.1353/sls.2006.0019

National Association of the Deaf. (2020). *Historic win: White House ordered to provide sign language interpreters for COVID-19 briefings.* https://www.nad.org/2020/09/23/historic-win-white-house-ordered-to-provide-sign-language-interpreters-for-covid-19-briefings/

National Association of the Deaf. (2021a). *Civil rights laws.* https://www.nad.org/resources/civil-rights-laws/

National Association of the Deaf. (2021b). *Emergency preparedness.* https://www.nad.org/resources/emergency-preparedness/

Racino, J. A. (Ed.). (2014). *Public administration and disability: Community services administration in the US.* Routledge.

Roy, C. B., & Napier, J. (2015). *Sign language interpreting studies reader.* Benjamins Publishing Company.

Stokoe, W. C., Jr. (2005). Sign language structure: An outline of the visual communication systems of the American deaf. *The Journal of Deaf Studies and Deaf Education, 10*(1), 3–37. https://doi.org/10.1093/deafed/eni001

Yin, R. K. (2015). *Qualitative research from start to finish* (2nd ed.). The Guilford Press.

Zavattaro, S. M. (2020). *City sextons: Tales from municipal leaders.* Routledge.

6

Unseen but Irreplaceable

The Role of Air Traffic Controllers

Sean A. McCandless

At any given time, thousands of aircraft are in the air. In the busiest airspaces in the world, namely North America, Europe, and East Asia, there is a good chance that an airplane, perhaps several, is within 10 miles of anyone standing on the ground (Petchenik, 2020). In the United States in particular, thousands of planes fly every hour (Federal Aviation Administration, 2021b).

While many may think of pilots and flight attendants as the faces of aviation, and they are, another class of worker is diligently working behind the scenes—air traffic controllers. Controllers are the guardians of air traffic safety. Anyone who has been on an airplane has been kept safe by numerous air traffic controllers. And anyone who has ever had the misfortune of being in (but with the good fortune of surviving) an air traffic incident can credit part of their survival to the dedicated work of air traffic controllers (Nolan, 2010; Smith, 2017). In fact, so important are air traffic controllers to public safety that the 2019 U.S. government shutdown ended "after only 10 air traffic controllers stayed home" (Kaufman & Marsh, 2019; see also Reich, 2019).

Despite the importance of air traffic controllers, as public servants, they largely remain unseen. As such, this chapter investigates these questions: How do air traffic controllers understand their work, and what values does their work bring to public service? This chapter addresses these questions in several ways. First, two vignettes—the Überlingen midair collision and the flight of Jim Lawson—showcase the differences air traffic controllers make. Second, the chapter examines where and how controllers' work takes place and what is required to work as a controller. Finally, the chapter ends with a discussion of future key issues controllers will likely face and the consequent effects on public service.

The Importance of Air Traffic Controllers: Two Vignettes

Before going further, it must be noted that, overwhelmingly, air traffic controllers perform their jobs with distinction, keeping millions of travelers safe. Despite some near hits and close calls, air traffic controllers succeed at promoting secure, navigable airspaces. They save lives. However, when air traffic control fails, the results are often catastrophic. This section presents two vignettes—one when air traffic control fails and another when air traffic control saves lives—to showcase the importance of controllers.

When Air Traffic Control Fails: The Überlingen Mid-Air Collision

On the night of July 1, 2002, two flights, Bashkirian Airlines Flight 2937 and DHL Flight 611, collided in midair over Überlingen, Germany (Bennett, 2004; Johnson, 2004). Flight 2937 was crewed by Captain Alexander Mihailovich Gross and First Officer Oleg Pavlovich Grigoriev. The flight was serviced by a Tupolev Tu-154 and had 69 passengers and crew. Most passengers on this chartered flight from Moscow to Barcelona were Russian schoolchildren and their parents, many of whom were high-ranking officials. Flight 611 was crewed by Captain Paul Phillips and First Officer Brant Campioni and was serviced by a Boeing 757 cargo jet. The flight originated in Bahrain with a stop-over in Bergamo, Italy, on the way to Brussels, Belgium.

Flight controllers were based in Zurich, Switzerland, and worked for Skyguide (which oversees a portion of German airspace), a private Swiss airspace control company. On duty was veteran air traffic controller Peter Nielsen. Nielsen was the only controller working at the time and was manning two workstations while his colleague was resting in another room. This entire work situation, a controller monitoring two stations alone and long work hours, was against company policy, but management had ignored these issues for years. Technical glitches compounded overwork in the control tower. Zurich controllers were forced to use a backup radar system because of maintenance concerns that were causing data delays on the primary radar. Additionally, Zurich's ground-based optical collision warning system was down for maintenance. No one had seemingly informed Nielsen of this last issue (Bennett, 2004; Johnson, 2004).

The two flights, both at 36,000 feet, were on a collision course. Nielsen, overworked and stressed, did not immediately notice this situation. However, a fatal outcome was not yet guaranteed. For one, modern planes are equipped with technology (called TCAS, or the traffic collision avoidance system) to warn of potential collisions, but these warnings should not be needed because controllers have already issued commands for pilots to avoid collisions. For another, with a properly managed work environment, most air traffic controllers have the time and space to order descents, ascents, and course changes to avoid collisions (Bennett, 2004; Johnson, 2004).

When Nielsen eventually noticed the danger, he immediately contacted Flight 2937, instructing a descent to 35,000 feet. At nearly the same time, Flight 2937's TCAS instructed an ascent while Flight 611's TCAS instructed a descent. Flight 611's pilots followed TCAS instructions but did not inform Nielsen because he was busy with Flight 2937. The pilots of Flight 2937 disregarded the TCAS climb instructions, descending as per Nielsen's order. Both planes were now descending, and Nielsen repeated the instruction for Flight 2937 to continue descent, yet he relayed incorrect information about the position of Flight 611 to Flight 2937's pilots. Gross and Grigoriev realized what was going on mere seconds before when they sighted Flight 611. Phillips and Campinoni seemingly realized a collision was about to occur and increased the descent rate. Mere seconds later, the pilots of Flight 2937 obeyed TCAS climb instructions. However, it was too late—the planes collided in the air, killing everyone on both flights and raining debris over a large area (Bennett, 2004; Johnson, 2004).

Nielsen experienced traumatic stress because of the collision, and his employer, Skyguide, had to pay restitution to victims' families. Yet the tragedy was not over. On Flight 2937 were the wife and two children of Vitaly Kaloyev. Kaloyev researched where Nielsen lived and on February 24, 2004, fatally stabbed Nielsen (Kramer, 2012).

WHEN AIR TRAFFIC CONTROL SAVES THE DAY: THE LAWSON FLIGHT

The vignette above was a low-frequency, high-impact event, and the reality is that air accidents, including those like the Überlingen midair collision, are rare (see Federal Aviation Administration, 2009). Controllers save lives every single day by safely navigating aircraft and by helping pilots during medical emergencies and difficult takeoffs and landings. During emergency situations, controllers clear traffic; guide pilots; help coordinate fire, rescue, and police services; and much more. The public often does not hear success stories (Nolan & LaRue, 2018; Smith, 2017). In brief, the examples of controllers saving lives far outweigh the numbers of instances in which controllers fail in their work.

One example of the lifesaving roles played by controllers is the 2012 flight of Jim Lawson (Brown, 2012). In 2012, Jim Lawson was piloting his Mooney M20D/C through perfect weather to deliver Christmas presents to his son who lived in Washington state. Lawson was heading to Ellensburg, Washington, but thick clouds quickly rolled in. He tried to go to nearby Arlington, but this airport was also closed. The clouds were still too thick to land, and Lawson's plane was running low on fuel.

As the plane's second fuel tank ran dry, Lawson contacted Seattle Center and was put in contact with veteran controller Ken Greenwood. Greenwood knew Lawson's plane was running low on fuel, and he helped Lawson descend through the clouds toward Auburn, Washington. The engine kept sputtering and cut out several times. Two other controllers—Josh Haviland and Ryan Herrick—helped clear space, coordinating with multiple aircraft centers like Renton, Boeing Field, and Seattle-Tacoma International Airport (the largest airport in the area), to allow an emergency landing for Lawson. As Lawson's plane proceeded through the cloud barrier at 2,200 feet and as the plane experienced turbulence, Greenwood, sensing how tense the cockpit situation was, reminded Lawson to put down the plane's gear on final approach. As Lawson said, "Gear down and locked. [. . .] Hey you know what? You just saved my life." Greenwood, Haviland, and Herrick were later given the National Air Traffic Controllers Association's Archie League Medal of Safety Award (Brown, 2012).

The Work of Air Traffic Controllers

As these two vignettes demonstrate, the work of controllers is stressful but necessary. The highest duty of a controller is to keep people safe, and as the air travel industry continues to expand, the need for safety is even more pressing. Like officers directing traffic when no stoplights are present, controllers oversee hundreds of cubic miles of airspace and at any one time are responsible for thousands of lives. However, to understand the complexity of controllers' work and the value they bring to public service, it is helpful to see more about *how* and *when* their work occurs and what it takes to even get a job as a controller.

AIRSPACE: CONTROLLERS' "OFFICES"

The world is divided geographically into airspaces overseen by different countries and guided by international law. While the United States has the busiest airspace in the world, other areas experience enormous amounts of traffic, especially countries in Western Europe and East Asia, such as China (Centre for Asia Pacific Aviation, 2021; Dong et al., 2019). Places like South and Southeast Asia, most notably India, are becoming aviation hotspots (Kundu, 2021). Overall, Africa and South America see reduced levels of overall air traffic compared with other areas of the world, but this is rapidly changing (The World Bank, 2021). Historically, as a *single* country, the United States has had the busiest air in the world (Cox & Wright, 2013), although this too is rapidly changing as air traffic across Asia increases (Fazzi, 2018). To simplify the discussion of the importance of airspace and the place of controllers in airspaces, this section focuses on the United States.

U.S. airspace is a multidimensional area divided geographically with nested layers of control. This airspace has 21 zones called centers. Centers are large, span multiple state borders, and are abbreviated by three-letter codes. For instance, "ZDV" refers to the Denver Center, which geographically covers Colorado as well as portions of Wyoming, South Dakota, Nebraska, Kansas, New Mexico, and Arizona. Each center, in turn, is divided into sectors. Another type of airspace is TRACON airspace (Terminal Radar Approach Control) within which lie airports, each of which has its own 5-mile radius airspace (Nolan, 2010).

The Air Traffic Control System Command Center (ATCSCC) oversees all air traffic control, guiding planes to safely navigate through or around problems like congestion, weather, and runway shutdowns. Each center has its own Air Route Traffic Control Center (ARTCC). ARTCCs manage traffic within a center except for areas designated for TRACON and local airports. TRACON, in turn, handles aircraft that are departing and approaching with its space. At airports, air traffic control towers (ATCTs) guide takeoffs, landings, and ground traffic (Nolan, 2010).

Air traffic controllers work in all these airspaces. Anytime someone flies, they are in the hands of teams of air traffic controllers across all these spatial divisions. If flights are long enough, planes pass between centers, and air traffic controllers successively hand pilots off to the next center's air traffic controllers (Nolan, 2010).

FROM PREFLIGHT TO POST-LANDING: WHAT CONTROLLERS DO

Any flight is guided in several ways by controllers as well as by different types of controllers. The various tasks and types of controllers can be understood by the roles each play in the major aspects of flights—pre-flight, takeoff, departure, cruise, descent, and landing.

Even before passengers are within visual range of an airport, they likely already see planes taking off and landing. Behind this flurry of activity, air traffic controllers are working unseen. Controllers are active even before a plane takes off from the ground. As passengers check their bags and head to their flights, pilots are already inspecting their planes, filing flight plans, coordinating the uploading of fuel and baggage, and briefing and prepping crews. After passengers board, pilots transmit vital flight and plane data to the ground controller, who ultimately approves planes pushing back from the gates and proceeding via taxiways to a runway (Nolan, 2010; Nolan & LaRue, 2018; Smith, 2017).

A local controller in the airport's tower watches the skies around the airport and monitors the surface radar that tracks aircraft. Local controllers must ensure that planes are able to take off safely. This controller also gives final approval for planes to take off. As wheels go up, the pilot turns on the transponder, which transmits much of the flight data used by controllers to guide planes safely. The local controller hands the flight off to the TRACON facility controller in charge of the departure airport. Still, the local controller's job is not done; they must monitor planes until they are beyond 5 miles from the departure airport. At TRACON, a departure controller monitors all airports and aircraft and airspace within its 50-mile radius. This air traffic controller tells pilots what to do to avoid traffic and bad weather, such as giving directions on heading, speed, ascent, and more (Federal Aviation Administration, 2006).

As planes reach cruising altitude, the TRACON controller hands planes off to the center controller, or an ARTCC controller. If a trip is long enough, ARTCC controllers will pass off the plane to numerous controllers across different sectors. Several traffic controllers monitor any given flight. The first are radar and associate radar controllers, who control communications, maintain safe vertical and horizontal distances between aircraft, and generally monitor all airspace in a given area. Next, ARTCC controllers advise pilots on weather, air turbulence, and traffic, giving directions on factors like speed, altitude, direction, and distance. Finally, a radar handoff controller assists the radar and associate radar controllers to coordinate heavy traffic. Across all of this, flight plans may need to change. For instance, dangerous weather can rapidly develop, necessitating multiple aircraft course changes and even diversions. Turbulence can make for a bumpy ride, and pilots may request a different altitude. There may also be issues at a flight's arrival airport, and air traffic controllers may need to put flights into holding patterns until the issue clears (Federal Aviation Administration, 2021c).

As flights near their arrival airport, or around 150 miles from the destination, the ARTCC controllers begin to order pilots to descend their aircraft and then line up aircraft in preparation for final approach. At 50 miles from the airport, ARTCC hands pilots off again to TRACON. At TRACON, an approach controller helps guide the plane into standard approach corridors, which can change dramatically depending on traffic conditions, weather, and situations at the arrival airport. When flights are about 10 miles from the airport, the approach controller hands the plane off to the airport's local controller. Like takeoff, the local controller monitors runways, taxiways, and traffic using both visual and radar aids. It is this controller who ultimately gives clearance to land and who guides aircraft safely into the airport and to the gate (Federal Aviation Administration, 2021c).

Thus, a safe flight does not "just happen." A safe flight involves extensive coordination between people, agencies, equipment, and procedural and legal requirements all within four-dimensional spaces. Without controllers' coordination, especially concerning timing and an ethic of care, safe airline travel would not be possible.

Education and Skills

The tasks described above are complex, with the lives of thousands in the hands of just a few. As such, it is essential that all air traffic controllers are exceptional workers in many ways. In the United States, air traffic controllers are Federal Aviation Administration (FAA) employees.

Controllers must demonstrate numerous competencies and skills even to set foot in a control center (FAA, 2021a).

First, all controllers must be competent in so-called "aviation English" as well as the phonetic alphabet (i.e., alpha, bravo, charlie) of the North Atlantic Treaty Organization (NATO). "Aviation English" is the default worldwide aviation language, and it is needed because everyone working in airline safety must be able to understand one another. For instance, at any international airport, pilots from all over the world take off and land, and without a common form of communication, disasters will occur (Trippe & Baese-Berk, 2019).

In fact, miscommunication, including between controllers and pilots, has been an important factor behind several aviation accidents. Perhaps the most famous example of how miscommunications between controllers and pilots can lead to disaster is the 1977 Tenerife Disaster, the deadliest non-terrorist related aviation incident in history (Ziomek, 2018). In this incident, two Boeing 747s, KLM Flight 4805 and Pan Am Flight 1736, collided on the runway of Los Rodeos Airport, resulting in 583 fatalities. A terrorist incident at nearby Gran Canaria Airport (Spain) resulted in copious diversions of aircraft to the much smaller Los Rodeos airport. After several hours and as a dense fog covered the airport, aircraft were cleared to depart Los Rodeos airport for Gran Canaria. However, Los Rodeos airport was small—it had a single runway and a small taxiway—and was so congested because of the flight diversions that aircraft taking off had to taxi down and then turn around at the end of the runway. Air traffic controllers gave nonstandard answers and confusing instructions to the pilots of both flights. As a result of many factors, including unclear instructions about the taxiway exit to be used by the Pan Am flight as well as confusing replies to the KLM pilots, KLM Flight 4805 collided with Pan Am Flight 1736, killing everyone on the KLM flight and most of those on the Pan Am flight. While the fault overwhelmingly lies with the captain of the KLM flight for taking off without explicitly confirming clearance, the lack of clarity and standard language by the air traffic controllers was a major factor leading to pilot confusion (Ziomek, 2018).

Second, in addition to competency in "aviation English," U.S. air traffic controllers must successfully navigate through the hiring in the federal civil service system (Federal Aviation Administration, 2021a). In addition to a written test to gauge understanding instructions as well as federal airline safety requirements, prospective controllers are tested on their skills in abstract reasoning and 3-D spatial visualization. Such tests are critical because at any one time, a controller must be able to memorize the positions of aircraft and understand and process numerous symbols, such as those assigned by the International Civil Aviation Organization for airline names and flight numbers, technical terms, and computer readouts. Thus, controllers must be able to take in and process information quickly and clearly; make decisions efficiently, effectively, and economically; communicate well; and be able to focus intensely for long periods of time. Further, even to submit an application that will be taken seriously, prospective controllers must have 3 years of work experience, a 4-year college degree, or some combination of the two (Kern, 2017; Nolan & LaRue, 2018; Smith 2017).

Third, if someone is selected to take the next steps, they will train at the FAA Academy in Oklahoma City for 7 months. After completion of the program and successfully passing the academy's various tests, junior controllers will work at various sites across the country, gaining competency in airports of varying traffic levels and types. Further, any controller must be specifically certified for any of the various types of positions mentioned above (Kern, 2017; Nolan & LaRue, 2018; Smith 2017).

Finally, on the job, controllers are regularly tested. Trainings form part of the regular routine, and controllers must pass physical examinations, undergo drug screenings, and participate in performance evaluations. Shifts are stressful and are broken up into blocks of 90 to 120 minutes with 30-minute breaks in between, and, as performance deteriorates rapidly if shifts go beyond 120 minutes, such breaks are essential. Finally, air traffic control never stops on any day of the year, and schedules must be established well in advance, often upward of a month (Smith, 2017).

STRESS ON THE JOB

Air traffic controlling is one of the most stressful but necessary jobs in the world. At times, this stress can be a factor in national-level issues, as shown in two exemplars. First, in August 1981, U.S. air traffic controllers went on strike (McMartin, 2013). The controllers' union, the Professional Air Traffic Controllers Organization (PATCO), was concerned about safety that resulted from overwork. The union called for a 32-hour workweek, a $10,000 per annum pay increase, and better benefits. When the federal government refused these demands, PATCO declared a strike.

President Reagan ordered controllers back to work under the provisions of the Taft-Hartley Act. Only 1,300 of 13,000 controllers returned. Reagan gave an ultimatum: Return to work or be fired. A federal court injunction ordered an end to the strike, which did not happen. A federal judge found workers to be in contempt of court, and Reagan fired the more than 11,000 controllers who ignored the order, and he banned them from federal service for life (a decision later reversed for some). The FAA scrambled to fill positions, which caused further concerns about safety and competency of the new controllers. PATCO was decertified in 1981 following the illegal strike (McMartin, 2013).

Second, the 2019 U.S. government shutdown underscored the dangers of on-the-job stress for controllers (Kaufman & Marsha, 2019; Reich, 2019). During the shutdown, the longest in history to date, air traffic controllers as FAA employees were not being paid. As was the case with many federal workers, the shutdown and the lack of pay caused significant levels of stress. On January 25, 10 controllers decided to stay home. The absence of just 10 controllers temporarily shut down travel at some of the busiest airports in the country, like New York City's La Guardia Airport, causing a ripple effect on the whole country's airspace. The National Air Traffic Controllers Association union president, Paul Rinaldi, noted that while the union did not endorse a strike or a coordinated action, controllers had "reached the breaking point of exhaustion, stress and worry" caused by the shutdown. The call-off helped tip the scales to encourage negotiations to reopen the government (Kaufman & Marsha, 2019; Reich, 2019). That just 10 people could call in sick demonstrates how important controllers are as public servants; they have such specialized skills and are so hard to replace that the absence of only a few can shut down an entire industry.

The Future for Air Traffic Controllers

Just as air travel is only getting more stressful for the average passenger, so too are the demands of air safety becoming more stressful for air traffic controllers. Despite that controllers' work occurs largely unseen, governments must address several emerging concerns if air travel is to continue to be safe (Federal Aviation Administration, 2017a).

Congestion problems are perhaps the most pressing issue negatively affecting controllers' work environments. Airspaces all over the world, including in up-and-coming crowded airspaces like South and Southeast Asia, will only get more congested. Congestion leads not only to issues during flights but also to on-the-ground issues such as flight delays, lack of gate space at airports, and even radio communication congestion (Adacher et al., 2017). Numerous airports in the United States have had to expand terminals and runways and, at times, massively redesign logistical procedures to handle increased traffic (Reid, 2019). As but one further example of the seriousness of the issue, the U.S. economy loses billions of dollars a year because of flight delays and congestion. Given that air travel contributes billions of dollars to the U.S. economy alone, such losses are grim (Airlines for America, 2021).

Another issue concerns the types of support, especially technological, needed for air controllers to conduct their work. To modernize air traffic control technology and processes, since 2007, the United States has been implementing the Next Generation Air Transportation System (NextGen), which is set to be fully implemented by 2025. As part of NextGen, the United States is collaborating with the European Commission to harmonize key areas, which is pressing given the extensive air traffic between North America and Europe (Federal Aviation Administration, 2020). In 2008, then-president George W. Bush issued Executive Order 13479, which mandates the secretary of transportation to establish NextGen support staff. In 2012, the U.S. Congress passed the FAA Modernization and Reform Act, which established deadlines for adopting existing NextGen computerized communications, navigation, and surveillance systems (Federal Aviation Administration, 2017b). Without such modernization programs to support controllers' work, issues of safety will only compound.

Conclusion: Return to the Questions

This chapter opened with two questions: How do air traffic controllers understand their work, and what values does their work bring to public service? As seen throughout this chapter, there are several answers.

First, to understand how controllers view their work, it is essential to understand the (air)spaces in which the work takes place as well as what constitutes their extensive everyday responsibilities. Controllers' work on any given flight occurs before the flight even takes off and continues until after it lands. Such work directly affects hundreds of flights and thousands of lives a day, ideally to ensure safe, navigable routes. Controllers coordinate technological systems worth trillions of dollars and safeguard lives whose values are incalculable. As was the case with both the Überlingen collision and the Lawson flight, among many other examples, air traffic controllers deal in matters of life and death daily.

Second, the discussion above exemplifies how controllers bring numerous values to their work, including those associated with public service. Above all, controllers work to promote *safety*. Controllers help government fulfill its first duty—to protect its people—and because people of all citizenship statuses can be on any given flight, this duty extends to *all* people. Further, one can understand controllers' work in terms of the four pillars of public administration. They must *efficiently* and *effectively* manage air travel; they must *economically* relay instructions; and they must work *equitably* to protect the lives of everyone in their care. Controllers' work implicates other values—*accountability* (to the profession, to the government, and to the public); *responsiveness* (especially to the needs of often rapidly evolving situations); and *transparency* (operating in trustworthy, open, and accessible ways).

Given controllers' importance to public service, and as issues of safety and congestion will only get more acute, it is incumbent on decision makers at all levels to do what is necessary to promote work environments conducive to controllers being able to embody these values above. In terms of the major aspects of public administration—law, politics, and management (Rosenbloom et al., 2008)—decision makers must pay attention to several areas. First, concerning law, the U.S. Congress must ensure that air traffic safety, especially projects like NextGen, are fully funded, expanded, and refined as needed. Second, concerning politics, decision makers, especially at the federal level, must collaborate to ensure that control centers have the resources and attention needed for controllers to operate efficiently, effectively, economically, and equitably. Finally, concerning management, control centers themselves must be led and managed in such ways that controllers are valued and supported, compensated and rewarded appropriately, monitored effectively, evaluated regularly and transparently, listened to (especially regarding concerns they raise about stress), and provided the space not only to work but also to rest and recuperate.

Literally millions of lives depend on controllers' service, and thousands of lives have been saved by their actions. While controllers may largely engage in unseen work, their work is, nonetheless, profoundly *felt*.

References

Adacher, L., Flamini, M., & Romano, E. (2017). Rerouting algorithms solving the air traffic congestion. *AIR Conference Proceedings, 1836*(1), 020053-1-020053-6.

Airlines for America. (2021). *Annual U.S. impact of flight delays (NEXTOR report)*. Airlines for America. https://www.airlines.org/data/annual-u-s-impact-of-flight-delays-nextor-report/

Bennett, S. (2004). The 1st July 2002 mid-air collision over Überlingen, Germany: A holistic analysis. *Risk Management, 6*(1), 31–49.

Brown, S. (2012, February 2). "You just saved my life": ATC aids pilots in a pinch. *Aircraft Owners and Pilots Association*. https://www.aopa.org/news-and-media/all-news/2012/february/02/atc-aids-pilots-in-a-pinch

Centre for Asia Pacific Aviation. (2021, March 18). *China domestic traffic grows; new Chengdu airport opens 2021*. Centre for Aviation. https://centrefor aviation.com/analysis/reports/china-domestic-traffic-grows-new-chengdu-airport-opens-2021-555104

Cox, J., & Wright, D. (2013, September 16). Ask the captain: Flying in the busiest airspace. *USA Today*. https://www.usatoday.com/story/travel/columnist/cox/2013/09/16/busiest-airports-air-traffic-control/2818733/

Dong, Y., Lu, Z., Liu, Y., Zhang, Q., & Wu, D. (2019). China's corridors-in-the-sky design and space-time congestion identification and the influence of air routes' traffic flows. *Journal of Geographical Sciences, 29*, 1999–2014.

Eurocontrol. (2010). *Human performance in air traffic management safety: A white paper*. https://www.skybrary.aero/bookshelf/books/1404.pdf

Executive Order 13479. *Transformation of the national air transportation system*. https://www.presidency.ucsb.edu/documents/executive-order-13479-transformation-the-national-air-transportation-system

Fazzi, R. (2018, April 10). U.S. dethroned as "busiest skies" capital of world. *Financial Advisor*. https://www.fa-mag.com/news/u-s--dethroned-as--busiest-skies--capital-of-world-38053.html

Federal Aviation Administration. (2006). *Fact sheet—Co-located TRACONS (Terminal radar approach control)*. https://www.faa.gov/news/fact_sheets/news_story.cfm?contentkey=4009

Federal Aviation Administration. (2009). *Risk management handbook*. https://www.faa.gov/regulations_policies/handbooks_manuals/aviation/media/FAA-H-8083-2.pdf

Federal Aviation Administration. (2017a). *Air traffic organization 2015 safety report*. Federal Aviation Administration.

Federal Aviation Administration. (2017b). *FAA Modernization and Reform Act (P.L. 112-095) reports and plans*. https://www.faa.gov/about/plans_reports/modernization/

Federal Aviation Administration. (2019). *Air traffic control order: JO 7110.65Y.* Federal Aviation Administration.

Federal Aviation Administration. (2020). *Modernization of U.S. airspace.* https://www.faa.gov/nextgen/

Federal Aviation Administration. (2021a). *Aviation careers: Air traffic control specialists.* https://www.faa.gov/jobs/career_fields/aviation_careers/

Federal Aviation Administration. (2021b). *Air traffic by the numbers.* https://www.faa.gov/air_traffic/by_the_numbers/

Federal Aviation Administration. (2021c). *FAR/AIM 2021.* Federal Aviation Administration.

Johnson, C. (2004). *Final report: Review of the BFU Überlingen Accident Report.* University of Glasgow. http://www.dcs.gla.ac.uk/~johnson/Eurocontrol/Ueberlingen/Ueberlingen_Final_Report.PDF

Kaufman, E., & Marsha, R. (2019, February 6). *The government shutdown ended after only 10 air traffic controllers stayed home.* CNN. https://www.cnn.com/2019/02/06/politics/ten-air-traffic-controllers-shutdown/index.html

Kern, R. M. (2017). *Air to ground: A guide to the world of air traffic control and aviation weather* [e-book edition]. Solar Ranch Publishing.

Kramer, A. E. (2012, June 30). Plane crash remembered; One mourner not welcome. *The New York Times.* https://www.nytimes.com/2012/07/01/world/europe/killer-of-air-traffic-controller-barred-from-crash-memorial.html

Kundu, R. (2021, January 26). Smaller cities, towns fuel rise in Indian air traffic. Aviation Pros. https://www.aviationpros.com/airlines/news/21207318/smaller-cities-towns-fuel-rise-in-indian-air-traffic

McMartin, J. A. (2013). *Collision course: Ronald Reagan, the air traffic controllers, and the strike that changed America.* Oxford University Press.

Nolan, M. S. (2010). *Fundamentals of air traffic control* (5th ed.). Cengage.

Nolan, M. S., & LaRue, S. L. (2018). *A career in air traffic control.* eAcademic Books, LLC.

Petchenek, I. (2020). Flightradar24's 2019 by the numbers. *Flightradar24.* https://www.flightradar24.com/blog/flightradar24s-2019-by-the-numbers/

Reich, R. (2019, January 29). Air traffic controllers defeated Trump. That's worker power. *The Guardian.* https://www.theguardian.com/commentisfree/2019/jan/29/air-traffic-controllers-defeated-trump

Reid, J. (2019, June 2). The 10 U.S. airports set for billion-dollar expansions. *Business Traveler.* https://www.businesstraveller.com/features/the-10-us-airports-set-for-billion-dollar-expansions/

Rosenbloom, D. H., Kravchuk, R. S., & Clerkin, R. M. (2008). *Public administration: Understanding management, politics, and law in the public sector* (8th ed.). McGraw-Hill.

Smith, R. A. (2017). *Life with a view: Memoir of an air traffic controller.* iUniverse.

Trippe, J., & Baese-Berk, M. (2019). A prosodic profile of American aviation English. *English for Specific Purposes, 53,* 30–46.

World Bank. (2021). *Air transport, passengers carried.* https://data.worldbank.org/indicator/IS.AIR.PSGR

Ziomek, J. (2018). *Collision on Tenerife: The how and why of the world's worst aviation disaster.* Post Hill Press.

7

Serving in Silence

The Emergency Manager

KYLE R. OVERLY

Across the nation, emergency managers provide the framework for disaster and emergency response. Leveraging their critical analysis and networking skills, emergency managers assemble teams of experts who collaboratively solve complex problems and implement policies that reduce suffering and disaster impacts. Emergency managers often work in the shadows, inside emergency operations centers (EOC), far away from the impacted communities and outside the lenses of the media.

Emergency managers build systems that flex to meet the needs of any threat or hazard; however, 2020 tested the capacity of even the most robust systems. The year brought with it a global pandemic, hurricanes, protests, earthquakes, flooding, tornadoes, severe weather, and a host of other challenges. These hazards, coupled with economic uncertainty, staff attrition, and existing duties that could not take a back seat to conse-quence management actions, created impossible situations for emergency managers across the nation.

This chapter tells the story of the emergency manager, often serving in silence yet creating the conditions that enable response and recovery from disasters. Told from the autoethnographic perspective of an emergency manager responding to the COVID-19 global pandemic, it presents the unique challenges that emergency managers face. 2020 and 2021 brought with them multiple cascading disasters, to which these unsung heroes coordinated response and recovery efforts in the background, with little or no praise or recognition, but because it is what they do and how they serve. Emergency managers focus on achieving the mission rather than on getting praise and accolades.

As an emergency manager myself, these are my observations, conclusions, and thoughts on how emergency managers build from the events of 2020 and 2021. It is my intent to give voice to emergency managers working tirelessly in the background to protect the communities they serve. Emergency managers deserve to have their voices heard, and to emerge from the shadows. This is their story.

Emergency Management in the United States

Since the birth of the United States government, officials have been responding to disaster. The nation's emergency management system includes a system of local, state, and federal emergency managers augmented by nongovernmental actors such as voluntary organizations active in disaster (VOAD) and the private sector. Leveraging an all-hazards approach, emergency managers have coordinated response and recovery activities for major disasters such as the September 11, 2001, terrorist attacks and Hurricane Katrina, as well as countless community-based emergencies and disasters. Modern emergency management organizations reflect decades of policy change that shaped focal areas, bureaucratic structures, and disaster politics (Sylves, 2008).

As a discipline, emergency management traces its roots to the civil defense era. As early as the War of 1812, U.S. officials sought ways to protect the nation from catastrophic disaster, primarily resulting from war and nation actors. In the post-Soviet era, civil defense organizations gradually expanded their missions to address natural hazards leading to the emergence of emergency management as a fledgling discipline (Sylves, 2008). Beyond the field's early roots, key policies and legislation (e.g., the 1979 National Governor's Association report on Comprehensive Emergency Management) have influenced emergency management as a field and the jobs of emergency managers.

The Role of Emergency Managers

Across the nation there is no standard job description or duties for an emergency manager. In general, emergency managers prepare for and respond to disasters and hazards, as well as facilitate recovery from and mitigate against the impacts of disasters and hazards (Sylves, 2008). Of these duties, response and recovery are those with the highest awareness of the public because they occur contemporaneously in the context of a major emergency or disasters impacting a community. While some emergency management agencies are large enough to allow staff to specialize in one subsector of the field, most local agencies are either small or part of "duties as assigned" to a local fire or police chief; thus many emergency managers are generalists familiar with a breadth of issues. Regardless of the composition of the agency, emergency managers complete their duties leveraging several broad-based skills.

STAKEHOLDER ENGAGEMENT

Emergency managers build consensus across stakeholder groups. Because emergency management functions occur both across government (horizontal) and at various levels (vertical), engaging the whole community is critically important to effectuate a complex web of disaster relief programs. A global growth in system interdependence further exemplifies the need for earnest stakeholder engagement. Broadly speaking, stakeholder groups consist of individual and families, business and industry, and government entities (Sylves, 2008).

Through network building and stakeholder engagement, emergency managers build coalitions to protect communities. From delivering services during a disaster to providing pre-disaster educational opportunities, these relationships form the basis for much of the emergency management system. These efforts are not easy; rather, they are the result of years of work. Emergency managers across the nation leveraged their carefully built relationships and stakeholder engagement efforts in response to the COVID-19 global pandemic (Tartaglia & Overly, 2020).

CRITICAL ANALYSIS AND PROBLEM SOLVING

Emergency managers are experts at leveraging their stakeholder network to solve complex problems. Dealing in ambiguity, often with incomplete or limited information, emergency managers make decisions that can have real community impacts. From deciding which community should evacuate from a hazard first, what segment of the population should receive a resource, or how best to communicate risk, emergency managers use critical analysis and problem-solving skills to solve wicked problems.

Given that wicked problems are novel and multifaceted with no quick solutions, where conventional methods will not solve them (Yankelovich, 2014), emergency managers use their abilities to assemble multidisciplinary teams of experts to propose solutions. While most issues are acute in nature, occurring during a disaster, emergency managers have applied their process and critical analysis skills to long-term problems such as homelessness (Le, 2016), the opioid crisis (Turque, 2017), and climate change (Stults, 2017). While they often create the conditions to solve many of these challenging issues, they receive little credit, taking a back seat to more visible agencies.

INFORMATION MANAGEMENT

In addition to engaging stakeholders and solving complex problems, emergency managers handle information for stakeholders and the public to keep them informed. This includes both warning the public of threats and hazards, as well as providing information to elected officials and stakeholder groups to make operational decisions. Information management also includes activities such as providing an accurate picture of what is happening, how severe the impacts are, and communicating what government officials are doing to resolve the issues. Emergency managers accomplish much of this work through the visualization of data that present key messages in graphic format (e.g., maps) and shows, rather than tells, what is going on. This is made possible by programs that convert impact data into easily shareable graphic format. Communicating messages graphically is even more important today, where much communication occurs through social networking platforms.

In the 21st century, engaging the public through social media has become an essential emergency manager task. Modern emergency management agencies both share information about disaster impacts as well as gather information and damage reports from citizens through crowd sourcing mechanisms (Chaves et al., 2019). Both the "push" of information to the public as well as the "pull" of information about what is happening in the community are essential components of an emergency management organization's information management practices. Skilled social media managers understand how to leverage different platforms to engage different target demographic groups within their community. While some emergency management agencies view this as a luxury, it is instead a vital component of a mature program.

RESOURCE MANAGEMENT

Finally, emergency managers support the on-scene disaster response activities through resource management. These actions include tracking resource status and filling requests for specialized personnel and equipment. Through a variety of mechanisms, emergency managers source, request, track, and deliver lifesaving equipment to those working to limit consequences from disaster.

In addition to managing the resource needs of on-scene responders, emergency managers assemble complex logistical networks and systems. This includes calculating resource burn rates, vetting prospective venders, and bulk purchasing of critical supplies. Supporting the direct on-scene needs of emergency responders is yet another way that emergency managers serve in silence, providing critical services to disaster survivors.

As noted in this section, emergency managers provide highly technical, analytical services supporting community-wide response and recovery. Emergency managers, when recognized, are often included in the general category of first responder agencies. This comparison, however, is not appropriate. The reality is that first responders only represent a fraction of the agencies involved in community response and recovery to disaster. Emergency managers have adjacent responsibilities, but the one-for-one comparison is not fair.

Emergency Management versus First Responder Agencies

Emergency managers provide vital support to frontline emergency responders during disasters. This group of dedicated public servants works tirelessly to support the communities they serve. Working long hours (12-hour shifts or more), for extended periods of time (months in the case of major disasters), often far away from the disaster scene at emergency operations centers, emergency managers rarely receive the recognition of their first-responder counterparts on-scene. Supporting the on-scene operations at disasters is a behind-the-scenes integrated network spanning government, nongovernmental, and private sector organizations.

Unlike emergency managers, first responders (e.g., firefighters, emergency medical services, and law enforcement) are the visible representation of government's response to disaster. They serve on the front lines and as a backdrop to live media reports and press conferences. Delivering direct survivor assistance, these response and recovery partners are a critical link in the overall disaster response system. Community members see first responders every day; however, few know what emergency managers do or who their local emergency managers are. I often describe what I do as similar to the Federal Emergency Management Agency (FEMA), but for the state. As emergency managers, we need to do a better job of marketing ourselves.

COVID-19 Global Pandemic

The COVID-19 pandemic fully emerging in the United States in 2020 and its continuation into 2021 brought years like none other. They tested the resolve of these unseen public servants in ways never experienced. From managing multiple disasters at once to mobilizing fragmented community-driven responses to COVID-19, emergency managers rose to the occasion in unprecedented ways. Before many in the public were aware of the looming pandemic, emergency managers across the nation were aware of what lay ahead in 2020 and were there working to address it.

As news of the COVID-19 global pandemic began to unfold in China in late 2019 (Reuters, 2020), emergency managers started considering the potential impact in their communities. By the time the first death occurred in China on January 11, 2020 (Reuters, 2020), emergency managers and public health officials started coordinating and preparing for the repatriation of American citizens abroad. Their response coordination increased substantially through January and February as cases began emerging in Europe, and the Diamond Princess cruise ship was docked in Japan experiencing a major outbreak (Reuters, 2020).

Eventually, COVID-19 made its way to the United States, prompting major selloffs in the stock market and widespread travel bans. On March 13, 2020, then-U.S. President Donald Trump acknowledged the severity of the crisis, declaring a national emergency. Throughout the rest of spring and into the summer, cases continued to soar (Reuters, 2020), presenting new challenges to emergency managers across the nation.

Throughout the summer and into the fall, regional outbreaks, coupled with political unrest and widespread protests (Reuters, 2020), stretched thin an already beaten-down emergency management system. As communities began to ease restrictions, planning was underway for a fall resurgence and mass vaccination campaign. The following section tells the story of emergency managers serving in silence throughout 2020 and into the spring of 2021, told from the perspective of emergency managers in Maryland who lived through the daily challenges with the nation's largest emergency management response in its history.

The Emergency Management Response to COVID-19

Pre-Pandemic—Monitoring and Early Coordination

Before the pandemic made its impact on the United States, emergency managers were coordinating efforts to protect those abroad and to prepare for direct impacts. In Maryland, our response story began long before the pandemic emerged from the daily noise of national headlines. Early response coordination efforts included coordinating with the Centers for Disease Control and Prevention (CDC) for plans to repatriate Americans through a limited number of airports in the United States, one of which is in the National Capital Region. Working across agencies and governmental levels, officials developed plans for transportation, providing housing for those in mandatory quarantine and medical care for expats returning to the United States. We did have previous experience with pandemics, recently with the response to Ebola in 2014 and H1N1 in 2007; however, even with those experiences, COVID-19 seemed like another pandemic false alarm, like Ebola in 2018. Little did we know that this incident was shaping up to far exceed the complexity of those responses.

Applying lessons learned to improve future response by developing plans, conducting training, and testing plans is a core function of emergency managers. In the years since those incidents, officials across the country developed plans, engaged stakeholders, and formed relationships with key response partners. However, as was the case with many past disasters (e.g., 9/11, Hurricane Katrina), the more time passes from the disaster, the less attention and resources it receives. As a nation, we have a short attention span, and the attention span for pandemics was no different from these disasters.

Despite the challenges of waning attention, in Maryland, emergency managers at all levels of government developed a response system capable of meeting the needs of any threat or hazard. This was the result of years of efforts to engage the correct partners through a variety of preparedness actions and engagement. The outcome was an emergency management system capable of flexing between civil unrest, extreme weather events, and even a global pandemic. The next several months would test not only our response system but also the entire nation's emergency management system in ways never imagined.

Immediate Response—Cancellations and Lockdowns

After 2 months of buildup, response activities reached an inflection point in late February when COVID-19 cases began to appear in the United States (Reuters, 2020). In Maryland, our response coordination efforts now pivoted to mitigating direct impacts from COVID-19 in Maryland communities. From past experiences and knowledge about pandemics, we identified immediate concerns related to supply chain, specifically personal protective equipment (PPE) and medical supplies needed for the response. These concerns materialized in early March 2020 as response efforts dramatically increased.

By March that year, amid widespread lockdowns, national controversy, and political posturing, emergency managers continued to quietly do their work in the background. Spreading the word and informing the public became one of the immediate priorities for emergency managers. This included mobilizing public information officers (PIOs) across Maryland state government into a systematic joint information system (JIS) to bring forth one consistent message and responding to the hundreds of media inquiries each day. These efforts, spread across both traditional media and social media platforms, provided vital information to an uneasy public whose lives had been thrust into chaos. Like other functions, we quietly provided the structure and systems to elevate the profile of public health officials as they communicated key messages.

In addition to the public, the initial months of the pandemic left the business community reeling. Maryland leveraged our Maryland Business Emergency Operations Center as a means to connect with the business community. Through active engagement and weekly conference calls, we provided direct interpretative guidance for executive orders, received and distributed scarce supplies, and provided updates about the governmental response (Tartaglia & Overly, 2020). Emergency managers leveraged both the JIS and the MBEOC to connect with external stakeholders. Our approach was not unique in Maryland. For those states that had established relationships with the private sector, the integration was seamless. Outwardly, we maintained a calm and collected presence, working diligently with the private sector even if internally we were encountering once-in-a-career challenges.

Early in the pandemic, several major challenges emerged for the teams of emergency managers coordinating response efforts. Working alongside subject matter experts, we facilitated resolution to these emerging cascading problems. The first, and perhaps most public, challenge was locating and purchasing enough PPE to serve hospitals, first responders, long-term care facilities, prison staff, and other essential services. With a nonexistent supply chain, procurement specialists engaged in bidding wars with other states. As PPE became available, vendors demanded large down payments or payments in full before they would process a transaction. Within minutes, millions of dollars of supplies would sell out, leaving staff to regroup and pursue other suppliers. Supplies were short and dwindling. As an example, at the height of the initial surge throughout Maryland, we were using more than 120,000 N-95 masks per day (Friend et al., 2020). Eventually, in late spring, piecing together several sources including the private marketplace, federal government, donations, as well as repurposed supplies, emergency managers stepped up and met the challenge of providing PPE to those in most need.

While the PPE crisis was dominating the news cycle, we were preparing for a major surge on the health care system. We watched as COVID-19 patients overran the health care systems in Italy and New York, and expert modeling from prestigious universities predicted that this was Maryland's eventual fate. Again, working across a stakeholder group of subject matter experts, emergency managers led a statewide effort to build surge capacity through construction of temporary structures, equipping the Baltimore Convention Center as a mass hospital site and taking other measures to ease the burden on the health care system. Physical space was only one component of building capacity; it also involved a massive undertaking of identifying retired doctors, nurses, and other health care staff to work in the newly expanded spaces. Like many other major undertakings, emergency managers coordinated these massive efforts quietly in the background.

Among the operational challenges emergency managers faced, building sufficient testing capacity to uncover the true extent of the pandemic proved challenging. Once again, our teams of emergency managers coordinated closely with officials across the government to build out the components needed for testing, facilities, equipment, staff, and lab capacity. Like PPE, the supplies health professionals needed to effectuate widespread testing were unattainable. From nasal swabs to viral transport medium to reactive agents used in laboratories, the technical components of testing simply were not available. What is worse, lab capacity was inadequate, and testing sites were scarce. In the initial months of the pandemic, emergency managers identified and purchased supplies, negotiated agreements with federal and private laboratories to expand capacity, and worked through the logistics of converting vehicle emissions sites across Maryland into drive-through testing sites.

While expanding testing and increasing hospital capacity were two of the major actions emergency managers undertook in the early months of the pandemic, the impacts of stay-at-home orders and school closures presented a number of cascading impacts. Augmenting widespread feeding activities for students who rely on school for meals as well as for the newly unemployed became a major operation. In addition to food distribution, emergency managers worked to support response to COVID-19 hot spots such as nursing homes and in critical services such as the poultry industry. Throughout the initial months of the pandemic, we quietly leveraged our multiagency collaboration and problem-solving skills to assemble teams of experts capable of meeting the demands of a rapidly developing situation.

SUMMER—PREPARING FOR THE FALL

Maryland was largely spared the horrific spring impacts in New York thanks to aggressive government action and a commitment by citizens to adhere to stay-at-home orders, capacity limitations at businesses, and masking requirements. This likely was due to Governor Larry Hogan's pragmatic approach to leadership during the response. Where some states hyper-politicized the pandemic, Maryland leaned on pragmatism to mitigate its effects.

As the calendar turned from spring to early summer, restrictions eased, and we paused to address some issues completely neglected in the previous 6 months. This "break" also included reducing response activity while preparing for a second wave in the fall. Thanks to the efforts of state and local agencies, Maryland now had an infrastructure in place to meet the demands of a fall surge.

While Maryland's COVID-19 response scaled back in the summer months, and with preparations for fall underway, we had new issues to contend with. The killing of George Floyd kicked off nationwide protests (Taylor, 2021) that yet again required the intervention of emergency managers. In addition, an overly active hurricane season (National Oceanic and Atmospheric Administration, 2020) challenged exhausted emergency managers along the Atlantic and Gulf coasts. Maryland was not immune from the overbearing hurricane season, as Tropical Storm Isaias cut through the state in early August (Campbell, 2020). This response, couched in the midst of COVID-19, required emergency managers to adjust their plans, such as the way they operated shelters. COVID-19 also changed the way stakeholders conducted preliminary damage assessment post-impact. It also involved doing things we never imagined, such as live media interviews from our living rooms and having a skeleton crew of four people physically at the State Emergency Operations Center during Isaias. Outside the Northeast, emergency managers grappled with the impacts of wildfires (Roman et al., 2020), earthquakes (United States Geological Society, 2021), and other hazards. Exhausted and stretched thin, emergency managers across the nation pushed forward toward a fall resurgence of COVID-19.

The Fall Surge

As predicted by top scientists, the United States experienced a fall COVID-19 surge that impacted communities across the nation (Davis, 2021). In Maryland, it was time to ramp coordination efforts back up, reactivate the MBEOC, and implement plans for mass vaccination. Through a multiagency coordination structure, Maryland officials carefully monitored case levels, hospitalizations, and deaths while elected officials implemented new mitigation measures.

In the spirt of reaching complete and utter exhaustion, we were called upon once again, this time to help coordinate public safety support for the 2020 general election. Responding to the needs of state election officials, staff worked to deploy critical supplies to polling stations (e.g., sanitizer, PPE) prior to the general election. We coordinated operational conference calls across the whole community and again activated the State Emergency Operations Center on Election Day. With little rest from an unrelenting year, emergency managers throughout Maryland worked through the holidays as cases surged, creating new challenges.

Beyond 2020—A New Year

As the world turned the page toward 2021, emergency managers were still overwhelmed battling the virus. Post-holiday case surges and hospitalizations tested hospital systems, and emergency managers continued work on building hospital surge capacity while simultaneously driving the push for mass vaccination. Despite challenges, 2021 briefly provided hope that the end of the pandemic was in sight; however, after a relentless year, emergency managers across the National Capital Region once again faced novel challenges.

Months of divisive rhetoric came to a head on January 6, 2021, when a mob of Trump supporters breached the U.S. Capitol while Congress was in the process of certifying election results. Within Washington, D.C., emergency managers were busy providing information and supporting resources needs before the day began. Despite a footprint of public safety resources in place, they quickly became overwhelmed, immediately seeking assistance from Maryland and Virginia. We took decisive action, sending resources immediately to Washington, D.C., much in the same way they had supported us during the 2015 Baltimore Civil Unrest that resulted in the wake of the death of Freddy Gray. Across Maryland, our emergency management partners were once again simultaneously responding to multiple major incidents. One report out on a call exemplifies the chaos that 2021 brought with it, where an emergency manager noted, "that concludes my insurrection report, now moving onto my COVID-19 report." The first week of 2021 brought with it the same challenges that had plagued emergency managers since early 2020. Despite our best efforts, we, like our emergency management colleagues across the nation, were unable to escape the relentless grind of 2020 and 2021.

As vaccine supply increased in early 2021, emergency managers in Maryland built out vaccination sites to ensure equitable access. These efforts included building out mass vaccination sites, working with public health on vaccine distribution logistics, and sending vaccination messages across the state. These efforts developed the structural framework for massive vaccine distribution.

The mass vaccination effort was as relentless, if not more so than the fall surge, PPE shortages, or any of the other problems we addressed throughout the pandemic. At one point, the Maryland Emergency Management Agency (MEMA), an agency of 110 people, had more than 100 staff members dedicated full-time to the vaccination effort.

Statewide, nearly 8,000 state employees contributed to the spring efforts to develop mass vaccination capacity. We converted amusement parks, convention centers, football stadiums, abandoned shopping malls, and pretty much any site capable of a high flow of vehicle traffic into mass vaccination efforts. Mass vaccination sites were established and operated by local, state, and federal emergency management teams throughout Maryland.

Equity was a major concern of ours in addition to the newly minted Biden administration. We partnered with FEMA to develop mobile vaccination teams that deployed into hard-to-reach communities, those without the resources to obtain a shot at a mass vaccination site. These efforts, coupled with a deliberate and well-coordinated public messaging campaign, propelled Maryland to the top of the list for state vaccination rates in the nation.

Implications for Emergency Managers

As this chapter described, emergency managers supported nearly every facet of the response to the global pandemic from 2020 into 2021. On top of this massive effort, they dealt with hurricanes, tornadoes, wildfires, elections, insurrection, riots, and other hazards. Meanwhile, these dedicated public servants largely go unrecognized for their efforts, serving in emergency operations centers usually far away from the cameras on the scene of incidents. The response to the COVID-19 pandemic highlighted several key issues for emergency managers.

Elevating the Profile of Emergency Managers

Emergency managers serve in silence, but this does not need to be the case. Originating from diverse cultural, subject matter, and geographic backgrounds, these dedicated public servants provide the backbone for the community response to disaster. To highlight the important role emergency managers play, elected officials, community members, and others involved in response activities should recognize the work of emergency managers publicly both in response and recovery.

Part of this task involves committing to professionalizing the field of emergency management and working to make these organizations indispensable to government. As a relatively young field, born with its roots in civil defense, and until recently seen as a second-career destination for retired public safety professional, emergency managers are now coming from different backgrounds and with college degrees, a major step forward for the field. Emergency managers must commit to education, training, and professional development to elevate emergency management as a field in the eyes of the public and elected officials.

Across the nation, elected officials are recognizing the skills of emergency managers, entrusting them to lead complex multiagency coordination efforts beyond traditional hazards. Emergency managers are more than the "hurricane people" and should be respected as such. Along with elevating the profile of emergency managers, communities need to adequately invest in their emergency management systems.

Investing in Community Emergency Management Systems

Local and state governments have historically underfunded emergency management agencies. Across the nation, agencies rely on federal homeland security grants for sustainment of basic activities. What this leaves is public administrators who work long hours for low pay without the recognition and support they deserve. The year 2020 showed how difficult it is to maintain response operations for months on end, relying on the same staff to fill key emergency operations center staff in perpetuity.

Investments in emergency management programs also allow for smooth response and recovery operations. This includes building systems and processes capable of rapid procurement of scarce commodities, integrating horizontally and vertically across response partners. In addition, states and local governments need to set aside funding for disasters as the federal government works to divest itself from funding small disasters. Building emergency management organizations and disaster relief funds will be critically important as disasters become more frequent and intense because of the impacts of climate change (Harvey, 2018).

Prioritize Disaster Risk Reduction

Disasters are not decreasing. Coupled with thinly stretched resources, explosive population growth in vulnerable areas, and increasing complexity/independency of critical systems, emergency managers will have their work cut out for them in the decades to come. The only way to break the cycle of disaster is to invest in transformative hazard mitigation and disaster risk reduction projects. Emergency managers can further demonstrate their value and apply the emergency management system to the implementation of hazard reducing activity.

Changes in federal hazard mitigation policy through the Disaster Recovery Reform Act provide an opportunity to implement widespread sweeping change in communities that will break the cycle of disaster. Coupling government investment with partners in the private sector will allow communities to make meaningful strides in stopping disasters from happening (Taraglia & Overly, 2020). Continued reliance on response and recovery mechanisms are simply unsustainable in the changing threat/hazard environment.

Conclusion

Emergency managers serve silently yet provide essential background services that drive community disaster response. Their service often goes either unnoticed or unrecognized in the broader context of community response to disasters. Rarely the ones highlighted on the scene of a major disaster, emergency managers instead work tirelessly in the background to effectuate operations.

The 2020 global pandemic challenged emergency managers across the world in ways only imagined previously. For more than a year, they responded to the changing demands of the pandemic, successfully building hospital capacity and a mass testing strategy, organizing a mass vacci-nation campaign, and solving dynamic problems as they arose. Meeting the needs of the COVID-19 pandemic would have been challenging enough; however, they also responded to several compounding disasters throughout the year.

Emergency managers have a unique opportunity to elevate their profession and continue to demonstrate their value. Emerging from the pandemic, they can emerge from silence as the field continues to professionalize. This, coupled with greater investment in emergency management programs at the state and local level as well as an emphasis on reducing disaster risk, will position emergency managers to meet the rising demands of a changing environment.

140 | Overly

References

Campbell, C. (2020, August 4). Timeline: Tropical storm Isaias brings heavy rains, winds to Maryland on its way up East Coast. *The Baltimore Sun.* https://www.baltimoresun.com/weather/bs-md-tropical-storm-isaias-timeline-20200804-ywmwyg4lrbe3njam6hlpdiucuy-story.html

Chaves, R., Schneider, D., Correia, A., Motta, C., & Borges, M. (2019). Crowdsourcing as a tool for urban emergency management: Lessons from the literature and typology. *Sensors, 19*(23), 5235. https://doi.org/10.3390/s19235235

Davis, W. (2021, January 3). *COVID-19 cases surge in U.S. as vaccinations fall below government predictions.* NPR. https://www.npr.org/2021/01/03/953045468/covid-19-cases-surge-in-u-s-as-vaccinations-fall-below-government-predictions

Friend, A., Christen, R., Vogel, R., & Fenley, A. (2020). *COVID-19 burn rate calculation methodology summary report.* Maryland Emergency Management Agency.

Harvey, C. (2018, January 2). Scientists can now blame individual natural disasters on climate change. *Scientific American.* https://www.scientificamerican.com/article/scientists-can-now-blame-individual-natural-disasters-on-climate-change/

Le, P. (2016, February 18). Seattle experiments with new solutions to ease homelessness. *AP News.* https://apnews.com/article/7015cb1ddb444274a4817d7d3c07cd1d

National Oceanic & Atmospheric Administration. (2020). *Record-breaking Atlantic hurricane season draws to an end.* https://www.noaa.gov/media-release/record-breaking-atlantic-hurricane-season-draws-to-end

Reuters. (2020, June 28). *Timeline: How the global coronavirus pandemic unfolded.* https://www.reuters.com/article/us-health-coronavirus-timeline/timeline-how-the-global-coronavirus-pandemic-unfolded-idUSKBN23Z0UW

Roman, J., Verzoni, A., & Sutherland, S. (2020). The wildfire crisis, November/December 2020. *NFPA Journal.* https://www.nfpa.org/News-and-Research/Publications-and-media/NFPA-Journal/2020/November-December-2020/Features/Wildfire

Stults, M. (2017). Integrating climate change into hazard mitigation planning: Opportunities and examples in practice. *Climate Risk Management, 17,* 21–34. https://doi.org/10.1016/j.crm.2017.06.004

Sylves, R. (2008). Disaster management in the United States. In *Disaster policy and politics: Emergency management and homeland security* (pp. 2–25). CQ Press. https://www.doi.org/10.4135/9781483330761.n1

Tartaglia, A., & Overly, K. (2020). COVID-19 case study: Public private partnerships in Maryland. *Journal of Critical Infrastructure Policy, 1*(2). https://doi.org/10.18278/jcip.1.2.9

Taylor, D. (2021, January 6). George Floyd protests: A timeline. *The New York Times*. https://www.nytimes.com/article/george-floyd-protests-timeline.html

Toque, R. (2017, March). Maryland governor declares state of emergency for opioid crisis.

The Washington Post. https://www.washingtonpost.com/local/md-politics/hogan-declares-opioid-state-of-emergency/2017/03/01/5c22fcfa-fe2f-11e6-99b4-9e613afeb09f_story.html

United States Geological Survey. (2020). *Significant Earthquakes—2020*. https://earthquake.usgs.gov/earthquakes/browse/significant.php?year=2020

Yankelovich, D. (2014). *Wicked problems, workable solutions: Lessons from a public life*. ProQuest Ebook Central.

Possibly Misunderstood Roles and Responsibilities

In this book, we have been placing the spotlight on public servants who are often ignored or underappreciated for the hard work they do. In this section, we are continuing this exploration by asking what happens to some of these public servants when attention does fall on them—their work may fundamentally misunderstood, demeaned, or stigmatized. There are many jobs in the public service that are important, noble, and necessary, but are perceived as negative in the eyes of the public and other stakeholders. We know what meaning and value can be socially constructed through iterative understanding processes and that this understanding can be manipulated (Ainsworth & Ghin, 2021; Gergen, 1985; Liebrucks, 2001).

While scholars in public administration have examined election administration over the past twenty years (with the presidential election in the United States in 2000 sparking renewed interest), the work done by professional public servants in election offices is misunderstood, underappreciated, and indeed actively questioned by many with little understanding of the work they do (Montjoy, 2010; Mohr et al., 2019). In chapter 8, Amanda Clark opens the door to an elections administration office in a setting of particular importance for understanding this complex environment—local governments where election administration is often fraught with political contention, misunderstandings, and even threats of violence (So & Szep, 2021).

There are many jobs in the public service that need to be done for the good of the state and citizenry but receive negative attention and/or stigma. It could be because the work associated with those jobs is tough (physically or emotionally), is not welcomed by citizens or viewed as punitive, or have shame or attached to them, with these jobs constructed as "dirty work" (Ashforth & Kreiner, 1999; Mastracci, 2021). As Mastracci (2021) argues, government often steps in to provide services when no one wants to do so, or people cannot afford services in the private sector. Therefore, when professionals work in those settings, they can acquire social constructed stigmas attached to their work—"dirt exists when people think it does" (Ashforth & Kreiner, 2014, p. 85). Dirty work can be "physical dirty work . . . handling foul material such as collecting garbage or performing autopsies . . . social dirty work places the worker in close contact with socially stigmatized populations as with addiction counselors and parole officers. Morally dirty work involves engaging in ethically questionable conduct and/or coming into contact with those who do" (Mastracci, 2021, p. 3).

In chapter 9, Adam Croft examines the public defenders who represent many criminal defendants in the United States, helping to ensure that people's constitutional rights are protected. While this should be perceived as a higher calling, these public defenders battle dirty work stigma, along with significant capacity and emotional labor challenges. In chapter 10, drawing on years of experience in the job, Michael Fouassier describes being a property tax assessor, a public servant few citizens are ever excited to see arrive at their door. However, local government could not accomplish any of its goals or serve its citizens without careful and thoughtful valuation and assessment of property for tax purposes. While tax assessment could be considered dirty work by some, Fouassier demonstrates how integral it is to the success of government and how those who do this work serve without fanfare or complaint, even when they are challenged by those with little understanding of the importance of this work.

Finally, in chapter 11, Maren Trochmann travels through the world of public housing and homelessness policy work, describing the many public servants who together work to ensure that those most in need have access to safe housing and seek to end homelessness in the United States. While housing is at the center of individuals' well-being, those experiencing homelessness or housing insecurity are often characterized negatively by policy makers and the public, making those public servants working this area subject to dirty work stigmas as they endeavor to change minds and policy on homelessness and affordable housing and help those in need.

Together these chapters showcase public servants who do work that is fundamental to a functioning state and democracy—running elections, providing people with representation in criminal cases, assessing property taxes to fund public services, and facilitating affordable housing—but is misunderstood and even stigmatized. We hope these chapters foster understanding of this important work and reflection on the many challenging jobs required to keep government running and citizens served.

Our Stories and Reflections on Section 3

Staci: *The chapters in this section highlight for me the importance of what some might think are the "simple" aspects of public service. Yet we really notice them when something goes wrong. Throughout each chapter, what struck me was the internal struggle the public servants experienced when simply trying to carry out their job functions. I noticed people discuss burdens such as time, resources, the political environment, funding. Maren's chapter here, I think, highlights all the themes so far in this book—life and death situations, contributions to a functioning democracy, and dual identities. Sadly, Amanda's chapter on election workers in the U.S. also shows the danger of doing again what some might think is the "simple" public service role. Amanda and I both live in Florida, and as I write this story Gov. Ron DeSantis has just signed into law the creation of the nation's first stand-alone elections police force, despite saying our Florida 2020 election was the best run, most efficient, and safest (Fineout, 2022).*

The stories in these chapters show public servants under stress, working in systems ever changing and sometimes crumbling under the weight of the pressure. The public defenders, as Adam's stories show, are tired. They are not always portrayed well or understood. He has a section on emotional labor in his chapter, and I can see that theme clearly throughout the other chapters in this section and the book. Emotional labor is a workplace response to the environment and often dictates how someone is supposed to behave. Solving these problems like homelessness or vaccine hesitancy or teacher overload while having to smile is taxing. These chapters do a nice job of bringing that to light, even if the language of emotional labor is not used.

Jessica: *I remember the first time I voted (not sharing the date). I was so excited, but I never really thought about what went into administering the election. I do have to admit—it was a little anticlimactic. I expected balloons to drop from the air when I left the polling booth (or at least an exit survey). Now I wish for those simpler, more innocent times when voting was a* noncontroversial process. When I worked in Cleveland, Ohio, several of my students worked in election administration and I got firsthand accounts from them of how important and stressful this work is, especially since Cuyahoga County often ended up making an actual difference for the national leadership of the country. As we move toward the next election and we all hold out hope that it is fair and without incident, supporting those who do this critical work is more important than ever.

Across these chapters, we see many areas of public service we take for granted (e.g., how our properties are assessed) or many that we never experience but will really appreciate if we need to (e.g., public defenders, affordable housing). Reading these chapters made me think about how much I really love seeing these stories told and how we can continue to collect these stories moving forward—for our students and for the field.

Alex: Many of the narratives or descriptions of street-level professions found in these chapters echo my previous professional and volunteer experiences in frontline, public-facing roles. Though the work I did in emergency services roles is often slightly better understood than those detailed here, many of the same assumptions about roles, contexts, and resources are at work here as well. Assumptions (especially those that are unexamined or untested) can be powerful in shaping public ideas of or sentiment about the work of public and nonprofit organizations. Taken together, this should serve as a call for all of us to actively avoid what may be comfortable assumptions about these types of potentially underappreciated roles, and indeed to actively seek out more and better information. This book is important in that it does just that—it continues conversations about the importance of street-level roles while also highlighting those that are often underexamined.

Lauren: When I worked in the City of Irving in Texas, one of my tasks was entering responses from our citizen satisfaction surveys. There was one department that always got the worst ratings—code enforcement! I worked with officers from the department on a neighborhood initiative and found them professional, hardworking, and, surprisingly, passionate about city codes. It turns out that somebody should be passionate about city codes! I saw firsthand how the public can build a negative perception of a department due to the impression that code enforcement is nuisance in their lives or based on rumors of their terribleness. However, I felt that the public would feel very differently if they saw what these professionals did or got to know them. The reality is that code enforcement often plays an important role in cities. In Irving, they often mediated neighborhood disputes that came up because of external paint colors or lack of lawn care, issues that do not require the police but have the *potential to snowball into much bigger problems. This dissonance is one of the reasons I think that this book is an important contribution to public service discourse. Making the hidden more visible.*

References

Ainsworth, S., & Ghin, P. (2021). Public servants in reflection. In H. Sullivan, H. Dickinson, & H. Henderson (Eds.), *The Palgrave Handbook of the Public Servant* (pp. 411–423). Palgrave MacMillan/Springer.

Ashforth, B. E., & Kreiner, G. E. (1999). "How can you do it?": Dirty work and the challenge of constructing a positive identity. *The Academy of Management Review, 24*(3), 413–434. https://doi.org/10.2307/259134

Ashforth, B. E., & Kreiner, G. E. (2014). Dirty work and dirtier work: Differences in countering physical, social, and moral stigma. *Management and Organization Review, 10*(1), 81–108. https://doi.org/10.1111/more.12044

Fineout, G. (2022). DeSantis signs bill creating one of the nation's only election police units. https://www.politico.com/news/2022/04/25/desantis-florida-election-police-units-00027577

Gergen, K. J. (1985). The social constructionist movement in modern psychology. *American Psychologist, 40*(3), 266–275. https://doi.org/10.1037/0003-066X.40.3.266

Liebrucks, A. (2001). The concept of social construction. *Theory & Psychology, 11*(3), 363–391. https://doi.org/10.1177/0959354301113005

Mastracci, S. H. (2022). Dirty work and emotional labor in public service: Why government employers should adopt an ethic of care. *Review of Public Personnel Administration, 42*(3), 537–552. https://doi.org/10.1177/0734371X21997548

Mohr, Z., Pope, J. V., Kropf, M. E., & Shepherd, M. J. (2019). Strategic spending: Does politics influence election administration expenditure? *American Journal of Political Science, 63*(2), 427–438. https://www.jstor.org/stable/45132487

Montjoy, R. S. (2010). The changing nature . . . and costs . . . of election administration. *Public Administration Review, 70*(6), 867–875. https://doi.org/10.1111/j.1540-6210.2010.02218.x

So, L., and Szep, J. (2021, November 9). Campaign of fear: A Reuters special report. *Reuters.* https://www.reuters.com/investigates/special-report/usa-election-threats/

8

When Silence Is Golden

Stories from an Elections Office

AMANDA D. CLARK

Varying levels of visibility are evident across the spectrum of public service. For some, the desire to be visible may also vary as the harsh limelight of criticism, warranted or not, shines on them. Elections offices around the country have experienced an increased level of attention over the past few major election cycles. How do those involved with administering elections perceive this attention? What would these public servants want the public to know about the task of running elections? For many public servants who do election work, there is a desire for the public to know that they care deeply about doing a good job. However, they also would express that while their job is extremely important, it is also routine and bound by laws over which election workers have little control. The phrase "serving in silence" can mean public servants who *prefer* to serve in silence because silence is a metaphor for having done a job well. More ominously in the world of elections, not being visible may also be preferable for safety reasons. For election workers across the country, both ideas hold merit and were particularly present in Palm Beach County, Florida.

For those of a certain age, Palm Beach County holds a special place in the history of U.S. elections (Hale, Montjoy, & Brown, 2015; Moynihan & Silva, 2008). I moved to Palm Beach County in 2018 as our family relocated for my spouse's job. The academic job market, challenging in the best of times, was particularly difficult for a new transplant from northeast Ohio with no local network to leverage. With my political science/public administration background, I reached out to the local supervisor of elections (SOE) office and was lucky enough to land an entry-level position as an elections specialist in June 2020. My peers back in Ohio were excited for me. We discussed my new experience in a podcast,[1] and the inevitable came up. "Isn't that the hanging chad county?" Indeed, it was, but Palm Beach County and the state of Florida have worked on both improving their images across the country and elections processes since 2000. The mantra around the office was absolutely "We don't want to be in the news," at least, not in a negative way. Overall, the 2020 elections in Florida were successful, albeit with some worrying signs of things to come with the 2021 state legislative session (Fins, 2021).

My experience with my colleagues at the elections office was one of the most enlightening (and exhausting!) of my life. Elections offices are interesting places. In presidential and gubernatorial election years, they are teeming with activity and people. Regular staff are but a small contingent of the thousands of poll workers, trainers, temporary employees, and volunteers who work during a presidential election cycle. Years without major elections bring fewer poll workers and temporary help, but the work that is left is handled by the small group of regular employees. How do these contributors feel about their role in delivering democracy?

This chapter aims to uncover how the need to be understood, but perhaps remain invisible, impacts the people who end up working in one of the most public, foundational, yet increasingly attacked cornerstones of our democracy: elections. Elections and voting behavior are often the purview of political science. We receive much information regarding polling, voter turnout, and other quantitative data. Even in public administration, research has focused on how elections are impacted by public budgets (Clark, 2019), the selection of elections' systems vendors (Gibson, 2020), and campaign financing (Garrett, 2016). In this chapter, I share stories, including my own, of the unique contributions that elections' staff share with their communities and how those contributions impact democratic practices (Dodge, Ospina, & Foldy, 2005).

My research found that everyone appreciated and was proud of the vital work they were doing to ensure the voters of our county were receiving the best service and opportunity to vote. They were also cognizant of the fact that, like the oft-heard phrase regarding our federal intelligence services, "we never get to hear about the good things we do, only the mistakes." The desire to change the reputation of the office and to have that reputation match the amount of work that goes into holding elections was palpable from day one. However, being seen and being appreciated can be two entirely different things. The idea that serving in silence can be a positive one is evident in stories uncovered during my time at the office.

The motivations of the staff can be framed by the mission statement of the organization: Integrity, Accountability, and Service. While these goals may seem antithetical to remaining somewhat invisible, I would argue that the achievement of those goals brings the office closer to being respected and not publicly maligned while fostering a sense of civic pride and support from the community. This chapter proceeds as follows: first, a short summary of the staffing needs of an elections office, followed by a discussion on how narratives can be used to uncover the lived experiences of public servants who are not always in the limelight, and, finally, an analysis of how the different stories of public servants impact their understanding of their own role in public service and the value of that service to the greater public. To conclude, I discuss how public administrators can use their own stories to help protect their work and shed more light on the vital services they provide.

It Takes a Village: Running an Election

As we talk about public servants who serve in silence and unpack their stories, we come across layers of unseen public servants within even that distinction. There are three categories of public servants who work during elections, and they have varying degrees of visibility (see Table 8.1).

Table 8.1. Visibility by Election Administration Role

Public Servant Role	Visibility Level
Poll Workers	Very visible
Election Office Staff	Somewhat visible (mostly the supervisor or head of the elections office)
Seasonal/Temporary Help	Very invisible

Source: Author-created.

Elections offices in Florida are staffed by regular county employees who serve under an elected supervisor of elections. Other states have different procedures or regulations regarding the administration of elections (NCSL, 2020). The number of regular employees varies by county, with smaller counties staffed with a small contingent of staff (<5) and larger counties with larger staffs (>50). However, regardless of the number of staff, there are several common tasks that all offices need to address. Whether these tasks are conducted by one person or departments with multiple people, they remain important and time sensitive, and require a certain level of expertise.

- Administration—elections offices are responsible for replying to public records requests; providing updated voter information via phone, fax, email, social media, and traditional news outlets; being accessible to the public with office hours; and providing voter education and outreach. Human resource and accounting functions also fall into this category.

- Poll worker recruitment/training—elections offices are responsible for keeping up-to-date with all changes in state and local law regarding the administration of elections. These changes happen regularly and require constant updates to training for even seasoned poll workers. Florida law requires poll workers to be trained prior to every election. So, for presidential election years where there is a presidential preference primary, a state primary, and a general election, poll workers must attend training three times. For large counties, the number of poll workers can run into the thousands, as the bare minimum for a staffing a precinct is five poll workers. Poll workers must also be trained anytime there is an equipment change or a change in security procedure.

- Vote-by-mail (VBM)—states have offered absentee (also known as vote-by-mail) for decades, but 2020 saw a surge in interest because of the COVID-19 pandemic. Vote-by-mail in larger counties often includes large, automated machines that help in stuffing envelopes, processing returns, and matching signatures. Smaller offices may do all or some of these tasks manually. Temporary help is necessary for large primary and general elections, as the percentage of participating voters increases. Record retention and storage of VBM ballots are also a function of this area.

- Voting equipment storage—elections require a vast number of supplies (more than I thought before I started working there). From voting equipment to ballots to orange cones for accessible parking to signage, all those materials need to be stored when not in use and dispatched efficiently during elections. The year 2020 brought a new category of personal protective equipment (PPE) such as gloves, face masks, and hand sanitizer.

- Information technology (IT) and cyber security—elections, while backed by paper ballots for audit and fraud purposes, are technical affairs where election data are stored and protected electronically. Elections offices must staff IT personnel to maintain equipment and prepare the office for cyberattacks.

Regular staff only account for a fraction of the people who work on elections. Months before the actual elections, elections offices hire temporary, seasonal staff to help with election processes. Temporary staff help in the warehouse by prepping supplies, serve as ballot openers in the VBM department, are trained by IT to help maintain voting equipment and run vote tabulation tasks, can be hired to work in the office to assist in answering phones, and can act as trainers and assistant trainers as poll workers are attending class. While many people barely are aware of the regular employees who are tasked with conducting elections around the country, these seasonal and temporary workers fly even more under the radar and help bring about democracy in the snippets of time they give.

Interestingly, the most visible category of public servants during elections are poll workers. Voters have the most interaction with poll workers at their precinct and may even be poll workers themselves. Numbers of poll workers vary by county and number of precincts. During the 2020 election cycle, poll workers were on the front lines of an unprecedented challenge, battling COVID-19 exposure and an emotionally charged, record-breaking voter turnout. All three of these categories of public servants came to these positions for a variety of reasons and have stories to tell about their journey. The next section outlines how narratives can provide scholars with rich data about the depth and breadth of government work.

Tell Me a Story: Narrative Inquiry in Public Administration Research

Narrative inquiry is an essential tool in the public service methods toolbox. Stories help us understand the world around us; as such, the "narrative as knowledge" approach (Dodge, Ospina, & Foldy, 2005, p. 291) is one that resonates when discussing public administration work. This approach also tracks with the idea that Stout and Love (2017) identify as "public encounters." Although they were discussing practices of direct democracy, it can also be interpreted as a practice in which public servants relate to each other. Elections offices in particular are populated by a unique blend of regular employees ("experts"), poll workers (highly skilled "laypeople"), and temporary help (many of whom have no election experience). These different groups reside both inside and outside the formal structure of the public administration office but form a single community when elections are being held. All these people use stories to express their skills, to teach others, and to make sense of the larger mission at hand and their role in it (Dodge, Ospina, & Foldy, 2005; Maynard-Moody & Musheno, 2003).

Storytelling is a way in which people can explain their motivations, their work, their struggles, and their hopes for their own future growth. Unlike van Hulst's (2013) assertion that it is difficult to access the "mundane frontline work through storytelling" (p. 522), in many instances storytelling becomes a language in which employees tell the newbies how *we* got to *here* and *why* it was done one way or another. In fact, in places where there were no written procedures or the procedures were scattered throughout the office, the stories were what helped connect A to B (Behn, 2009; Levin & Sanger, 1994; Swap, Leonard, Shields, & Abrams, 2001; White, 1999). Stories can lead to enhanced collaborative innovations as many actors work together to provide the best level of public service (Sorensen & Torfing, 2011). Herzog and McClain (2011) posited that stories from public administrators could be assessed on seven criteria: relevancy, application, factual/lifelike, social construction, effectiveness, has a point, and goodness. While this chapter does not delve so deeply into assessing whether one storyteller was better than the rest, the criteria are important to assessing how well stories relayed the work happening on the ground and how they fit into the overall mission of the office.

The stories that came to me during my time at the elections office, in addition to my own evolving understanding of my role, were an inductive process of learning. Charmaz (2014) states that, "increasingly, a major purpose for ethnographic study focuses on learning about events and actions in specific settings and situations as they unfold" (p. 36). Like Michel's (2007) study of investment banks, I had prior experience with elections and democracy from my PhD studies, which gave me insight into some of the processes about which I wanted to learn more. As such, I was coming into election administration with a set of basic understandings, but no practical experience. Constructive grounded theory posits that theory is derived from constructed data and researcher involvement (Charmaz, 2014).

As an employee at the Supervisor of Elections office, I was more than a casual observer. My role was deeply embedded within the service of the organization. I ran early voting for both the primary and general elections of 2020. My job duties included training of poll workers, managing the logistics of supplies, on-demand support for all poll workers during the 2-week early voting period, and reporting/record retention functions after the election. My participation was overt, as everyone knew that I was an adjunct professor of political science, and natural, as I was in the field doing the actual work and not in a simulated environment (Flick, 2014). My data are my field notes, taken during meetings, my own reflections, and the interesting conversations I had with my coworkers along the way. My story is my own, and it not intended to replace anyone else's or suggest that my story is the only viable interpretation of these events.

I do not divulge any of my colleagues' actual names or job functions. One, this serves to protect them and not bring them undue scrutiny. Two, the motivations that brought them to public service often have very little to do with the functions they do once they are in the office. I know from experience that in elections, while we may belong to one department or another, it is often all-hands-on-deck when the work of the office demands it. My definition of colleagues also extends to those outside the formal structure of the office, such as poll workers and temporary staff.

Although my experience was unique and focused on one county's elections office, the lessons learned from this fieldwork can be applied to other unseen public servants across a spectrum of services. Indeed, the "sample of an inductive study is never purely random nor convenient" (Nowell & Albrecht, 2019, p. 353). The drive to provide good service to the public, the pride in the work that is being done, coupled with a desire to be judged on their "real" work is likely mirrored across the country. In addition, the idea that "serving in silence" might be becoming more desirable for certain classes of public servants, many of whom are being unfairly targeted as inept or nefarious because of partisan attacks on their work, may resonate across sectors.

"We Run Elections": Integrity, Accountability, and Service[2]

After the appointment of a new supervisor, Wendy Sartory Link, in 2019 (followed by her successful election campaign to be elected supervisor in 2020 for a 4-year term), the Palm Beach County SOE office took on the challenge of revamping its procedures, updating its voting equipment, and reviewing its poll worker training to rectify some of the reliability issues that had sullied the reputation of the organization since the infamous hanging chad debacle of 2000. Antiquated voting equipment, bad ballot design, and a host of issues have been well documented throughout the past 20 years (Beall, 2018; Hale, Montjoy, & Brown, 2015; Washington, 2018). These stories, while certainly having more nuance than there is space to evaluate here, impacted the feelings of the employees and poll workers.

Employees keenly felt the weight of the responsibility to "get it right" and felt their personal reputations would be impacted if mistakes were made. When wearing my name badge or SOE staff shirt, I was often stopped by members of the public imploring me to "not make *us* look bad." Poll workers, the most visible of the three groups working on elections, related the same interactions to me as well. Many of them had been working the polls for years and had many stories to share about friends, family members, and often complete strangers asking them to not "mess it up" or asking them if certain procedures were reliable or secure.[3]

The phrasing of the requests often took me aback, but also made me realize how the public views itself as part of a larger whole. While recognizing that the elections office staff was "responsible" for the administering of the election, the use of the word "us" also indicated a sense of belonging, or being attached, to that public process. As an employee, this shared credit would sometimes chafe. Being an armchair quarterback is never received well by those on the field. However, as a social scientist, it was thrilling to see members of the public still care about democratic processes and their impact on the broader community.

The value of *Integrity*, both as it pertains to election administration and the employees/poll workers, was important to reinstating trust in the office and in democracy itself at the local level. The employees and seasonal workers at the elections office wanted to be recognized for working hard and trying their best to do the right thing. This never meant that everything would be perfect; however, the intent of trying to get it right was an important value that many wanted the public at large to see and appreciate. *Integrity* is also an important part of creating a positive culture within the office; studies have shown that higher levels of trust within the organization can lead to better quality of work and effectiveness (Lee, Oh, & Park, 2019).

The office regularly updated the revamped website and increased its accessibility for the public. *Accountability* and transparency were values that were shared by many within the office. As procedures were revised and written, care was taken to remember the impact of the change on both employees and the voters. Adherence to state and local law drove many of the changes, particularly those regarding security of ballots and equipment. However, employees also tried not to lose sight of how changes may impact the voters. In addition, elections officials rely heavily on the cooperation and service of members of the public during elections as poll workers, so any massive changes to procedure or paperwork must be communicated clearly. A key function of any elections office is good training, as voters' perceptions of how well the office handles its responsibility starts with their experience in the polling place or with the response they receive when asking questions, either via phone or in person at the office.

Effort was also made to keep social media accounts updated, providing pertinent information in a timely manner. Palm Beach County held multiple Facebook town halls, Zoom calls, and other press events to provide maximum transparency to questions regarding the voting process. With increased usage of VBM ballots, members of the staff came up with postcards that could be handed out to voters when they turned in their ballots. These postcards gave voters information on how to track their ballots as they traveled through the system. Staffers and poll workers alike commented on how this transparency was important. As one poll worker mentioned, "you could just see the voter's shoulders relax as we handed them the card to show them how to track their ballot." Staffers would discuss how they wanted voters to be assured that the office cared about their ballots and they were not "just being thrown out or stored in a back closet somewhere."

These conversations about accountability happened daily. For example, Florida law allows a voter to request a VBM ballot but surrender it if they want to vote in person instead. However, voters cannot take a marked-up VBM ballot as a reference in the voting booth; it is required to get a clean ballot to vote. The system also automatically counts the first ballot cast (whether in-person or VBM) and disregards any second ballot from the same voter. The handling of these surrendered VBM ballots was a hot topic, as the office did not want voters to see a box or open container of surrendered VBM ballots at the polling site and misconstrue what they were. Procedures were created to require the voter to mark their own VBM ballot as "spoiled" or "canceled," and then the voter could place them into a specially marked box that was labeled "canceled vote-by-mail ballots." Poll workers often walk a thin line between following procedures and providing good customer service, as the definition of what good service is lies with the voter and their perceptions or opinion of what the process "should" be. The blend of visibility to the process and voter privacy was a delicate balancing act, but necessary to support the *accountability* goal.

Accountability is crucial for creating trust with voters and even members of the nonvoting public. Elections workers play a vital role in providing goods and services. Outside of counting votes, providing training, and staffing polling places for election day, the public at large knows very little about what election administrators actually do and the work that is required to do it. *Service* to the public and other departments is the third goal of the office's mission statement. As outlined in section 2 of this chapter, elections are an administrative juggernaut that require personnel trained in information technology, warehousing, human resource management, and public relations; and then there is the need to keep up with ever-changing laws and local ordinances that impact the running of the office and elections. The employees, poll workers, and seasonal staff expressed pride in their work, even when frustrations were present.

Employees at the elections office were cognizant of how everyday decisions could impact the delivery of secure, accessible elections. One employee stated, "I could go somewhere else to work, but no one will care about what I do more than me. This is about *voting*." The emphasis on the word voting was evident and clearly a motivating factor for this employee. As is often the case with public agencies, salaries are not commensurate with those that can be earned in the private sector. This can make recruiting a particular challenge. It also illustrates the need for employee retention, as the skill set for long-term employees is difficult to replicate. However, in an organization with a history of controversial events, retention can be a double-edged sword.

After a smooth 2020 election cycle in Florida, one might think that the work done by these public servants was finally paying dividends in the form of visible appreciation from the governor to members of the public. However, despite the transparency and credibility restoring execution of the 2020 elections, many elections office employees continue to feel attacked as restrictive changes to the Florida voting rules were made by Florida Republicans in 2021 (CBSmiami.com, 2021; Fins, 2021; Moline, 2022). Conversations with employees ranged from incredulity that elected officials would impugn the work done by the SOEs around the state to resignation that no matter what improvements were made, it would mean little in an increasingly hostile partisan environment (Webb & Miller, 2020).

Elections offices are nonpartisan in practice and by law; poll workers must sign a nonpartisan agreement to serve at the polls. Yet partisan attacks on the administration of elections have been very public since 2020. These attacks are hard on the morale of the people who do the work. Most often these attacks are baseless and driven by conspiracy theories, and they drive members of the public to, at the very least, harass elections officials, and, much more worrisome, threaten them with violence (Lee & Brown, 2020). This new climate has altered the desire of many workers to be more visible. In fact, polling shows that the hostile environment is leading to an exodus of experienced election workers (Brennan Center, 2022). Yet visibility and transparency are perhaps the only ways to counter the accusations hurled at election officials across the country. Staff members, poll workers, and seasonal staff all care about the work they do to facilitate elections. Democracy depends on fair and accessible elections.

Conclusion

My colleagues expressed the desire for the public to understand that what they do is not easy. Long hours, trying to perform at a high level with low budgets, and the terrible pressure of knowing that what you do means a fellow voter may have their vote questioned or, worst case, thrown out on a technicality are all constantly present. Yet they would also say that they are proud of the work they do. One long-time poll worker told me, "Every time, I say this is my last election . . . and then I sign up for the next one." However, it is worrying that many staff members and poll workers are beginning to question whether they can be safe doing this job in the future. What happens when dedicated, experienced public servants can no longer serve? How can democracy thrive under the double assault on voting rights and intimidation at polling sites?

Organizations with fraught histories have a unique challenge in balancing the need for visibility to restore trust with a desire to be trustworthy and avoiding undue scrutiny. The stated goals of the Palm Beach County SOE—Integrity, Accountability, & Service—all require quite a bit of visibility. Yet appreciation of good work does not always require constant accolades or attention. In addition, public servants should not be threatened for doing their jobs based on unsubstantiated and, more often, completely disproved conspiracy theories about election integrity. The mission and goal of the elections office in Palm Beach County echoes the call for public servants to "serve, not steer" (Denhardt & Denhardt, 2015) as it navigates the complicated waters of administering democracy on the ground. In the rush of our own lives, we often overlook the amount of skill and dedication that it takes to keep our democracy going through the routine functioning of elections. Elections workers are permanent employees, volunteers, and temporary workers with varying degrees of visibility as they work to provide everyone the space to make their voices heard. Their knowledge and experience should be valued and appreciated for the vital service it provides to their communities. Their stories matter, and we would all be better off for having listened and, perhaps, joined them in their work.

Notes

1. Growing Democracy Ohio (growingdemocracyoh.org/podcasts)

2. The section title comes from the team name the office used for the annual Halloween 5K health event (held virtually due to COVID-19).

3. After the November 3, 2020 elections, members of the public were just as vocal about thanking us for our work and they were thrilled that Palm Beach County "did it right" and was not in the news.

References

Ashworth, R. E., McDermott, A. M., & Currie, G. (2019). Theorizing from qualitative research in public administration: Plurality through a combination of rigor and richness. *Journal of Public Administration Research and Theory*, 29(2), 318–333. https://doi.org/10.1093/jopart/muy057

Beall, P. (2018, November 17). Palm Beach County voting hardware has storied history of snafus. *The Florida Times-Union*. https://www.jacksonville.com/news/20181117/palm-beach-county-voting-hardware-has-storied-history-of-snafus

Behn, R. (2009). *Leadership counts: Lessons for public managers from the Massachusetts welfare, training, and employment program*. Harvard University Press.

Brennan Center for Justice. (2022, March). Local Election Officials Survey. https://www.brennancenter.org/our-work/research-reports/local-election-officials-survey-march-2022

CBSMiami.com Team. (2021, February 19). Despite "Transparent & efficient" 2020 election in Florida, DeSantis pushes for changes. CBS Miami. https://miami.cbslocal.com/2021/02/19/florida-governor-desantis-pushes-election-changes-florida/

Charmaz, K. (2014). *Constructing Grounded Theory*. SAGE.

Clark, A. (2019). The cost of democracy: The determinants of spending on the public administration of elections. *International Political Science Review*, 40(3), 354–369. https://doi.org/10.1177/0192512118824787

Denhardt, J. V., & Denhardt, R. B. (2015). *The new public service: Serving, not steering* (4th ed.). Routledge.

Dodge, J., Ospina, S. M., & Foldy, E. G. (2005). Integrating rigor and relevance in public administration scholarship: The contribution of narrative inquiry. *Public Administration Review*, 65(3), 286–300. https://doi.org/10.1111/j.1540-6210.2005.00454.x

Election Administration at State and Local Levels. (2020). National Conference of State Legislatures. https://www.ncsl.org/research/elections-and-campaigns/election-administration-at-state-and-local-levels.aspx

Fins, A. (2021, March 7). Florida was a 2020 election star. So why are lawmakers messing with success? *The Palm Beach Post*. https://www.palmbeachpost.com/story/news/politics/2021/03/07/florida-2020-election-star-so-why-gop-messing-success/6918050002/

Flick, U. (2014). *An introduction to qualitative research*. SAGE.

Garrett, R. S. (2016). Administering politics: Rediscovering campaign finance and public administration. *Administrative Theory & Praxis*, 38(3), 188–205. https://doi.org/10.1080/10841806.2016.1202079

Gibson, N. S. (2020). Privatized democracy: The role of election services vendors in the United States: Part of special symposium on election sciences. *American Politics Research*, 48(6), 705–708. https://doi.org/10.1177/1532673X20920264

Hale, K., Montjoy, R., & Brown, M. (2015). *Administering elections: How American elections work*. Palgrave Macmillan.

Herzog, R. J., & McClain, K. C. (2017). Assessing stories managers tell. *Administrative Theory & Praxis*, 39(3), 222–237. https://doi.org/10.1080/108418 06.2017.1345508

Lee, H. J., Oh, H. G., & Park, S. M. (2019). Do trust and culture matter for public service motivation development? Evidence from public sector employees in Korea. *Public Personnel Management*, 49(2), 290–323. https:// doi.org/10.1177/0091026019869738

Lee, M. Y. H., & Brown, E. (2020, December 2). Election officials warn Trump's escalating attacks on voting are putting staffs at risk. *The Washington Post*. https://www.washingtonpost.com/politics/election-workers-threats-trump/ 2020/12/02/d3e14d78-34c2-11eb-8d38-6aea1adb3839_story.html

Levin, M. A., & Sanger, M. B. (1994). *Making government work: How entrepreneurial executives turn bright ideas into real results*. Jossey-Bass.

Maynard-Moody, S., & Musheno, M. (2003). *Cops, teachers, counselors*. University of Michigan Press.

Michel, A. A. (2007). A distributed cognition perspective on newcomers' change processes: The management of cognitive uncertainty in two investment banks. *Administrative Science Quarterly*, 52(4), 507–557. https://doi. org/10.2189/asqu.52.4.507

Moline, M. (2022, February 15). Testimony: FL's new elections restrictions are driving local supervisors from office. *Florida Phoenix*. https://floridaphoenix.com/2022/02/15/testimony-fls-new-elections-restrictions-are-driving-local-supervisors-from-office/

Moynihan, D. P., & Silva, C. L. (2008). The administrators of democracy: A research note on local election officials. *Public Administration Review*, 68(5), 816–827. https://doi.org/10.1111/j.1540-6210.2008.00923.x

Nowell, B., & Albrecht, K. (2019). A reviewer's guide to qualitative rigor. *Journal of Public Administration Research and Theory*, 29(2), 348–363. https://doi. org/10.1093/jopart/muy052

Sørensen, E., & Torfing, J. (2011). Enhancing collaborative innovation in the public sector. *Administration & Society*, 43(8), 842–868. https://doi.org/ 10.1177/0095399711418768

Stout, M., & Love, J. M. (2017). Integrative governance: A method for fruitful public encounters. *The American Review of Public Administration*, 47(1), 130–147. https://doi.org/10.1177/0275074015576953

Swap, W., Leonard, D., Shields, M., & Abrams, L. (2001). Using mentoring and storytelling to transfer knowledge in the workplace. *Journal of Management Information Systems*, 18(1), 95–114. https://doi.org/10.1080/0742 1222.2001.11045668 van Hulst, M. J. (2013). The search for credible stories in the public sector. *Journal of Public Administration Research and Theory, 24*(2), 519–526. https://doi.org/10.1093/jopart/mut050

Washington, W. (2018, November 16). Here's why Palm Beach County is saddled with slow

vote-counting machines. *The Palm Beach Post.* https://www.palmbeachpost.com/news/20181116/florida-election-recount-heres-why-palm-beach-county-is-saddled-with-slow-vote-counting-machines

Webb, K., & Miller, K. (2020, November 2). Palm Beach County businesses, officials are ready for any post-election unrest. *The Palm Beach Post.* https://www.palmbeachpost.com/story/news/politics/elections/2020/11/02/palm-beach-county-stores-officials-prepare-post-election-unrest/6127358002/

White, J. D. (1999). *Taking language seriously: The narrative foundations of public administration research.* Georgetown University Press.

9

Public Defenders as Constitutional Pariahs, Surrogate Deviants, and Emotional Laborers

Adam Croft

In *Gideon v. Wainwright* (1963), the United States Supreme Court ruled that the Sixth Amendment guarantees criminal defendants accused of a felony legal counsel regardless of their ability to hire an attorney. In the majority opinion, Justice Hugo Black wrote, "any person hauled into court, who is too poor to hire a lawyer, cannot be assured a fair trial unless counsel is provided for him. This seems to us to be an obvious truth" (p. 344). Prior to the ruling, 36 states had some form of public defender office (Lentine, 2013). Following the ruling, federal, state, and local jurisdictions established them in accordance with Black's obvious truth.

Public defenders since the ruling neatly fulfill Rohr's charge that public administrators "run a constitution" (1986, p. 172) by ensuring all criminal defendants' right to counsel is preserved. Today, public defenders represent roughly 80% of all criminal defendants in the United States, and while the current provision of public defense is certainly an improvement from the piecemeal regime it replaced, no reasonable legal scholar could argue that poor defendants receive adequate representation (Baćak et al., 2021; Baxter, 2010). Research from journalists and scholars alike shows that a general lack of financial support for indigent defense from policy makers has resulted in public defenders who are overworked, underpaid, and subsequently ineffective, rendering the *Gideon v. Wainwright* ruling little more than "a ghostly shadow prowling the halls of criminal justice throughout the country" (Baxter, 2010, p. 341; see also Jaffe, 2018; Oppel Jr. & Patel, 2019).

The American Bar Association (ABA) introduced state-by-state reports in 2017 that used survey data from public and private attorneys to determine the amount of time lawyers need to provide reasonable representation in different types of criminal cases. The goal of the research was to provide an estimate of how many cases public defenders can handle in a year before they become ineffective. In every state examined thus far, public defenders have handled at least double the recommended workload, and in some states such as Mississippi, public defenders worked as much as five times the recommended caseload (Oppel Jr. & Patel, 2019). In Colorado, the focus of this chapter, public defenders typically worked at least double the recommended caseload (American Bar Association and RubinBrown LLP, 2017).

Working conditions such as these represent an unconstitutional and inequitable criminal justice crisis. Overworked public defenders frequently lack the time necessary to properly evaluate and argue clients' cases, forcing them to settle for suboptimal outcomes for clients (Baxter, 2012; Jaffe, 2018). Additionally, public defenders often fail to communicate effectively with clients during the limited amount of time each case is allocated (Campbell, Moore, Maier, & Gaffney, 2015; Dean, 2016). The failures of public defense tied to underfunding and overwork disproportionately harm non-White defendants, who are more likely to face criminal charges generally, use a public defender, and who may receive less attention from an overworked public defender because of implicit racial bias (Alexander, 2010; Blakemore, 2016; Marcus, 1994; Richardson & Goff, 2012). In addition to worsening inequities, the present state of public defense also results in violations of public defenders' ethical and constitutional mandates to provide competent, zealous legal representation to their clients (Baxter, 2012).

Public defenders themselves are also suffering from overwork, driving many to burnout or employment outside public defense. One study found that public defenders in the United States deal with intense and chronic stress driven by "the social and psychological demands of working in a punitive system with laws and practices that target and punish those who are the most disadvantaged" (Baćak, Lageson, & Powell, 2021, p. 1). Other studies highlight that high levels of occupational stress increase defender burnout and turnover rates (Ogletree, 1993; Welch, 2019). However, the costs of working in indigent defense are not just professional. Numerous studies of public defenders indicate that working in close proximity to trauma with staggering caseloads is associated with a number of recurring issues like insomnia, depression, and even physical illness (Levin et al., 2011; Levin, Besser, Albert, Smith, & Neria, 2012; Molvig, 2011; Norton, Johnson, & Woods, 2015; Steinberg, 2006).

This chapter is guided by a desire to better understand how public defenders make sense of their work and their place as public servants at a time when public defense is clearly in crisis, a crisis that may not be readily apparent to the average citizen but is no less urgent. It seeks to advance an understanding of how street-level public defenders are drawn to and value their profession, despite its reputation for overwork and limited resources. It is inspired by the efforts of Maynard-Moody and Musheno (2003) and other notable scholar who studied policy implementation at the street level, advancing a citizen-agent understanding of policy implementation with work stories and worker commentary (Lipsky, 1983; Riccucci, 2005).

Collecting Public Defense Narratives

The stories and statements from public defenders in this chapter come from six interviews with attorneys who work for the Office of the Colorado State Public Defender (OCSPD). The attorneys interviewed were at varying stages in their careers. Some had just begun working in public defense; others had been in public defense for as long as 10 years. OCSPD policy dictates that junior attorneys handle less severe cases, while more senior attorneys handle appellate cases and felonies. One of the attorneys interviewed was still handling misdemeanor cases, while the remainder handled appeals or felony-level cases. All the attorneys worked and lived in the city of Denver, and all the attorneys interviewed were White. The latter is particularly troublesome given the role of race and racial profiling in public defense, and future research will focus on collecting perspectives from non-White public defenders (Marcus, 1994). Respondents were equally divided along gender lines with three male and three female interviewees.

The prevailing themes and connections from these interviews are discussed alongside stories in four sections. Each section focuses on a different core aspect of public defense and is driven by responses from public defenders. The stories indicate that public defenders are motivated by values like fairness, equity, and freedom, and many believe their work is about disrupting a criminal justice system that is inherently biased against the poor and non-White. Their work is a dominating force in their lives. Vast caseloads mean work-life balance is often difficult to attain, and stress and burnout are the norm. They also feel little support or understanding from lawmakers, or the public at large, and regularly confront misconceptions or even outright disdain for their work and their clientele. In this way, public defenders act as a kind of constitutionally mandated pariah, preserving the Sixth Amendment's guarantees for those who might otherwise pass silently into jails and prisons without a day in court.

Careers in Public Defense

The path to a career in public defense is similar to most legal careers. Every public defender interviewed attended law school, took an internship in public defense, and passed the bar exam before ultimately entering what they refer to as the "PD system." In some ways, the career trajectory of a public defender in Colorado is fairly fixed. Most of the public defenders interviewed began the job trying misdemeanor cases and worked their way into full-time positions trying more severe felonies or handling appeals. As they became more senior, the severity of the charges their clients faced increased. One senior public defender mentioned that handling murder cases is a significant portion of their caseload, meaning the stakes for their clients are typically a life sentence. While the prospect of representing someone accused of murder might not appeal to many, all of the attorneys interviewed mentioned both client interaction and the stakes of their work as the main appeals of public defense, at least initially. Managing the risk of a life sentence is not only a typical day on the job for some, but it also makes the work meaningful.

Some went into law school planning to work in public defense; others came around to it after an internship or time spent in a legal clinic. All of the attorneys went straight from law school into the Colorado public defender system. As one public defender put it:

> All through law school, I kind of felt like my work was missing the human element. I wasn't doing much client interaction, and I knew that I wanted to go into some kind of public interest law. I wasn't totally sure what that looked like, I just knew I wanted to work with people and help people. I landed

an internship with a public defender and it all just kind of clicked. I loved the PDs I worked with. I went straight into the [public defender] system after graduation.

Several public defense values become apparent through this quote. Public defenders are driven by the relational aspects of their work. Unlike some attorneys who may be content to read case law all day and keep client interaction to a minimum, all of the public defenders mentioned client interaction as one of the joys of their work, at least in the beginning. Moreover, they are all driven by the idea that they might be a source of positive change for their clients, that in some small way they might make a difference in their lives. Making money is not even mentioned as a career motivation. This comports both with public administration's notion of public service motivation and more recent scholarship that indicates that public service professionals are often motivated and affected by the relational characteristics of their work (Ritz et al., 2016; van der Voet & Steijn, 2019).

Arriving at a career in public defense entails an acknowledgement that the criminal justice system is not functioning equitably. As another public defender put it, "I came into law school knowing the system was unfair and racist and that poor people in this country don't stand a chance, but during law school I just became more aware. This career was the only real way to fight back with the skills I have." This idea, that public defenders are somehow agents of disruption in the very system that employs them, was common throughout each interview. For all public defenders interviewed, this role as a constitutionally mandated disruptor is articulated as their main contribution to society at large. As another public defender said: "I have a commitment to ensuring that a person's story is told, and they have their day in court. I try not to be paternalistic, but I am in a position where if the client is innocent or the plea bargain on the table is trash, I can do something. I can tell them 'don't just roll over for this, we can do better.' Doing better means slowing down the wheels of justice." This notion comports completely with Justice Black's majority opinion in Gideon v. Wainwright (1963), in which he noted that public defenders are vital to maintain an adversary system in which "Governments, both state and federal, quite properly spend vast sums of money to establish machinery to try defendants accused of crime" (p. 344). The real triumphs for public defenders come from beating this machinery and helping a client beat a tough case, as in the following stories.

Story 1. Office of the Colorado State Public Defender

"Rolling and Rolling and Rolling"

We have a lot of cases and clients that stick with us, and this was one. I was still working in county court, and it certainly wasn't my toughest case, wasn't my hardest trial or anything like that. It was a woman who was charged with child abuse, and she was a Black woman. A really sweet woman. The allegation was that she beat up her son, who had no injuries at all. But they [the prosecution] kept making offers, and the offers were getting better and better, but she would not take an offer and she kept saying to me, "no, I didn't do that, nothing like this ever happened." We got to trial, and she was acquitted. It was a huge relief, because we had taken such a risk declining every offer to that point. A juror afterword said something that stuck with me, and it's something I think about a lot. He said, 'It seems like the system got started here before anyone took the time to see if something had really happened. And it just kept rolling and rolling and rolling until this point.' He was right.

When the system starts, the cops get involved, the prosecutors get involved, child protective services get involved, everybody's getting involved and investigating and trying to do what they think it right. And the assumption becomes that the client is guilty. But no one is slowing down to say, 'Did this happen?' The fact that a juror could get that at all, let alone after a one-day misdemeanor jury trial is huge. But I think it's exactly what our job is all about, disruption. Forcing the system to stop and actually evaluate if a person is guilty. Without us, it might not actually pause for long enough. That same person, if she had been charged with felony child abuse because it was alleged a deadly weapon was involved, may be incarcerated pre-trial, and may be forced to take a plea for something she didn't do, just because she needs to get out to take care of her family. Those cases shape your practice and the way you approach a situation and this job.

Story 2. Office of the Colorado State Public Defender

"Double Carjacking"

This case was easily my most memorable. I think about it all the time, and it becomes motivational for me when a case is tough, or I think we might not have a path to acquittal. The client was accused of carjacking, double carjacking. And the client was positively identified by a witness, found in one of the stolen cars, but was adamant he didn't do it. We went through a long argument in court about how the identification of the client by the witness, which she was 100% certain of, was unduly suggestive and shouldn't be used. The judge ruled against us, but a couple weeks later we were still able to exonerate the client with DNA evidence that proved it was somebody else. I remember throughout the client kept getting offered better deal after better deal and was facing mandatory prison. We were pretty clear to the client, and I kept saying, "it's a risk if you reject this" to every deal. But the client trusted us and was adamant that they were innocent, so we never took a deal. It's easily the defining moment of my career as an attorney.

What was especially important was that I got to know the client. I got to see him go from this bottom point, this difficult low of being in jail, to helping him with the resources to get clean, because he was struggling with addiction, but even eventually relapsing again. I learned a lot through that relationship, through the ups and downs, even the things that didn't relate to the trial were important to our relationship and our success. I think that will stick with me throughout my entire career, the importance of that relationship for both of us and the fact that we were able to triumph together and achieve some improvements to the client's life that wouldn't have been possible if we hadn't built a relationship.

These stories are indicative of what public defenders believe they contribute to public service. As "Rolling and Rolling and Rolling" shows, the machinery of prosecution that Justice Black talked about gets going and seldom stops to assess the case in favor of the defendant. Without a public defender, a defendant would surely end up charged with a crime and face sanctions that they may never recover from. This story also shows that combating racial inequity matters to public defenders. The defendant's identity as a Black woman is implicitly conveyed as part of why the case kept progressing even though abuse likely did not occur. As one public defender put it:

> There must be a recognition that most of my clients are not privileged. They've had significant life trauma. They've grown up as minorities in a society that doesn't value minorities and have had experiences that I can't understand due to my own privilege. And it's more than just their race, there are so many issues our clients face. We have to slow down the court and say, "This is their life experience. This person has been sexually assaulted, or they've been forced into homelessness, they haven't had the resources of a good education or real economic opportunities." We have to keep the system from just incarcerating and hiding a portion of our population. We have to make it known that that portion of our population matters.

In addition to trying to fight intersectional inequities in the courtroom, public defenders also bring value to public service by building relationships and helping clients navigate other public services. In "Double Carjacking," the attorney notes that the real value of the case was relational. They won in court because they built a positive relationship on the basis of mutual trust, and that mutual trust also meant the attorney was able to help the client navigate the resources available to those struggling with addiction. Each of the public defenders interviewed noted that their role often involves helping their client find and use other important public services. Attorneys noted that they direct almost all of their clientele to a social worker and that a great deal of their clientele need housing support or help with recovery from an addiction. In this way, public defenders operate as a navigator at the center of a web of available services. Though the client starts with them because of pressing legal needs, they may ultimately find another vital resource in the process. This work often takes place outside the boundaries of a public defender's job description, in the hours before or after they address the legal demands of their caseload. Though these efforts often go unnoticed by supervisors or the general public, each public defender noted that providing additional assistance to a client made their job more rewarding.

Through these stories, it is clear Justice Black was right. Policy makers should invest in a team of attorneys who can balance and slow the vast machinery that is criminal prosecution in the United States. Without this balancing force, countless defendants like those mentioned would face unjust sentences that would almost certainly render permanent damage to their ability to lead meaningful, happy lives. Still, public and lawmaker perceptions of public defense are a long way from this ideal, and the policy process has subsequently devoted little resources to ensuring the kind of balance the Sixth Amendment ensures.

Public Perceptions of Public Defense

Common stereotypes of public defenders are that they are second-rate attorneys unable to attain employment outside public interest lawyering or that they are somehow immoral actors without the compunction necessary to decline defending heinous criminals (Dean, 2016, p. 38). Each of the lawyers interviewed felt the public either lacks awareness of or does not support their work. One public defender noted that friends and family routinely ask, "Do you even have to pass the bar exam to be a public defender?" All of them noted that friends, family, and the public generally fail to grasp the constitutional import of their career and instead condemn public defenders for their willingness to represent the worst in society. As one public defender noted, "I represent people accused of murder or child molestation. The worst crimes. And it's important. But I often think about how horrified and offended my mother-in-law would be if she heard the things I say in court or knew about the kinds of crimes my clients are facing." Another public defender put it even more directly: "People think public defenders are just shitty, overworked attorneys who couldn't get jobs elsewhere. On TV shows when a character gets assigned a public defender, he comes in and he doesn't know what he's doing. He's bumbling. And it's the opposite. We do better jobs on balance than the private attorneys that poor defendants can afford." Combating these stereotypes can be difficult. Clients sometimes become reluctant to trust their public defender as a result (Dean, 2016). Every public defender interviewed lamented that the public did not understand their work more: "At the end of the day, most people need us if they end up in criminal court. Most people can't afford a private attorney. I wish the public knew how important we are, and how good we are at our jobs so we could start out with more mutual trust." The questions of public defender competence are especially frustrating to those interviewed because many come from renowned law schools and beat out stiff competition to become public defenders: "I work with attorneys that come from top, Ivy League schools. They could work anywhere, but this is where they want to work, and they're great at their jobs." This was a common theme across interviews with public defenders, who feel slighted by a general public that can regard them as subpar or incapable even though they are often well-trained and educated professionals in the top of their selected area of legal practice.

Lawmaker Perceptions of Public Defense

In a 2010 statement, then–district attorney for Colorado's Ninth Judicial District Martin Beeson proclaimed, "Public defenders are not defenders of the public. They are not serving the public good. They are taxpayer-funded attorneys for criminals" (Travers, 2010, para. 15). Beeson later ran unsuccessfully for Congress, and if the state of indigent defense funding in the United States is any indicator, his attitude is somewhat common among the lawmakers who determine how public defenders are funded.

One theoretical basis for understanding why public defenders receive so little funding from lawmakers comes from Schneider and Ingram's (1993) theory of social construction and policy design, which posits that the ways in which a population is socially constructed couples with the power the group wields to dictate whether they are rewarded or punished by the policy process (Pierce et al., 2014). Notably, the group in the least advantageous position in Schneider and Ingram's hypothetical quadrant of target populations is criminals, a group with little power over the policy process that is frequently punished because of their negative social construction. Though public defenders are not themselves criminals, the fact that their budgets force them to work as much as five times the recommended caseload is clearly a de facto punishment from lawmakers. Those who work in indigent defense are a kind of surrogate deviant in terms of social construction, receiving treatment from the policy process as though they are criminals and not revered public servants.

The public defenders interviewed know this attitude all too well, and it pervades more than just the funding they get from policy makers. Said one interviewee: "There is such an ideological difference between what we think is a just outcome and what the state legislature or the district attorney thinks is a just outcome. We start out with the belief that the prison system is fundamentally unjust, but most lawmakers and district attorneys don't think that way. They keep us afloat because they have to, but we're not a priority."

Still, the tide may be turning. On the campaign trail, Vice President Kamala Harris, herself a former prosecutor, advocated for pay parity between public defenders and prosecutors to alleviate criminal justice inequities (Kamala D. Harris: U.S. Senator for California, 2019). The public defenders interviewed welcomed the idea of improved pay, but each noted that their top policy priority would be better resources for their clients. As one of the public defenders interviewed noted:

I make enough money; I'm actually thrilled with my salary. What we need are more resources to support our clients. We need more social workers in our offices, we need immigration specialists, we need more resources for investigation, and we need to be able to hire expert witnesses as often as district attorneys do. District attorneys have the full police force to help their investigations and they always hire all of the expert witnesses in a criminal trial. We have a great investigation team, but it's just not enough. That would be my wish list if our budget improved. That's what I want lawmakers to know we need.

Though the wish list varied across defenders in small ways, nearly all of them came up with the same list. None of the attorneys mentioned reducing their caseload as a legislative priority, though the Office of the Colorado State Public Defender noted in its most recent performance report that reductions in caseload would be an immediate goal if more resources were available for indigent defense (Ring, 2020). This shows that while many public defenders may be overworked and underpaid, their priorities typically revolve around improving advocacy and resources for their clientele both in and out of the courtroom. As guides to the array of public services criminal defendants often require, most public defenders acknowledge that even the best legal services will fail to improve a client's well-being if additional community resources are unavailable to them.

Public Defenders as Emotional Laborers

All of the public defenders interviewed noted both that they are highly satisfied with their work and that they frequently experience burnout. While these trends seem contradictory, they are both hallmarks of public service work that requires emotional labor (Guy, Newman, & Mastracci, 2008). Emotional labor, defined as labor that "requires one to induce or suppress feeling in order to sustain the outward countenance that produces the proper state of mind in others" (Hochschild, 2012, p. 7), is already a noted component of lawyering generally and public defense specifically (Westaby & Subryan, 2020; Yakren, 2008). The work of a public defender is highly emotional. Public defenders are expected to be a source of competent legal strategy for their clients, but often end up providing much more:

> Frequently, when a client is in jail, I'm the only person they can talk to. When they're in jail, I tell them don't talk about your case to anyone. It can be used against you. So, I end up being their only outlet, and we usually end up talking about a lot more than their case.

As this quote shows, public defenders provide care and comfort to their clients beyond the realm of legal advice.

Work with clients is not the only emotional component of public defense. Their work is also emotional when working with opposing counsel, judges, or a jury. Said one interviewee: "There are times in court where you want to scream at the [district attorney]. Early in my career, I did. And it always cost me, so I learned not to, for the client. You learn the rules of the game, how you should present yourself to the jury, to the client. And sometimes that means bottling things up and dealing with them later." The "bottling" discussed in this quote is a hallmark of jobs that require emotional labor. Practitioners suppress the emotions that are not conducive to professional competence and display those emotions that aid their goals. This suppression has consequences. All of the public defenders interviewed said they deal with burnout routinely and that it often makes them question their career choice. For these attorneys, the office is a safe space to vent the feelings that are not permissible in a courtroom or in front of clients. Camaraderie becomes its own kind of coping mechanism: "We all get back to the office and if you have a client or a judge or something that's pissing you off or made you cry, you bring it to your coworkers because you're all going through the same thing."

Conclusion

Public defenders have a somewhat paradoxical relationship with public service. While they are part of systems of criminal justice and, more broadly, public service, they view their role as disruptors of that system and are driven by an anti-establishment ethic. They believe in equity, fairness, and the freedoms afforded to all by the Constitution. Though they are overworked and undersupported by lawmakers and the public, they find tremendous fulfillment in their work and their clientele. Still, the state of public defense creates many difficulties for its workers. All of the attorneys interviewed deal with burnout, and each attorney readily produced a wish list for policy makers that is unlikely to be fulfilled given current perceptions. They all feel the pangs of a public that typically considers them incompetent, immoral, or forgets them entirely. In some ways, public defenders are the constitutional pariahs of public service, fulfilling a vital requirement that every citizen might need but few appreciate. Still, they rise above suboptimal working conditions and stereotypes to ensure every criminal defendant has their day in court, though their workload may render them less effective at times. In many respects, they should be celebrated as champions of equitable public service rooted firmly in the jurisprudence of the Constitution.

References

Alexander, M. (2010). *The new Jim Crow: Mass incarceration in the age of colorblindness*. The New Press.

American Bar Association and RubinBrown LLP. (2017, August). *The Colorado project*. https://www.americanbar.org/content/dam/aba/administrative/legal_aid_indigent_defendants/ls_sclaid_def_co_project.pdf

Baćak, V., Lageson, S., & Powell, K. (2021, January 19). *The stress of injustice: Public*

defenders and the frontline of American inequality. SSRN. https://www.njchs.org/wp-content/uploads/Stress-of-Injustice-article.pdf

Baxter, H. (2010). Gideon's ghost: Providing the Sixth Amendment right to counsel in times of budgetary crisis. *Michigan State Law Review, 2010*(2), 341–368.

Baxter, H. (2012). Too many clients, too little time: How states are forcing public defenders to violate their ethical obligations. *Federal Sentencing Reporter, 25*(2), 91–102. https://doi.org/10.1525/fsr.2012.25.2.91

Blakemore, J. (2016). Implicit racial bias and public defenders. *Georgetown Journal of Legal Ethics, 29*(Current Developments 2015–2016), 833–848.

Campbell, C., Moore, J., Maier, W., & Gaffney, M. (2015). Unnoticed, untapped, and underappreciated: Clients' perceptions of their public defenders. *Behavioral Sciences and the Law, 33*(6), 751–770. https://doi.org/10.1002/bsl.2182

Dean, M. D. (2016). Public defender communication advice. *Criminal Justice, 31*(2), 38–40.

Guy, M. E., Newman, M. A., & Mastracci, S. (2008). *Emotional labor: Putting the service in public service*. M. E. Sharpe, Inc.

Gideon v. Wainwright, 372 U.S. 335 (1963). https://supreme.justia.com/cases/federal/us/372/335/

Hochschild, A. R. (2012). *The managed heart: Commercialization of human feeling* (3rd ed.). University of California Press.

Jaffe, S. (2018). "It's not you, it's your caseload": Using Cronic to solve indigent defense underfunding. *Michigan Law Review, 116*(8), 1466–1484.

Kamala D. Harris: U.S. Senator for California. (2019, May 8). *Harris introduces EQUAL Defense Act to boost pay and resources, limit workload of public defenders*. https://www.harris.senate.gov/news/press-releases/harris-introduces-equal-defense-actto-boost-pay-and-resources-limit-workload-of-public-defenders

Lentine, J. A. (2013). Gideon at fifty: The broken promise. *American Journal of Trial Advocacy, 37*(2), 375–392.

Levin, A., Albert, L., Besser, A., Smith, D., Zelenski, A., Rosenkranz, S., & Neria, Y. (2011). Secondary traumatic stress in attorneys and their administrative support staff working with trauma-exposed clients. *The Journal of Nervous and Mental Disease, 199*(12), 946–955. https://doi.org/10.1097/NMD.0b013e3182392c26

Levin, A., Besser, A., Albert, L., Smith, D., & Neria, Y. (2012). The effect of attorneys' work with trauma-exposed clients on PTSD symptoms, depression, and functional impairment: A cross-lagged longitudinal study. *Law and Human Behavior, 36*(6), 538–547. https://doi.org/10.1037/h0093993

Lipsky, M. (1983). *Street-level bureaucracy: Dilemmas of the individual in public service.* Russell Sage Foundation.

Marcus, R. (1994). Racism in our courts: The underfunding of public defenders and its disproportionate impact upon racial minorities. *Hastings Constitutional Law Quarterly, 22*(1), 219–265.

Maynard-Moody, S., & Musheno, M. (2003). *Cops, teachers, counselors.* University of Michigan Press.

Molvig, D. (2011, December 1). The toll of trauma. *Wisconsin Lawyer, 84*(12), 4–10.

Norton, L., Johnson, J., & Woods, G. (2015). Burnout and compassion fatigue: What lawyers need to know. *UMKC Law Review, 84*(4), 987–1002.

Ogletree, C. J. (1993). Beyond justifications: Seeking motivations to sustain public defenders. *Harvard Law Review, 106*(6), 1239–1294.

Oppel Jr., R. A., & Patel, J. K. (2019, January 31). One lawyer, 194 felony cases, and no time. *The New York Times.* https://www.nytimes.com/interactive/2019/01/31/us/public-defender-case-loads.html

Pierce, J. J., Siddiki, S., Jones, M. D., Schumacher, K., Pattison, A., & Peterson, H. (2014). Social construction and policy design: A review of past applications. *Policy Studies Journal, 42*(1), 1–29. https://doi.org/10.1111/psj.12040

Riccucci, N. (2005). *How management matters: Street-level bureaucrats and welfare reform.* Georgetown University Press.

Richardson, L. S., & Goff, P. A. (2012). Implicit racial bias in public defender triage. *The Yale Law Journal, 122*(8), 2626–2649.

Ring, M. A. (2020). *Annual performance report.* Denver: Office of the State Public Defender.

Ritz, A., Brewer, G. A., & Neumann, O. (2016). Public service motivation: A systematic literature review and outlook. *Public Administration Review, 76*(3), 414–426. https://doi.org/10.1111/puar.12505

Rohr, J. (1986). *To run a constitution.* University Press of Kansas.

Steinberg, R. G. (2006). Beyond lawyering: How holistic representation makes for good policy, better lawyers, and more satisfied clients. *New York University Review of Law and Social Change, 30*(4), 625–635.

Travers, A. (2010, October 22). Local public defender operates on one-fifth of the DA's budget. *Aspen Daily News.* https://www.aspendailynews.com/local-public-defender-operates-on-one-fifth-of-theda/article_5d5f7032-042d-51a8-9eb8-27c69a90eeac.html

van der Voet, J., & Steijn, B. (2019). Relational job characteristics and prosocial motivation: A longitudinal study of youth care professionals. *Review of Public Personnel Administration, 41*(1), 57–77. https://doi.org/10.1177/0734371X19862852

Welch, T. (2019). The sources and extent of occupational stress in Utah public defenders. *Utah Journal of Criminal Law, 4*, 28–58.

Westaby, C., & Subryan, A. (2020). Emotional labour in the legal profession. In J. Phillips, C. Westaby, A. Fowler, & J. Waters (Eds.), *Emotional labour in criminal justice and criminology* (pp. 34–53). Routledge.

Yakren, S. (2008). Lawyer as emotional laborer. *University of Michigan Journal of Law Reform, 42*(1), 141–184.

10

New York City Property Tax Assessment

Public Employees Serving in Silence

MICHAEL J. FOUASSIER

It is said by those who work in the field of local property taxation that few young people grow up wanting to be a property tax assessor. It is not the kind of career path most are aware of at an early age. Unlike firefighters, police officers, teachers, and other street-level bureaucrats (Lipsky, 1980), there exists a wide knowledge gap about local property taxation and the professionals who carry out the work of this essential function. This knowledge gap is exacerbated by the enormously complicated set of real property tax laws that govern the work. Yet despite its long history and importance to nearly every local government throughout the country, very little is taught in schools about how democracy is expressed and buy-in achieved when local residents pay their property tax bill.

In New York City, assessors and valuation modelers value approximately 1.1 million parcels citywide with an aggregate market value of $1.3 trillion each year. This figure rivals the GDP of many developed nations; represents hundreds of thousands of homes, businesses, and jobs; and is used to levy the single largest source of revenue for the city. This revenue, more than $30 billion or 47% of all collected tax revenue, is used to fund police and fire, as well as sanitation, education, and transportation agencies. The importance of this tax notwithstanding, New York City assessment professionals, a group of dedicated and highly trained individuals, are seldom seen by taxpayers. Unlike the Department of Building or Department of Health Inspectors, identified by their uniforms, assessors wear no outward signs that they are local government employees when deployed to the field. They are the very individuals for whom the expression serving in silence is appropriate. That became particularly true during the worst of the COVID-19 pandemic.

While I serve as Senior Director of Property and Tax Map Operations, with a background in analysis and project management, I find myself in a position of admiration for those practitioners who dedicate themselves to assessment administration. This appreciation has deepened in the years since I began a career in property tax policy. I began working in this field approximately 16 years ago while pursuing an MPA in Albany, NY. Working full-time during the day at a small business incubator, I was interested in a career change and began looking for a professional-class position in government. When multiple opportunities presented themselves after I passed a New York State civil service exam, I had a decision to make between the Office of the State Comptroller or the New York State Office of Real Property Services (ORPS). I had been studying public policy and finance in my MPA program, so it felt like a natural fit when I was offered a traineeship position with ORPS. In November of 2006 I began at agency headquarters as a real property analyst trainee and learned how to code in SPSS, analyze data, and manage various projects. It was at this time I began taking courses in assessment while familiarizing myself with the complex laws and policies that govern its administration.

Throughout my tenure at ORPS, which later became the Office of Real Property Tax Services (ORPTS), I developed many professional skills and an appreciation for the importance of collecting a local property tax to fund essential programs and services. ORPS promoted best practices in assessment, encouraged the professionalization of assessment staff, and offered analytical and IT support to assessing authorities across the state. I had an opportunity to travel to various parts of New York on advisory appraisals, learning from professionals in the field. I worked for six months in the Computer Assisted Mass Appraisal unit, populating test databases and providing feedback to developers. I even had an opportunity to travel to the Adirondacks and Great Lakes regions to inspect hydroelectric and steam-generating plants. This valuable experience led me to the next step in my career, one that would allow me to work directly for local government where property tax policy is effectuated. And where better to begin working in an assessment office than in one of the most diverse and interesting real estate jurisdictions in the country? What I did not anticipate, and what would open my eyes to the amount and complexity of assessment, is the quality of the professionals I encountered when I began working at the Department of Finance in 2011. The New York City assessors and valuation modelers I met at that time had decades of experience, both formal and informal professional training, often held designations from various organizations, and valued tens of billions of dollars of real estate each year.

Who Are New York City Property Assessors?

As I learned when I began working in the Quality Assurance unit, New York City property assessors come from various backgrounds and all walks of life. This includes academia, appraisal, technology, banking, and the arts, among other fields. They are multicultural and represent not only a cross-section of New York City but of the world. The most experienced assessors at the New York City Department of Finance today include individuals who began their careers as college aides or assistant assessors in the 1980s and 1990s. It is fair to say the field of assessing is homegrown, as there are few if any higher education programs in the United States that confer academic degrees in appraisal and property tax assessment.

Although many Americans are largely averse to paying taxes, a certain collective action ethos remains in our society that serves as the foundation for taxation. Individuals expect that roads will be paved, garbage collected, and that the water they drink is safe. Residents of New York City expect that their children will receive a quality education, have access to parks, and that roads are maintained and safe to drive on. Despite these expectations and the realization that taxes fund essential services, assessment professionals who work to fund these programs often are not viewed in a positive light. That is particularly true when property taxes seem to increase every year. Common misunderstandings about property assessment do not allow taxpayers to see that it is the budget that is nearly always responsible for tax increases, something not set by assessors (Haveman & Sexton, 2008). On an annual basis, the City of New York determines the total amount of taxes and tax rates required to fund essential programs. This is the domain of the Mayor's Office, the New York City Council, and the Office of Management and Budget. The assessment roll, by contrast, provides a mechanism to assign each property owner a share of this tax based on value. In instances where the local levy is the stable or is reduced over time, even as assessments increase, tax bills may fall. Educating the public on these facts is an ongoing effort, one that New York City assessment professionals endeavor every year. Despite the complexities and structural inequities built into New York State Real Property Tax Law, the assessor works to apportion tax liability in as equitable a way as legally permissible.

For example, during the COVID-19 pandemic, assessors and valuation modelers were entrepreneurial as they developed workflows and leveraged technology to meet the needs of the public. With the advent of new technology and an increasingly professional staff, New York City assessment became a prime example of evolving governance in the 21st century. This has been the case for years but never more so than during the pandemic. The Department of Finance ushered in not only aerial and oblique imagery but also street-level tools to capture detailed images of storefronts and the condition of homes and other properties. Assessors were able to perform desktop review work from the comfort and safety of their homes and still record critical changes in value and use that would not have been possible five years ago. It is because of this buildup of skills and ushering in of new technologies that New York City was prepared when the COVID-19 pandemic hit. Had the agency not invested in these transformational workflows and modernization efforts, relying on the hard work and perseverance of staff, the Department of Finance would not have been successful in producing a quality assessment roll in 2021.

In terms of governance, there has been a great deal of interest in the field of public affairs on those who serve at the front line of public service delivery, what Lipsky referred to as street-level bureaucrats (Birkland, 2020). In the absence of legislation, administrative codes, and other statutory provisions that guide local property tax administration, assessment professionals have had significant discretion in setting policy and implementing programs. One such innovative approach during the first few months of the pandemic was the creation of a virtual inspection program. This endeavor, one that provided a view into the interior of properties, was a way of not only conducting mission-critical work but also transforming taxpayer compliance into taxpayer participation. Virtual inspections have proven to be a first step in a greater move toward participatory governance that cannot be understated. Taxpayers, representatives, religious, and community leaders worked hand-in-hand with assessment professionals to inspect the interior of properties.

While the pandemic encouraged innovation in field inspections, it also provided assessment modelers with an opportunity to pioneer new approaches in their statistical analyses. The Department of Finance Modeling and Research team had to manage change quickly, working long hours in the first few months of the pandemic on developing valuation guidelines to ensure the agency could publish a Fiscal Year 2021/2022 assessment roll. One of the most significant challenges for the Modeling group was that real property income and expense statements, submitted each year on June 1, reflected an economy that no longer existed. Approximately 90,000 properties reported their prior year 2019 income and expense data that ultimately proved unusable. Instead of freezing guidelines and assessments as seen in neighboring municipalities, Modeling employed exploratory data analysis to account for the ongoing crisis of vacancy, collection loss, and risk that was clearly present in both residential and commercial real estate markets. Macroeconomic variables were considered, observing co-movement in both residential and commercial properties. The wage index, unemployment, interest, and absorption rates were examined with care to establish property value trends. These time adjustments, in turn, were applied to income and expense filings and used to assign market values to some of the most valuable real estate in the world.

As time passes, staff have returned what one might describe as the new normal. Assessors and valuation modelers, along with analysts and support staff, will inevitably look back on the COVID-19 pandemic and wonder how they managed to produce all that work from home during such unprecedented times. As someone who has dedicated the better part of two decades to this field, I will not soon forget the stories of individual sacrifice, hard work, and commitment of those serving in silence.

References

Birkland, T. A. (2020). *An introduction to the policy process: Theories, concepts, and models of public policy making*. Routledge.

Haveman, M., & Sexton, T. (2008). *Property tax assessment limits: Lessons from thirty years of experience*. Lincoln Institute of Land Policy.

Lipsky, M. (1980). *Street-level bureaucracy: Dilemmas of the individual in public services*. Russell Sage Foundation.

11

Affordable Housing and Homelessness Policy Professionals

MAREN B. TROCHMANN

Many public servants working in affordable housing and homelessness are not frontline service providers, yet they play an essential role in setting policy, overseeing funding and implementation, and providing technical assistance. Civil servants in federal, state, and local governments in the United States are sometimes several layers removed from the families, individuals, homeowners, residents, and tenants who ultimately benefit from the services, policies, and public programs they oversee. Nonprofit and private technical assistance providers work under government contracts to support the frontline workers implementing programs and utilizing data management systems to serve people experiencing homelessness. These individuals are rarely considered "street-level" public servants, and they may not be classified as "essential" in the now-common pandemic parlance of 2020. However, their work undoubtedly informs both citizens' and frontline service providers' experiences and ability to access necessary shelter and stable, affordable, and inclusive housing.

Federal government involvement in housing policy began in the 1930s and in the decades since has grown to many fragmented programs across three major federal agencies: the U.S. Department of Housing and Urban Development (HUD), Department of the Treasury, and U.S. Department of Agriculture (USDA) (McCarty, Perl, & Jones, 2019). According to the Congressional Research Service: "The modern [federal] housing assistance programs include both relatively flexible grants to state and local governments to serve homeless people, build affordable housing, provide assistance to first-time homebuyers, and promote community development; and more structured, direct assistance programs that provide low-cost apartments and rental vouchers to poor families, administered through local public, quasi-public, and private intermediaries" (McCarty et al., 2019, p. 1).

The field of housing policy is highly specialized and complex. These stories are a snapshot of the complex roles in this realm. From the research directors of state housing organizations whose work informs local governments' affordable housing development decisions to the officials at HUD whose oversight ensures local housing authorities can serve low-income families, these professionals play crucial roles in the provision of a vital component of the social safety net.

The stories these public servants tell highlight how housing provides the foundation for many aspects of a healthy and fulfilling life; it links citizens and families to education, jobs, transportation, community networks, and countless public services and economic opportunities. They work behind the scenes and influence policy decisions and program delivery daily. How they understand the value of their work and talk about their mission to others—whether the public or elected officials—can provide insight to academics and researchers, to citizens and politicians, and to anyone hoping to pursue a career in this field.

This chapter is organized as follows: First, a brief section outlines the methodology and describes the individuals whose stories inform this chapter. Next, three sections detail key findings, drawn from the embedded knowledge of public servants themselves. The concluding section, which may be most pertinent for MPA students and future public servants, outlines key applied lessons drawn from the lived experiences of these professionals.

Methods

Inductive, qualitative research methods inform this chapter, including open-ended interview prompts and narrative inquiry to connect the work of academic research to practitioners (Ospina & Dodge, 2005). As a former manager and civil servant with almost a decade of experience in affordable housing in the federal government, my own knowledge of and connections to this work informed these discussions and provided a point of entry in participant recruitment. The interviewees' responses were coupled with a critical auto-ethnographic approach to provide additional depth and nuance to the findings (Roth, 2005). The semi-structured interviews explored (a) how and why the public servant chose to work on affordable housing or homelessness issues; (b) how they believe the public understands the value of their work; and (c) how they think about the value of their work and explain that value to the public or political principals. Interviews took place between February and March 2021 and lasted an average of 30 minutes. Once completed, interviews were transcribed and analyzed using a thematic open and axial coding technique (Saldaña, 2015) in NVivo12 qualitative data analysis software (see Figure 11.1).

Of the 22 total participants, eight were government officials (36% of participants), including four at the federal level, two at the state level, and two at the local level. The largest group represented is the nonprofit sector, which included 11 individuals (50% of the sample). Interviewees also included two individuals currently working for private for-profit consulting firms (9%); both individuals had previously worked in the affordable housing and homelessness at various levels of government. Women represented the majority of participants (77%), which is typical for the field; and participants also represented a mix of racial and ethnic identities. Table 11.1 details the demographics of interviewees.

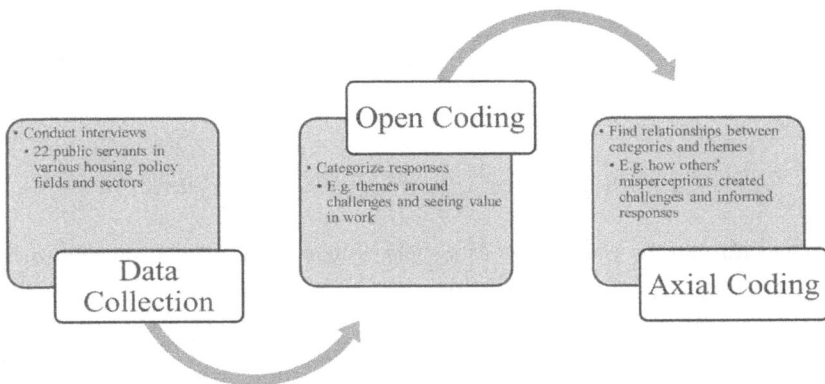

Figure 11.1. Data Collection and Analysis Process. *Source:* Author-created.

Table 11.1. Demographic and Organizational Characteristics of Interviewees (N=22)

	Government		Sector		
	Federal	State/Local	Nonprofit	Private	Total
Gender					
Female	3	3	9	2	17 (77%)
Male	1	1	2	0	4 (18%)
Nonbinary	1	0	0	0	1 (4.5%)
Race/ethnicity					
Black	1	2	2	0	5 (23%)
Latinx	0	0	1	0	1 (4.5%)
AAPI	0	0	1	0	1 (4.5%)
White	4	2	7	2	15 (68%)
Total	4 (18%)	4 (18%)	11 (50%)	2 (9%)	22

Source: Author-created.

The remainder of this chapter outlines key findings and narratives from these interviews in three broad sections. The first findings section turns to common themes in how these public servants understand the value of their roles. The following section dissects how these public servants believe the public views their work and how they find common ground with those who may be unaware of—or even unsympathetic to—the imperatives of affordable housing programs and homelessness services. Finally, the last section synthesizes applied lessons the interviewees shared after years of working in the field.

The Value of Housing and Homelessness Policy Work

Across all sectors, public servants spoke about housing as a foundational necessity and a right. Indeed, since the U.S. Housing Act of 1949, the goal of "a decent home and a suitable living environment for every American family" has been an unfulfilled promise of U.S. housing policy (Bratt, Stone, & Hartman, 2006, p. 237). The idea of housing as a right for all and a foundation for healthy, thriving communities motivated their work. While seeing the impact of systemic work can be difficult, these public servants consistently came back to the mission. They drew a connection between their more mundane, technical tasks and the overarching goal for a more just, equitable system in which all people have access to shelter and affordable housing.

When asked one thing they might share about the value of their work, these professionals asserted that housing is both a foundation and a right. As a federal employee stated, "Having access to safe and accessible housing and improving neighborhoods, I view those as fundamental building blocks to improving people's lives." These public servants held firm to the belief that housing is crucial and should be a right that every person in our country can access, regardless of income or circumstance. As another nonprofit employee asserted: "Housing is a right for all. Doesn't matter who. It doesn't matter what their past was. It doesn't matter what their future is. There is a basic human right to have a place to call home, and we as neighbors, as a community, as a society, we need to work to ensure that everybody has a place to call home." Some iteration of housing and shelter as both a foundational need and/or a right was present across all sectors.

Much of this work, particularly for the technical assistance providers, was system-focused and tied to macro-level analysis. In explaining the value this systems-level work adds, a federal civil servant stated: "I think that we as humans tend to think a lot on the individual level, like, 'Well, parents should do better with their kids on this.' And it's systems. It's huge structures that need intervention, and that is the point of the government. The scope and scale of societal needs are so great that it's not possible to [address them] on a really small scale." A nonprofit worker put it this way, "We are the connectors between 'we have this idea' which I think leaders develop, you know, Congress [or policymakers] and then the implementers. We are the connectors and the translators in a lot of ways." This systems-level work serves as the bridge that allow policies to be realized in an effective and equitable way. However, that long-term, systems-level change work also made it difficult to always see the value. As a nonprofit employee stated, sometimes "you don't see [the outcome or value] for six months, a year, two years." This time horizon often meant there were days and weeks with few explicit policy "wins" or readily apparent positive outcomes. Thus, these practitioners knew they needed to be intentional about centering the people ultimately benefiting and remind themselves often of the patience required to see progress.

Many noted that the value of this work—and their ability to *see* this value—ebbed and flowed depending on *what* they were doing that day. A federal employee expressed:

> A lot of time, we're so far removed, and we're, you know, like, the stereotypes—we ourselves are going through bureaucratic layers and red tape. It's kind of hard to see the end goal of what you're doing, sometimes you just get kind of trapped in the weeds. So, I think a lot of times, I don't necessarily get the value, sometimes I get it at work . . . A lot of times . . . it's kind of hard to see it when you're stuck in your current role.

Some of those frustrations stem from the slow-moving nature of the bureaucracy, the perceived lack of attention or political support, or the nature of day-to-day work that may seem far removed from the outcomes. As one state government employee noted:

> I'll be honest. I would say that the level of job satisfaction has swung back and forth. Certainly, there have been times when I was in a position to sort of move the ball forward and do something . . . and there was all this attention, and people were really thinking about these issues. I've been involved in some discussions on policymaking when I can see that what I've been doing is making a difference in the real world. You know, that's what's important. You know, not surprisingly, in bureaucracy, there's a lot of things you do that *aren't that*. There's a lot of times where you are frustrated, whether it's by the constraints of being a public employee, whether that's, you know, political or financial.

These frustrations were pervasive in the narratives and stories, but particularly for those who worked in government. They grappled with the nature of this work and the roadblocks to achieve housing as a right for all. Work in large bureaucratic agencies was predicated on implementing the laws and policies that may be limited in scope and funding, constraining the ability of these public servants to achieve the kind of housing justice and transformative social policy that initially drew them to the field.

Whether value was harder to see because of the long-term nature of systems-level work or the slow-moving bureaucracy, these professionals came back to the mission and their end goal. They addressed frustrations by, as one nonprofit employee put it, "just being centered in very specific values about housing and equity and those types of things and . . . letting that be the center of the work." Another federal employee noted, "I've always been able to sort of talk myself back to the mission, even when it's not obvious." And a state government leader shared: "It's about being mission-focused and hearing stories of—whether I'm the CFO, or whether I'm scanning documents in for record retention at the agency—that everybody is connected with the mission of our agency. And helping every child in [our state] not know what it feels like to be homeless."

This centering was essential to understanding the value, even amid frustrations, opposition, or lack of short-term policy wins. These public servants knew that they had to be intentional about the ultimate goals of this work daily. Mission focus becomes even more important when explaining the importance of this work to those who may not understand it, which is where this chapter now turns.

Finding Common Ground Across (Mis)Perceptions

In defining the public value of this work, it is helpful to understand general perceptions—and misperceptions—these professionals confront. To frame the value propositions, they often thought about how to speak to the many citizens, community members, and even politicians who carried prejudice against—or general lack of awareness of—affordable housing and homelessness programs. In confronting public perceptions, they sought common ground and directly addressed misperceptions about program beneficiaries and public policies. This allowed for them to talk about their mission and frame the need for their work so that even the most opposed individuals could see the value.

Across sectors, most public servants working in housing expressed some version of "I think that the vast majority of people don't know what we're doing." From their own families to the general public, they knew that many people could not quite wrap their heads around their systems-level work and public service that was *not* direct service provision. One nonprofit technical assistance provider reiterated how many conversations go: "[My family is] like, 'Oh, so you work at a shelter?'—'Nope. I don't work at a shelter.' "

There was also an inherent paradox and tension in how these public servants spoke. On the one hand, they wanted to be behind the scenes, as a technical assistance provider shared: "If I'm doing my job well, they may not know I am there." Alternatively, they knew that this lack of awareness and understanding could lead to a lack of public and political support for their work, which they knew was so essential to progress and success.

Other misperceptions of their work were more ardently grounded in philosophical opposition. Many misconceptions fall along partisan lines about the proper role of government in providing benefits. There are, as a state employee notes, "People who don't think there is a role for the public sector in housing." However, as a federal employee notes, this may simply be due to lack of awareness and an "underappreciation for how omnipresent the [Federal Housing Administration] is in housing infrastructure and financing across the nation." The average citizen may think of HUD as an agency that provides housing subsidies for impoverished people; they do not realize the historic and current impact of FHA on expanding access to homeownership, bolstering the national economy, and local economic development. Whether because of ignorance or beliefs about the appropriate role of government, there is a lack of knowledge of the history and reach of housing policy, which has been tacitly interwoven with so many aspects of the modern economy for people across income brackets.

These public servants also spoke about misperceptions that people experiencing homelessness or in need of affordable housing were simply lazy or not working hard enough. As one state government worker shared, "There are people who believe in a social safety net and people who don't. But maybe not just on principle, maybe just because they've never had to personally experience [that kind of hardship]." The belief that beneficiaries and recipients of affordable housing subsidies and homelessness services were somehow *different* from their own families and communities in meaningful ways was one reason for this opposition. As a nonprofit affordable housing developer explained: "We have a steep hill to climb . . . around the notion of, you know, affordable housing and . . . you know, it's like '*those* people'—that they get into that circumstance, whether it's homelessness, whether it's low-income people we're trying to house." This mentality was one of the major hurdles to garnering public and political support for their work.

A federal civil servant noted: "It's those, you know, terrible stereotypes about beneficiaries of some sort of subsidy where 'They're just lazy; they don't want to work.' . . . There's a lot of misconceptions about the work that we do and the people who receive not just HUD, but any sort of public assistance. I think everyone just assumes it's just fraud-ridden and, you know, that does exist, but that's not the vast majority of the recipients."

These public servants felt passionately that this mindset, which vilifies recipients of these programs, misrepresents the complex factors that lead someone to need to access affordable housing or shelter. Moreover, this stance fails to understand that "those people" are also members of the community.

The interviewees felt strongly that the work toward safe, stable housing and shelter for all benefits *everyone*. As a nonprofit leader asserted, "I think there is an underappreciation for [the fact that] if we are successful in our efforts, it benefits *the entire community*." Another nonprofit leader added, "Housing inequality really costs everybody."

The way many of these public servants think about demonstrating value and changing minds is simple: Continue to do the work, do it well, and educate people around the realities of these program outcomes and *who* ultimately benefits from them. As a nonprofit affordable housing professional asserted, "The best way to change that stigma around affordable housing is to do good projects and show people how different affordable housing—and low-income residents who benefit from it—is in reality." These public servants believed that, ultimately, even the most combative stances might be softened by how the reality of affordable housing diverges from their preconceptions.

Whether talking to the public, political appointees, or elected officials, these public servants spoke about the importance of education. One way to demonstrate the value is through providing data and evidence. A federal employee noted how data and evidence-based policy decisions could overcome these philosophical differences:

> I don't think ideology should ever take precedence over the reality that's in front of you. I found it very useful to, you know, when we would get correspondence or we would get proposals for policy changes, to just ground my responses in, "What does the research say? What does the data say? What do we know about this?" And to just serve that back to say, "These are facts. These are realities." I was very happy that I had those skills. Because without that, I think it does become just kind of a tussle over orientation to an issue. I think orientation to finding the data and finding the research is always a really strong approach.

A leader of state agency had a similar approach: "We had to come up with—to devise—a plan. And I thought the first part of that plan should be data-based, data-driven. You can't argue with facts and figures. You can try, but I think you lose out." Another federal employee spoke about how they talk to friends, family members, or general public who perpetuate these misperceptions:

> When I'm thinking about the public housing programs, [I'm] trying to give a snapshot of what the actual demographic of the population we're serving is. Because there's this notion, you know, of able-bodied individuals who make the choice not to work. And . . . that is a very small piece of the pie. And certainly, you know, you can find an individual or anecdotal story anywhere across America, where someone is gaming the system, but it's so the exception, and not the norm.

Other state and local officials noted that they spend a lot of time educating elected officials about their complex programs, the outcomes they accomplish, the varied funding mechanisms, and how their programs address constituents' concerns and needs. Some of these approaches are pragmatic, tapping into fiscal, economic, or social concerns. As one public servant noted: "Some don't understand on a philosophical plane, so you have to put it on an economic plane." As a local government leader explained:

> I think it's just essential that elected officials who I report to understand and are educated [about] "Why is housing important? Why do we need housing?" And so literally starting at the basic level with getting them to understand that . . . economically and socially enables me to navigate better. That is a process . . . I literally made it a mission of mine to educate each of our council members about the importance of housing, getting them data. Even though I know they're pretty inundated with information all the time, I got on the phone with them before any of my items came on the floor to say, "This is why this is important. This is who this is going to impact." . . . And it's excessively time-consuming, but I realized that it was pivotal.

Whether using data and evidence or providing detailed education about the complexity and breadth of these programs and policies, these public servants are adept at navigating the many stereotypes and potential opposition that plagues their work. They know how to ask the right questions and frame their work to lead toward dialogue and common ground.

Sometimes the use of data and evidence does not demystify the complex systemic work or change hearts and minds. In those cases, as a nonprofit employee shared, "It is the translation between the work that we do at a systems-level. Typically . . . people connect more with the individual story, the emotional . . ." For those who do not understand the purpose or value of policy work, they may be more inclined to relate on the personal level. The power of building relationships across difference was another antidote to the public opposition and misperceptions about this work. As a federal housing official noted:

> There's so much work to be done in our country to break the stereotypes that plague the people that have less than the others, and just find ways to get people outside of their bubbles, because it is so easy for us to live in our own world and think that because everybody in my bubble is okay and we've found a way to make it happen, it is so easy to think that others can do the same. But if we were to step one foot into these people's worlds, to see what they deal with on a day-to-day basis, I really believe the minds of others would change.

Another federal civil servant noted that her approach was to start conversations and ask questions: "How I kind of relate to them is to be like, 'You have a grandmother? You have anyone in your family who's disabled? Do you have any anyone in your family who is a single parent? Do you know [anyone] who has children who has lost their job?'" These approaches tap into shared human experiences and empathy over data and facts; they were more conversational than confrontational. They asked questions and started a dialogue rather than leading with data.

For those who cannot imagine relying on temporary shelters or subsidized housing, other stories can tap into their lived experiences. A nonprofit program manager shared his perspective:

If everybody could wrap their heads around what a big problem it is, and how it's coming for all of us, eventually . . . we
could pretty easily fix it. We could throw off the bounds of
this scarcity issue, because we'd never tolerate—we don't, we're
not tolerating it—with vaccines, right? We're losing our minds,
right? Because there's not enough vaccines for us. Imagine if
we lost our minds that there's not enough housing for people.
There's not. There's just not and that's crazy, because we can
afford it. We can afford it, and it would save us money.

Underneath the frustration of such widespread misperceptions, there was
an inherent underlying optimism in this approach. They believed even
those most opposed to their work had the capacity to understand and
support it eventually.

For many of these public servants, demonstrating the value—especially across political conflict—meant "playing the long game." They
worked hard on building relationships, particularly in communities
that may oppose affordable housing programs. As a current for-profit
technical assistance provider noted, "We worked really hard on a good
neighbor process. And part of it was just showing up and being willing
to sit through tense times and to say, 'We're not going to walk away. If
you're having problems, we're going to be part of it. We're gonna listen
to you. We want you to be part of this.'" Another nonprofit leader
shared this approach:

When I get the question "Are there people who just don't
want to be housed and would like to remain homeless all
the time?" That's a legitimate question from that person. [It]
makes my blood curl just a little bit . . . [But] how I meet
that person where they're at is by honoring their humanity
in their questions and thought process, and then try to bring
new information forward in order to recalibrate that. And
sometimes, like, there are some people who [get it right away].
And [with] other people, it's a super long game.

The way these public servants spoke about addressing resistance was
sitting through tense conversations. To get to consensus, relationship
building and vision and hope for long-term possibilities are required.

This is particularly true for those technical assistance (TA) providers coming into a community as an outside expert. As one TA provider shared: "[It is about] seeking entry into a community and finding your key informants . . . I have to attend more meetings and listen for somebody who sounds like they're asking good questions and schedule a separate conversation with them through video chat. And I think that mentality of like, trying to step back and start sort of mentally mapping community dynamics is really critical right now."

Another nonprofit housing coalition leader shared: "There's all of these political dynamics that impact priorities. The ways in which we overcome that is really figuring out who the *champion* is on the issue that can help us utilize their influence in their community, their political will, to help move the needle, right? Because I can't do this a lot of times, as an outsider coming into a community that I don't live [in] or don't have those relationships forged." This relationship building and understanding *what matters* to those who hold the political power within a given community was essential to implement policies.

Much of this work is about finding common ground and tapping into shared goals. A nonprofit leader shared her approach:

> I always like to start with the fact that in [our state] we need more affordable housing. I think there's really not an elected official that wouldn't nod and agree with that. Now, what for sure is different is *how* we might define affordable housing; how we might define the role of government in affordable housing; how we might define the path to get to a place where we have more—and/or access to—affordable housing. But I think to me, when we *set the table with people nodding*, people understanding that we love our communities. We don't want to see them hollowed out with people who can't live there anymore. We want our children to be able to live here, right? It's one where everybody nods. And after that, we can start having some more of the difficult conversations and get into the weeds.

Setting the table with common goals was a helpful and widely used approach. They grounded themselves in the conviction that, even across conflict, there was always agreement on some of the nonpartisan issues like love of community and a desire to ensure children have access to opportunities.

Finally, many of these public servants expressed an optimism about this moment in 2021, where there are more public conversations around the historic impacts of unjust, inequitable housing policies like redlining. Despite the resistance and the widespread lack of knowledge, they also saw this moment as an opportunity where people were beginning to engage in dialogue around housing, equity, and systemic challenges. The next section outlines some lessons for this moment.

Applied Lessons

From their years of experience in housing policy across different sectors, communities, and organizations, these individuals shared various lessons. The themes repeated most often and with the most force were twofold. First, they expressed how vital it is to understand and reflect on one's impact in this field—both good and bad. To make meaningful and positive impact, one had to first acknowledge the legacy of explicitly racist housing policies *and* reconcile the unintended negative consequences of misinformed policies. Second, they spoke about how public servants in this field must learn to approach this work with a sense of humility, admitting all they do not fully understand. Both lessons led the interviewees to underscore the imperative of working in collaboration with communities they ultimately serve.

Part of comprehending the importance of housing policy is about recognizing the impacts it has—both currently and historically—on people and communities, including the disproportionate benefits and burdens provided to specific demographic groups. This means not solely celebrating policy successes and victories, but also honestly grappling with policy failures. As one nonprofit employee with prior federal government experience stated:

> There is an opportunity for every government agency to own the wrongs that they created. So, when I say that, [I mean] addressing how they've played a role in creating racism, and that they now have to take a larger role to undo that wrong. Making that commitment, driving the change, and

then seeing it through with actionable [steps], and being accountable to the community in which they serve. That's a huge undertaking, because many may not want to admit that they did a wrong, but it's definitely needed, because you can see the institutional racism and structural racism that exists and [the opportunity that] is not [available now] for [people] of color . . . they have to own that. They created it, so how can they play a large role in making the change?

This lesson is about being candid about the lasting harms of explicit policies of segregation and discrimination. To be a public servant in housing policy requires historic accountability; to work toward housing justice requires eschewing an ahistorical vision that denies moral responsibility.

Relatedly, these public servants must be honest about how good intentions may still lead to harmful impacts. As one former federal employee who now works for a private government contractor explained when asked about the value of this work:

> I feel like it's easier to explain *the harm* that can be done. You know, you write a good policy, write a good regulation. You spend money; you can talk about the impact . . . when I think about kind of the impact that we can make as public servants, I think that often we take our jobs *too lightly* . . . I think that we forget the repercussions that can happen. We sit in a room; we come up with good ideas. And we're not often interested in hearing—or we don't know that it's necessary to hear—other opinions or to hear from, you know, others in the field to kind of challenge those perspectives.

Speaking about the field of affordable housing and homelessness policy work, they continued:

> I do think that we definitely have a listening problem. Sometimes, I think that we have gotten really bad at [listening] . . . And this is universal. This is public servants. This is [technical assistance]. This is philanthropy. This is all of us. I don't think that we do enough to listen to both the direct service providers that are doing the work, or the folks that

are having to navigate our programs. I think we talked to
one community, and suddenly that feels *representative enough*
to create policy.

The need to engage the communities, families, and individuals who
themselves benefit from—or are burdened by—these policies was a key
takeaway from many interviews.

There is a tension and paradox inherent in this assertion. These
are the experts, but doing this work also requires a healthy amount of
humility. As a technical assistance provider said: "I think that a big
lesson to me to learn over the years is like, I might be relatively smart.
I might understand certain things. But I'll never have all the answers.
I've never experienced homelessness. I've never experienced housing
instability." These public servants, although sometimes removed from
the program recipients or frontline service delivery, must constantly
strive to co-create solutions with those most impacted by housing
instability.

Conclusion

These public servants' stories underscore what Schwartz (2010) asserts:
"Housing policy is seldom just about housing" (p. 6). These individuals
shared a belief that housing is the foundation which links people to community and opportunity. Their work is grounded in a mission to realize the
unfulfilled promise of housing as a right for all. While much of this work
was about creating systemic change, it was just as much about changing
the vision of what is possible. As one nonprofit employee asked, "What
can we do to stop this cycle of poverty *and* impoverished thinking?" To
be successful, they knew they had to find common ground across political
and philosophical differences, use evidence-based approaches, and build
relationships. In this moment of focused attention on housing justice
and racial equity, they reminded us that this work entails recognition
of the great responsibility of this work, a sincere understanding of the
good *and* the harm that these policies and programs can foster. Doing
this work well has the potential to reshape communities in a more just
and equitable manner, to address entrenched patterns of segregation and
discrimination, and to unlock opportunities for all.

References

Bratt, R. G., Stone, M. E., Hartman, C. (Eds.). (2006). *A right to housing: Foundation for a new social agenda.* Temple University Press.

McCarty, M., Perl, L., & Jones, K. (2019, March 27). *Overview of federal housing assistance programs and policies.* Congressional Research Service. https://crsreports.congress.gov/product/pdf/RL/RL34591

Ospina, S. M., & Dodge, J. (2005). Narrative inquiry and the search for connectedness: Practitioners and academics developing public administration scholarship. *Public Administration Review, 65*(4), 409–423. https://www.jstor.org/stable/3542638

Roth, W. M. (2005). *Auto/biography and auto/ethnography: Praxis of research method.* Sense Publishers.

Saldaña, J. (2015). *The coding manual for qualitative researchers.* Sage.

Schwartz, A. F. (2010). *Housing policy in the United States* (2nd ed.). Routledge.

Section 4

Unexpected Realms of Democracy

We end our exploration of the frontline, street-level bureaucrat focusing on public servants who contribute to the functioning of our democracy even more than their titles would suggest. The line connecting politics, the policy process, and the implementation of public programs is not a straight line or even a dichotomous barrier separating the various parties (Svara, 1998). Democracy is messy, and the outcomes of democracy are imperfect and complex. Public servants have roles, small and large, in decision-making throughout the policy process, not limited to the administration of political choices, as noted by Kaufman (2001).

Though not a recent development, our current discourse often disparages public servants as part of the "swamp." There is more to this denunciation than the usual remarks about pay or laziness. Such attacks get at the very nature of what public servants are meant to do—they play essential parts in the functioning of democracies. Rather than being a subversion of democracy, the inclusion of public servants is an intended and necessary part of democracy. Sometimes these roles are unexpected and without fanfare or public disparagement, like that described in Clark's chapter on election officials.

There are so many positions that are vital in a working democracy. We often get to teach some of the most interesting public servants with jobs we had not thought of yet! The stories in this section highlight how we might think of a career as one thing, but these public servants carry a much larger democratic load than we first imagined, such as the photographer using his camera to document ecosystems, arts, culture, and humanities professionals committed to maintaining a record of society and creativity and providing access to books, art, and music—something that may be particularly needed during tough times like the end of the beginning of the 2020s, and public servants connecting the work of environmental agencies to those in other contexts for the good of the public.

We begin this section in the U.S. Fish and Wildlife Service with photographer Ryan Hagerty. In chapter 12, Maja Holmes describes how Hagerty's work as a photographer can raise public awareness for conserving important ecosystems and habitats with an image in ways that words cannot. He can show people our changing environment without them even leaving their laptops, contributing to the public discourse through careful photography and curation. Likewise, we are struck by the role arts and culture professionals and librarians play in democracy by providing the space and time for community connections, civic engagement, and civic discourse in chapter 13. Sarah Berry, Dutch Reutter, Judith Millesen, and Maren B. Trochmann focus on the role of museums, arts and culture agencies, and libraries during the pandemic and powerfully demonstrate that libraries and arts organizations were more "essential" than given credit for pre-pandemic. In chapter 14, Nandhini Rangarajan, Aroon Manoharan, and Bianca Ortiz-Wythe explore a similar occurrence in India, where they share stories from three community health workers trying to navigate rules, community health, safety, and their own well-being.

Our final chapter in this section focuses on the complications that can arise for public servants when they are expected to navigate the messiness of democracy. JoyAnna Hopper describes the role of public employees in combined environmental agencies and the frustrations that arise for those that serve as liaisons between agencies at all levels, politicians, and the public. These positions, though complicated, are vital for ensuring that critical policies and regulations are met.

Our Stories and Reflections on Section 4

Staci: *What I really like about this section is the focus on public servants in seemingly unexpected places. Clearly those places are not unexpected to those people in the roles, but I hope readers stop to think about the breadth of public service work. As trust in government in the U.S. and abroad continues to erode, finding people to fill these unseen yet critical roles will be paramount.*

The theme throughout these chapters of government in unexpected places reminds me of being in high school working for my local government in Florida. There, my friend and I were hired to work in the communications and marketing department as creators of a teen website to attract more young people into government service. When you are young, you never think being a teenage writer for a local government is even an option, but it was such a great job! We got to review concerts, makeup products, and a company even sent us prom dresses to wear and review. The website lasted several years after we graduated, but it was an innovative (at the time 20 years ago—yikes!) way to get people into public service. I never thought about a way to bridge my two interests, journalism and politics. The job helped me dual major in college, and today I pride myself on being a qualitative researcher privileged to tell stories from public servants.

Jessica: *As we finish this book in 2022, the United States, the country in which I live, is experiencing a lot of political division, to a level I never thought I would witness in my lifetime. I cannot lie and say it does not concern me greatly, but one area that keeps me filled with hope is thinking about the many public servants out there—in the U.S. and other countries—who are the anchors that keep the state going even when it seems that the politicians may just want to light it all on fire. The chapters in this book, from my point of view, show the hope that these public servants bring to people in big and small ways. It may sound overly poetic, but what really struck me about these chapters was how they captured the <u>beauty</u> of the public service—how government can really be a force for good. Government can help document and preserve the beauty of our lands, the cultural heritage of our people and places, the health and well-being of the citizenry. Individual dedicated public servants are a candle to light the darkest corners and times, and I personally think that is pretty amazing. I am excited to use these chapters to help remind myself and my students of this hope and keep it alive in the future.*

Alex: *These several chapters in section 4 resonated with me for a number of reasons, most notably because they describe professions that sit at the intersection of culture, art, knowledge, stewardship, and public service. We often associate the concept of government or public service with more visible functions like law enforcement, public works, and others (and often those that are much more expensive), and neglect to see to see other realms where the work of frontline public servants is critical. Those working in areas of arts and culture are particularly critical in that they provide support and public access to creative works and means of expression that explore or document the human condition (though presidential photographers like Pete Souza are an exception—his work is both creative and prominent). As with others, I find* more than a bit of joy and hope in these chapters and in the contributions of these authors in highlighting these public and nonprofit services.

Lauren: I do not play favorites among these chapters, but these were some that I keep coming back to and I cannot wait to assign in classes. There is a real power to the route that Maja Holmes took in chapter 12 in telling just one person's story. I have even started following the U.S. Fish and Wildlife Service's Facebook and Instagram. The pictures are truly stunning. I was struck by the idea that one can combine their passion for an interest, art, or task with their passion for serving the public, whether that is photography or the arts. These positions, even in the routine of day-to-day work, can have a lasting impact that is far more reaching than their job descriptions. They can open up dialogues in a community or broaden how citizens see the world around them.

References

Kaufman, H. (2001). Major players: Bureaucracies in American government. *Public Administration Review, 61*(1), 18–42.

Svara, J. H. (1998). The politics-administration dichotomy model as aberration. *Public Administration Review, 58*(1), 51–58.

12

Making in the Invisible Visible

The Photographers and Videographers in Public Service

MAJA HUSAR HOLMES

In the 1930s, 11 photographers set out across the United States as part of the Works Progress Administration (WPA). The Farmer's Security Administration deployed the photographers to capture the faces, environments, and emotions of Americans during the Depression. The photographers were public servants who reshaped the national narrative about the human experience in the United States (Library of Congress, 2021). Almost a century later, these images remain indelible reminders of the public value of making the invisible visible. Today, a new generation of photographers and videographers, employed by the U.S National Park Service, U.S. Fish and Wildlife Service, U.S Forest Service, and other conservation management agencies, continue to serve an essential role in painting a picture of public values. The photographers represent a distinct class of storytellers who bring the implementation of public policy to life through the mission of the public agencies.

This chapter highlights the distinct role of these public servants. Photographers bring a visual narrative to public policy. Conservation management agencies represent the implementation of myriad federal policies including the preservation and conservation of ecological, natural, and recreational resources in the public domain. Federal photographers and videographers craft the image of how the American public experiences the impact of these policies. The images captured by publicly employed photographers connect local contexts to national agendas to generate a more complete picture of the scope of public policy. Public service photographers leverage evolving technology (e.g., drones, underwater cameras) to generate and share a more nuanced story of our public values. They ensure access to our public resources through publicly available databases of images. In essence, the work of these individuals serves to promote the availability of the images that allow Americans to engage in a continuing conversation about our collective public values through policy choices.

Based on an interview with U.S. Fish and Wildlife Service photographer Ryan Hagerty, this chapter defines the role of the image creators who support the mission of U.S. Fish and Wildlife Service (USFWS). Hagerty brings 24 years of experience working for the National Conservation Training Center (NCTC), which serves as the primary training facility to support the U.S. Fish and Wildlife Service (USFWS) employees and conservation partners. His path to public service started as an intern when the NCTC facility first opened its doors in Shepherdstown, West Virginia, in 1997.

In his role as photographer of conservation resources, Hagerty contributes to the mission of USFWS in employing images to promote conservation practices for future generations of public servants and conservation partners and illuminate the habitats, wildlife, and ecosystems USFWS is charged with protecting. In the decades that followed, Hagerty honed a niche in conservation imagery focusing on habitats and species that were generally not accessible to the public imagination. Hagerty brought the underwater experience to the surface in capturing the wildlife hidden from public view in the rivers, streams, and wetlands, such as freshwater mussels, non-game fish species, and amphibians. Through a reflection on his role as a public servant who strives to make the invisible visible, the interview offers key aspects of the lived experience of a public administrator to advance public policy and values. Using illustrative examples, the chapter highlights specific practices and norms adopted by the photographers and videographers to frame their work in public service.

Creating Portraits of Species to Frame Policy Implementation

One of the primary missions of the U.S. Fish and Wildlife Services is to administer the Endangered Species Act (ESA). The 1973 landmark legislation recognized the rich natural heritage of the United States and its territories of "esthetic, ecological, educational, recreational, and scientific value to our Nation and its people" (United States, 1983). The purpose of the ESA is to protect and recover imperiled species and the ecosystems on which they depend. USFWS has primary responsibility for administering policies to protect endangered and threatened terrestrial and freshwater organisms. The photographers and videographers of USFWS generate the images that facilitate how biologists and conservationists implement the mission of U.S. Fish and Wildlife Services to "work with others to conserve, protect and enhance fish, wildlife and plants and their habitats for the continuing benefit of the American people" (USFWS, 2021).

The unique perspectives of the photographers and videographers of USFWS capture both highly visible species, such as the American bald eagle, monarch butterfly, and salmon species, and bring the less visible species, such as the candy darter fish and hellbender salamanders, to the limelight. The photographers, however, are more than just passive image creators. They work collaboratively with biologists and conservationists to create portraits of species that reflect their role in the ecosystem, the distinct challenges in ensuring their survival, and the practices that mitigate their extinction. In a way, the work of the photographers and videographers brings the rationale of the ESA to life. Hagerty reflected on this distinct role in the policy process, which involves getting ahead of the policy implementation and creating a meaningful visual of the policy:

> Shining a light that these species are important and getting ahead of some of these stories is important. When we designate animals that need protections, we have to have imagery to back up the reason why the public should care. Sometimes you are contacted by the press when a species is designated as protected. At least with fish, which were out of sight and out of mind, you may only have a photograph of a dead specimen, or a pickled specimen, which is not ideal. It may have lost all its natural coloration or its ability to do something unique in its environment.

Given the power that visuals can have on reflecting meaning and significance, the photographers serving in public agencies have an active role in contributing to the policy narrative. They adopt emerging technology that presents a fuller portrait of the distinctness of each species.

For example, the advent of digital photography and more sophisticated camera housings provide an unprecedented view of species that were previously hidden from public interaction. In bringing the camera below the water surface, photographers capture vibrancy and natural activity of the species underwater. Out of water, fish species may appear dull and flat. They may not capture our imagination of what the species are capable of. As he explained:

> From a conservation standpoint [the images] allows the viewer to see the fish in the habitat. The technology has grown in leaps and bounds in the past decade . . . capturing conservation imagery. Because really the general public cannot care about what goes on underwater unless they can visualize or see it. **Caring equates to conservation** [bold added] and unless we have a public consciousness of endangered species that live underwater that are out of sight and out of mind and therefore not funded.

Photographers also pay close attention to the composition of these species through the portraits. They understand that images are messages. They can affect the awareness of an issue and promulgate even minor changes in practice with significant consequences. Hagerty's perspective is that the way species are captured through images may have an impact on the overall survival of endangered and threatened species:

> I want to keep preaching to the biologists. When we photograph any species, the image reflects a moment in time, but it also sends messages. In the case of the mussels, when you want to show "hey look at this really neat mussel" . . . we take it out of the water and photograph it. They may have only pulled that mussel out of the water for a minute [but] **its psychological effect** [bold added] is to give people the idea that you can treat mussels like living rocks . . . That it is fine to get them out of the water. But it is not. So, what I have tried to do is to start photographing all these aquatic species, in or near water. If they are not underwater, they are at the water surface. When photographing mussels, I try and show them bathing in water to keep them cool and moist.

So that the idea that you do not take them out of the water
is perpetuated.

The result is that the image, even if it is just a moment in time,
sends a message. The work of the photographer is to make intentional
choices about how the species are portrayed and how we should interact
with the species. Collectively, the practices and norms adopted by publicly
funded photographers have a considerable impact on the implementation
and understanding of public policy.

Publicly funded photographers create visual representations of the
conservation policies. The species portraits and the ecosystems they
inhabit reflect both the promise and outcome of public policies. Specifically, they shed light on the practices and contexts to conserve both
the most visible and hidden species. In a way, the images generate a
visual language for the public, policy makers, conservation agents, and
scientists to meet the mission of USFWS "to work with others to conserve, protect and enhance fish, wildlife and plants and their habitats for
the continuing benefit of the American people" (USFWS, 2021). The
next section examines the unique role of the photographers to curate
the individual portraits to generate a fuller picture of the significance
of conservation practices and policies.

Curating Enduring Images for the Public Domain

An understated value of the work that photographers and videographers
do is that they curate images for the American public. The work and
products of any federal employee belong to the people of the United
States. In the case of the photographs generated by the federal employees, the images belong to the people. The images created by publicly
funded photographers not only are used to support the direct work of
public agencies and augment the implementation of public policy, such
as Endangered Species Act, but they also serve as a repository of reliable
images of wildlife and habitats. The public can use the images. The result
is that the general public connects to the images based on their specific
interests, conservation and wildlife groups rely on the images to convey
their initiatives, and federal, state, and local policy makers disseminate
the images to highlight localized natural resources. The accessibility of the

images generates new opportunities for public impact that goes beyond the scope of public agencies, like the USFWS. The key is for the public to be able to find the specific images, as Hagerty said:

> That is your reward, when people are seeing your image and using it . . . our images are being used by a lot of people who are searching out ways to illustrate the natural resources but do not have a large budget to bring forth. For example, the conservation organizations, such as the American Fisheries Society, use the images so that they can find a reliable source of good images of species in their area of conservation (in this case fish), they are eager to use and happy when you post more on your library. I have seen the images used in some very interesting places. You never know which photograph of yours is going to get very popular. For example, some of my images of invasive species have been used quite a bit. Especially the Asian Carp that are jumping in the rivers.

This means that an integral public service that photographers and videographers provide is a reliable, curated source of conservation-related images organized in a publicly available digital library. The photographers play a critical role in the life cycle of how the images become part of the public domain. First, they serve as producers. Partnering with USFWS and state biologists, conservation experts, they advocate for funding of specific photographic projects. Second, they are the visual artists. In the field, the photographers make choices about how they want to portray the species and their habitats. Third, they select the images that reveal the context of the species. In the digital age, innumerable images are created. The expertise of the photographer is to curate the images to generate a variety of quality images accessible through the digital libraries, as Hagerty notes: "I am very forgiving in which images I present, but I have also realized that when people are given many choices, they may not pick the best image to represent the content. I have started to be more judicious in selecting the images to publish publicly."

Finally, the photographer facilitates the creation of the metadata connected to each image. The metadata is what makes the images accessible to the public. Working with biologists and librarians, the photographers articulate the search functions that include the species common name, Latin name, habitat descriptions, and other aspects that contextualize the endangered the species (e.g., level of pollution, presence of invasive species, viruses). Interestingly, USFWS does not note the specific location of the image to protect the endangered or threatened species. The metadata connected to each image provides complementary information to contextualize the species and illustrate its habitat, distinct features, and how the species interacts with the broader environment. Hagerty explained:

> I try to put in a descriptive title that is not too flowery and has tags to lend themselves to a search. For example, if you are photographing someone restoring a stream, you might add in "cold water." A single species may have a few other subject areas that are complementary . . . The species is only one part of it. Critical habitat is part of the story, including [descriptions] of the things that will help or harm a species . . . such as the invasive species, or some disease a fish or animal might have.

Collectively, the production and dissemination of the images in the public domain play a critical role in narrating the policy and generating emergent areas of consideration for public discourse. As in the case of freshwater mussels, where access to the image is combined with the biological metaphorical description of the value of mussels as the "Brita filters" of freshwater ecosystem, there is a more direct connection from the policy adoption to practices mitigating the extinction of threatened species, demonstrating the positive impact of focusing public resources. He explained:

> I can capture what is going on underwater more extensively. The result is that pictures become more prolific in the public domain and caring contributes to conservation. The images pop up on social media posts. The most popular NCTC footage is the eagle using 4k camera. This winter an eagle was incubating in the snow and stood up, shook [its] feathers, and NCTC sent out the picture and several million people viewed that post. Buzzfeed and Reuters reached out. A 4-sec video raises public consciousness.

The photographers bolster the connection between the generation of the images and the diffusion of the images. They are the fulcrum that bring the images into the public domain through the collaborative work of the biologists, conservationists, and librarians. The curated collection of images available in the public domain is the platform for the public to continue to participate in the policy process. Through this commitment, photographers recognize the impact of their work in the development and implementation of conservation policies. The next section details how the images and the public domain of curated images generate the foundation for an evolving discussion of adoption and implementation of conservation policies to protect fish and wildlife for the American public.

Generating an Ecosystem of Visual Policy Narratives

What was most striking in reflecting on the work of the photographers and videographers of USFWS is their commitment to collaborations and partnerships with biologists, conservation officers, and state and local natural resource managers to generate a visual policy narrative. The photographers help the biologists create a vision through imagery. Hagerty noted that individuals working in the conservation space need help in translating what they are doing and how they are doing it into an accessible narrative for the general public and future generations of conservationists. A key part of the job is filming conservation techniques to train others and leveraging the network of federal, state, and local conservation managers to highlight practices that implement the policy intention.

Maintaining consistent communication within the ecosystem of conservation specialists across the United States and its territories is critical to producing visual policy narratives. The photographers make choices about which species to focus on. The process of selecting the projects reflects a collaborative and generative process that acknowledges new conservation techniques and species that are not prominently documented. For example, the candy darter, a vibrant freshwater fish species that looks as if it belongs in a coral reef, was recently designated as endangered under ESA (USFWS, 2017). The challenge is that the candy darter is being hybridized out of existence when anglers release similar fish in the streams, and they propagate with the threatened species. The photographers leveraged their networks to produce a visual narrative of the significance of the candy darter to the ecosystem and practices to support its survival. As Hagerty explained, the aim of one recent photo project was to capture darters, propagate them in hatcheries, and release them to the stream: "Through my contacts in the Fish and Wildlife biologist community, we had heard that a fish hatchery was in the process of propagating the candy darter. Filming the process is a great way to capture training footage for propagation of species, specifically non-game species. Most of the fish hatcheries have historically focused on game species [like] trout, but but non-game species propagation is a new area of interest."

The result is that the photographers are the catalysts in activating partnerships that generate the visual policy narratives. Federal photographers buttress the work of state and local conservation managers. The state conservation agencies are usually the first point of contact for getting into the field. Keeping a close eye on acute and ongoing conversation efforts reflects the generative role of the federal photographers. Awareness of the conservation activities is the foundation for proposing specific projects. This has become even more important as the landscape of state conservation work is evolving with volatile state funding structures of conservation efforts. For example, in many states, conservation activities, including the work of biologists, are funded through hunting and fishing license fees. With the decline in hunting and fishing, conservation efforts at the state level are in peril. This means that proposing discretionary projects becomes a significant part of the photographers' public service ethos. As Hagerty shared:

> When I do have the opportunity to make discretionary recommendations for projects, I focus on areas that are not well documented. For example, a new process for training or a new biological process. But ultimately it is linked to training, given the mission of NCTC as a training center. I see my role as training the next generation of biologists. I want to be able to convey potential mistakes that may ultimately have an impact on the mortality of a species.

The consequence is that the photographers in the public service context are not passive actors. They are actively contributing to and facilitating a discussion of policy practices through visual narratives. Their ability to see the broader picture of conservation initiatives and apply their discretion to visually capture emerging policies that impact conservation goals are a critical dimension of what it means to be a public servant.

Conclusion

Public servants representing many different professions and serve essential functions in implementing public policies and programs. They add their expertise to the policy process and contribute to the mission of public institutions. Many of these public servants not only apply their professional skills but also actively contribute to public discourse that shapes our collective values through policy choices. Federal photographers and videographers craft the image of how the American public experiences the impact of these public policies.

Photographers as public servants first came to prominence in the early 20th century. The United States was at an inflection point in the 1930s, facing massive social and economic challenges. The federal response was a creative and transformational initiative to not only implement policies to address social and economic needs, but also capture the landscape of the policy need. The legacy of the WPA photographers as early pioneers in crafting images of public policy continues to resonate. The work of the photographers, videographers, and producers that generate the narrative of various policy domains is just as important today. The images created, curated, and shared through the public domain by the publicly funded photographers create an enduring, catalytic, and reliable resource to add meaning and context to public policy. It is a testament to how these public servants silently make the invisible visible by crafting a visual narrative of public policies.

References

Hagerty, R. (2021, March 1). Personal communication.

United States. (1983). The Endangered Species Act as amended by Public Law 97-304 (the Endangered Species Act amendments of 1982). G.P.O.

United States Fish and Wildlife Service. (2021). About the U.S. Fish and Wildlife Service. https://www.fws.gov/help/about_us.html

United States Fish and Wildlife Service. (2017, June). *Candy Darter fact sheet.* https://www.fws.gov/sites/default/files/documents/508_candy%20darter%20 fact%20sheet.pdf

U.S. Library of Congress. (2021). *Documenting America, 1935–1943: The Farm Security Administration/Office of War Information photo collection.* https:// www.loc.gov/rr/program/journey/fsa.html

13

Arts and Cultural Management During the Pandemic

Introducing the Observant Servant

SARAH BERRY, DUTCH REUTTER, JUDITH L. MILLESEN, AND MAREN B. TROCHMANN

It's the artists who can lead. It's not about creating and registering a [website] domain and saying, "Let's put up stuff here." It's about artists having ideas and being inspired to want to share something.

—City Office of Cultural Affairs Director

During the last few decades, arts and cultural institutions have grown significantly in scope and reach, as well as in revenue, attendance, and participation. Interestingly, in the United States between 2015 and 2017, the arts and cultural sector grew at more than twice the rate of the national economy (National Endowment of the Arts [NEA], 2020); engaged millions of both domestic and foreign tourists in communities across the country (Americans for the Arts, 2018); and employed more than 5.1 million people (U.S. Department of Commerce, Bureau of Economic Analysis, 2020). Cultural institutions now encompass both formal and informal settings: theaters, museums, and concert halls, but also libraries and educational institutions. With this growth comes challenges for arts managers and other cultural institution professionals as they navigate a tumultuous climate of change in their practices. These changes have led to the blurring of genres, traditions, and categories amid constant competition for and reliance on a dwindling network of external funding sources and financial support (Woronkowicz, Nichols, & Iyengar, 2012).

Funding for arts and cultural institutions has always been under threat (Woronkowicz et al., 2012). And this trend continued throughout the COVID-19 pandemic as historically underfunded and underappreciated arts and cultural programming continued to be overlooked in favor of other public services deemed "more essential." While certain administrations hold the arts in higher regard than others, there has always been an underappreciation of the arts as a factor of economic development and a disregard for the importance of the arts in education (NEA, 2020). In South Carolina, the location of this qualitative study, arts and cultural institutions account for 2.5% of the state gross domestic product (GDP), more than 50,000 jobs, and bring in more than $6.2 billion to the statewide economy (National Assembly of State Arts Agencies, 2020). Despite the economic value added from public investment in arts funding, the argument is often made that private funds can, and should, support the arts. Some argue if people want a theater or a museum, they can support it without using taxpayer dollars. While private donors do in fact support the arts, the larger issue is that most arts organizations also provide educational opportunities, and public funding for education has deep roots in modern government. Policy makers are encouraged to understand why defunding the arts is detrimental and why arts and cultural institutions are vital in supporting a thriving society (NEA, 2020; Woronkowicz et al., 2012).

The funding network is diverse and complex, and sometimes arts organizations do not survive economic downturns (Woronkowicz et al., 2012). However, the flexibility and even uncertainty of this system might be the reason behind the increase in art making and arts participation in the last few decades. New arts organizations are constantly emerging and bringing new styles and perspectives to communities big and small. It is difficult to set one artistic agenda for the nation because the contrasting values and preferences of different funders ensure a rich diversity of artwork and programs (Woronkowicz et al., 2012).

For many who are not patrons, arts and cultural organizations may seem frivolous or unnecessary, which arguably contributes to the arts being underfunded and underappreciated, and therefore overlooked in favor of organizations deemed "more essential." However, as we demonstrate, the hidden and behind-the-scenes work offered through the creative economy provides essential public and civic education, fosters community connections, and serves many groups of people—from children to the elderly, from rural to metropolitan, and across all levels of income and socioeconomic status. While it is imperative to recognize and acknowledge the public servants on the frontlines of any disaster, it is equally important to celebrate all essential workers, including arts and cultural professionals, who work behind the scenes to keep our communities strong, healthy, and safe (NEA, 2020).

We started our chapter with a quote from a city director of cultural affairs to demonstrate how arts and cultural management professionals think about not only what it means to share what they love with the broader community but also to introduce a curiosity about how these public servants developed innovative strategies to minimize any interruptions to scheduled programming and service delivery during the pandemic. Guided by an ethic of public value and grounded in a commitment to helping people in their communities, we use the term "observant servant" to describe how those in the broader arts and culture community regularly interpret cues from the external environment so that they may hone their craft in service to others. While the COVID-19 pandemic, associated closures, and stay-at-home orders arguably shifted the stage for people around the world, the professionals we talked with seemed to interpret the disruption as a new venue to which they needed to adapt so that their cultural institutions could continue to share the things they loved with their communities.

The story we share is organized in the following way. We begin with a brief explanation of the methodology used to collect, analyze, and interpret the data that inform the narrative. We then offer an analysis of what drew these professionals to their work, highlighting the fact that while the notion of "helping" was essential, in many cases it was not the service that attracted them, but rather the opportunity to share something they loved with the broader community. Moreover, they are keenly aware of the fact that very few understand their work. Their reasons are deeply personal and rooted in a desire to share with others the things that bring them joy, whether that be music, dance, art, community activism, or the solace offered by a good book. Arguably, these personal motivations inform how arts and cultural management professionals understand the value their work brings to public service. Each interviewee had a remarkable ability to listen to what was important and tailor their craft in ways that resonated with individual audiences, thus inspiring the title "observant servant." We conclude with several important observations that celebrate the unique contribution of artisans in every genre who graciously share their gifts and talents with others.

Methods

During an unprecedented pandemic where patriotism and promotion of the public good entailed self-isolating and social distancing for most, it was also a time when public servants and others whose work we seldom notice or appreciate became our lifelines, including librarians, those working in performing and visual arts, and museum workers. We set out to tell their stories and used narrative inquiry to explore research questions centered around recognizing, uplifting, and remembering heroic acts of behind-the-scenes public service.

The data were collected as part of a master of public administration (MPA) degree summer class on storytelling. The research team, consisting of two instructors and nine graduate students, conducted more than 90 interviews. The storytellers (i.e., the research participants or interviewees) were public and nonprofit sector employees who worked in some capacity across the state of South Carolina before and during the COVID-19 pandemic. Ten of those interviews were with people who work under the broad heading of arts and cultural management, such as librarians, arts coordinators, cultural affairs officers, museum directors, and outreach coordinators. Those 10 interviews along with the experiences of the authors informed the story we share in this chapter. Specifically, two of the authors have work experience in the arts, one in a cultural institution that also functions as a circulating library and the other in numerous roles in the arts and culture sector. These coauthors were employed at the time of the pandemic and were able to recognize and relate to many of the stories that were shared, employing a critical approach of auto-ethnography to further inform the narrative (Roth, 2005).

The narrative inquiry approach allowed for both interactional and relational aspects of storytelling, rather than bracketing off the researcher as a "neutral observer" and/or objective collector of others' stories (Trahar, 2013). As Reissman (2008) puts it: "Stories don't fall from the sky . . . they are composed and received in contexts—interactional, historical, institutional, and discursive—to name a few" (p. 105). Thus, recruitment for interview participants drew a purposive sample from the connections of the MPA program: its faculty and staff, advisory board, and students. This allowed for the foundation of relationship, as public servants entrusted the stories and their retelling to the researchers.

The class co-created a semistructured interview script to allow for emergent findings and flexibility (Fontana & Frey, 1994; Merriam & Tisdell, 2013). The research design, scripts, and outreach methods were reviewed and approved by the College of Charleston Institutional Review Board. Interviews were completed over the course of 1 week via Zoom or phone to maintain social distancing. Interviews were first transcribed via the Otter.ai software and subsequently reviewed, cleaned, and coded by the four authors. A process of thematic and axial hand coding was used to determine overarching themes using an inductive process (Saldaña, 2015). The four authors held several meetings to both refine codes and concepts (Gerring, 2012; Saldaña, 2015) and interpret the data in ways that captured the essential work performed during the pandemic.

Professional Motivations for and the Value Created from Working in the Arts

Not unlike many other public service professionals, each of the 10 people we spoke with told us they were attracted to the arts and cultural management field by an inherent need to "be of service" or to "help people." The "help" offered by these public servants is fueled by a desire to share something personal flowing from their own life experiences and passions. One interviewee linked a love of books with desire to help others, "[and] not just those who can afford it but the public, [people experiencing] homeless[ness], others who need free access." Another noted a long history in the arts and being "drawn to the diversity of the public sector and serving multiple people and their interests." Another spoke of "community activism and organizing [and an] interest in studying African American history in higher education," which naturally led to work in a research center that had a mission to elevate the cultural achievements of Black people in the United States and the South.

Whether it was a long-standing love of the library, memories of attending local performances and working with artists, or community activism to elevate the oral history and rich traditions of marginalized groups, the people we spoke with outlined their personal connections to the arts alongside their motivations to serve. Arguably, reflecting and sharing these motivations provided an opportunity for arts and cultural workers to better articulate the value of their work. Perhaps it should come as no surprise that the people we spoke with described libraries, museums, and other cultural venues as "community hubs": places where lives are enriched through education, the arts, and community building; places where neighbors support neighbors; and, during the pandemic, a place where individuals and families could occasionally seek solace—even virtually—from the challenges associated with unprecedented solitude. As one person reminded us, "the arts reside in the community, they may be a schoolteacher . . . an auto mechanic, but they perform musicals, they are visual artists, or community theater actors . . . so being supportive of the arts is being supportive of your neighbors."

Three recurrent themes emerged as those we spoke with shared their personal motivations for working in the arts and the way they understood the value of their work. First, like many who tied their professional lives to the physical space in which they worked prior to the pandemic, after the mandatory stay-at-home orders were issued, these artisans were quick to recognize that sharing what they loved transcended the buildings in which they worked. Second, our storytellers appreciate that the creation of art, in all of its various forms, embodies innovation, creativity, and imagination often in response to constituent (i.e., audience) demand. So when the pandemic hit and building doors were locked shut, arts and cultural workers had a rich skill set from which to draw to make programming accessible and equitable for their various constituent groups. And finally, each of our storytellers talked about the continual challenge of communicating the value of the arts to skeptics.

More Than a Physical Space

One of the librarians described the library as more than a physical space but also a place for connection and community. She said, "I think of libraries as a platform. We're not just a place. We connect our community to lifelong learning for sure, but we also connect community to each other, to people." Another librarian shared, "I think that a public library service is one of the greatest services that our government provides to its citizens. It is key to a democracy." From this standpoint, learning and access to information took on a different kind of importance during the pandemic, in which in-person civic engagement became difficult, even detrimental and dangerous from a public health standpoint. A librarian collections coordinator was reminded of the important role she played in disseminating information: "[The COVID-19 pandemic] has reminded me just how important education is" and "how important critical thinking is. It really helps to be able to critically evaluate information and where you're getting it from." Each librarian underscored the importance of their work to support resilient, informed, and engaged citizens, particularly in turbulent times; and not one tied the obligation to provide information to the building in which the information is housed.

Similarly, a museum liaison described his organization as a hotspot for organizing, community programs and gatherings, and educational outreach; and as a museum and archive space. "You'll be hard-pressed to find people, museums, and repositories doing as much research, public programming, and community outreach as we are doing right now." And a librarian added, "We welcome everyone, and we get everyone. I love how diverse my job is as far as people's information needs, their diverse age groups, and everything in between." Another chimed in, "My favorite thing about this job is that we get to touch so many different parts of the community and expand on digital equity, literacy, workforce development, educational success, community engagement, all these things that libraries naturally do. But I really love that we are able to bring the modern library to the community and empower our patrons to use their library cards in different ways, and also get new users as our message continues to spread."

If anything, the pandemic further emphasized the need for these hub organizations to serve the diverse needs of their community in unique and innovative ways; and for some that meant helping everybody take their mind off the pandemic by doing what they did best. One museum employee stated, "we had to be more creative and find a way to keep our community engaged and help get their minds off of what is going on with this pandemic." They added, "People are looking to us for some sort of programming to help them get past whatever the hell is going on throughout the country. COVID has really put people in some dark places and with us being able to help them get through this gave us greater responsibility inside of the programming we had."

Two work-related legacies of the pandemic are likely to be an explicit acknowledgment that service delivery is not dependent on having a physical gathering place, and that public value is not created within the walls of a building. As the Office of Cultural Affairs Director reminded us, "artists are resourceful [and know] about working with limited resources." Those who worked in the broad field of arts and cultural management took steps, which mirrored that resourcefulness and adaptability, to ensure that the public continued to benefit from the services provided. Like so many other public services, arts and cultural workers transitioned to a digital space, which ultimately provided more opportunities to reach a wider audience. One library worker said: "I hope that the patrons think of us as a continual resource, even though they weren't able to come into our buildings, that we were still there for them. We worked very hard on meeting our patron needs wherever we knew their technology capacity was. So of course, we had a robust digital platform. I'm very, very proud of that. I hope that people appreciate and remember the digital platform and that it was helpful and a wonderful resource." Another expressed the positives of reaching a wider audience: "It's nice that all these programs can be done online. You can have a story time online with 500 people. You couldn't do that in the real world because you couldn't have that many people in a room. It's almost kind of neat to see that we're reaching more people."

Creating Accessibility and Equity through Innovations

While thinking about digitally reaching a wider audience, some participants talked about what this might mean for accessibility in the future. "We're going to be offering the services that we can, but they have to be offered at a safe distance." Others acknowledged that more of their budgets and efforts would continue to focus on digital resources and programming. "I think virtual programming is not going to stop even when we get the vaccine." Many questioned the degree to which technology will continue to influence the future of arts, as well as what it will look like to be a resource and ally for a wide array of people in the future. As one arts director said, "The other thing we've learned is, no matter what it is, you're going to need to have a way for people to engage in a virtual setting. Not everybody's gonna feel comfortable coming back and can't make it an obligation that you have to risk your life to see a show." This acknowledgment underscores how the adaptability in the midst of the pandemic will extend beyond vaccine rollout and change the shape of arts and cultural management work into the future.

The COVID-19 disruption also inspired innovation and creativity in service of creating more equitable access. Library workers in particular acknowledged that many they serve are without easy access to the internet. To solve this issue and continue serving the needs of their communities, many libraries decided to keep the Wi-Fi on in their parking lots, even after hours, so that patrons could still benefit from using the library. Others made Wi-Fi hotspots available to patrons. And some specifically considered how programming might address the current needs of those suffering most. For example, one organization partnered with a pro bono law firm to offer legal assistance to lower-income individuals.

ARTICULATING VALUE TO THE SKEPTICS

Despite the many benefits provided to the community, demonstrating value was much easier for regular users of the library, museum, or arts center. In these instances, conversation revolved around innovative ways to use a library card; new exhibits, displays, or events in museums; or how new programming in the performing arts might expand the public's appreciation and support. However, many did not have this foundational knowledge or appreciation.

When members of the community are not patrons, they often have difficulty expressing value beyond commonly held notions of what happens in a library or museum or performance hall. This challenge is exacerbated when elected officials, who facilitate public support, control budgets, and provide resources, do not feel a connection to the work in the arts and cultural field. As one library administrator put it:

> County council really didn't understand, for the most part, what the public library did. We were an unfunded mandate. And I met with all the county council members and [was] just asking "Do you have a library card?" Some did. Most of them weren't really library users, most of them fundamentally understood that libraries are wonderful and good and tax based. But they couldn't . . . articulate what we did beyond checking out books, and they weren't really sure about the return on investment. And that is something that I think public libraries everywhere struggle with is that when you are a public library user, or a school media user, or if [you] use a library, whatever form it takes, you know it, and you probably love it, and you can talk about how great it is. But if you aren't a library user, then you might not understand.

These public servants were well aware of the political values of small and limited government, which often led to resistance to funding arts, cultural institutions, and libraries, particularly in times of fiscal austerity like 2020.

Although the interviewees were from a deeply red state, the threat of withdrawing public funding and support for arts-based programming throughout all 4 years of the Trump presidency (Bowley, 2021) meant these arts and cultural professionals were regularly concerned that their programs were "first on the chopping block." A director of the Office of Cultural Affairs confirmed, "if you're not at the table, you are on the table." He went on to explain that despite any rhetoric about how much the local economy is related to arts and culture, it is the arts and cultural managers who are expected to remind policy makers and budget offices of the values these institutions bring to the community. These public servants are politically savvy; they know that building relationships and engaging in conversations to underscore both their institutional and community value are essential to their long-term sustainability and offer lessons about how to do just that.

Making the Invisible Visible

The COVID-19 pandemic changed the way we live, work, and socialize almost overnight. Arts and cultural organizations, like many other public sector organizations, encountered accessibility, technical, financial, and operational challenges that could have easily overwhelmed the workforce. Yet the stories we heard revealed a rich tapestry of observation, innovation, creativity, and reflection focused on making rapid adjustments so that those in the arts could continue to share their talents with audiences of every type. Specifically, the pandemic provided time to reflect and time to think about how best to communicate the value of their work through storytelling and quantifying their work. It also provided these dedicated professionals a glimpse at the future, a future that calls into question the very reason some were drawn to the field.

REFLECTION AND COMMUNICATION

One of the library workers we spoke with shared, "I will [say] that I've had time to slow down to rethink a lot of things that I do and put a lot more thought into things that I do. And I can't underestimate the thoughtfulness and energy in everything that you do in programming." Another added, "I think this time has been self-reflective. I think that I learned that it's important to slow down, it's important to do less things. I think it's better to put a lot of thought into a few things, do them very well, and do them in an accessible manner, rather than to just do a bunch of things at once to feel the rush of being busy."

The slowdown of 2020 and the COVID-19 crisis also highlighted the value of storytelling and being able to communicate the value of their work. These stories were used to share ideas with others and to provide political leaders the tools needed to articulate the importance of arts-related programming. A librarian noted, "[We have] lots of best practices—story times, ESL [English as a second language classes], etc., but not a lot of time to share and highlight that. [The] pandemic allowed for this deeper appreciation and reflection and elevation of those stories." An executive director (ED) of a library system confronted elected officials who didn't necessarily understand the importance of the county-mandated library system and the benefits of the community it creates. The solution was explained to them in terms they understand—return on investment. The ED shared, "I quantified what we did into what I call our core four: literacy, workforce development and educational success and community engagement and that's how we track our statistics. So I can quantify that impact for the county council and show them their return on investment with our libraries. And it's been really powerful in helping them understand." Public servants took the opportunity to communicate their value in responsive ways, which allowed them to build trust and support for their own sustainability.

Reconciling What Was with What Might Be

These reflective practices also uncovered challenges the field will need to address when the public is invited back inside the buildings. For example, one of the theater folks we spoke with talked about the tension between mission and reaching new audiences through technology. He told us he believed that scrambling to build multiple digital platforms was neither sustainable in the long run nor constructive in building an audience. He also shared that moving in this direction would require a purposive exploration of their mission to assure the same kind of quality that was promised in live performances.

A library professional also shared concerns related to how a commitment to service and helping is likely to be compromised when the libraries open to the public:

> And when we reopen, you know librarians and librarian staff are very giving, they want to help people, but I think we are going to have to be a little more muted in our reach out to people. We typically would be standing over a patron's shoulder, assisting them with their use of a PC or homework help or something of that nature. In fact, it's been a movement that's even informed library architecture that you eliminate the large service desks, replace the large bank teller style service desks, and in some cases have no service desk, and I think we're really going to be rethinking that. We're going to offer the services we can, but they have to be offered at a safe distance. And we are putting up plexiglass shields that are at our service points . . . and so much of library collections are based on a model of everybody sharing them . . . So, I think there are going to be some changes.

This idea of not just reverting to the way things were done previously was reflected across interviews as well. One arts director spoke about their stakeholders' decisions and noted how they "are all predicated on the assumption that we'll get right back to where we were." Instead, the stories we heard emphasized the need to think critically to acknowledge challenges, adjust course, and incorporate lessons learned.

The tension for these professionals is twofold—questions about what helping might look like in the future and reconciling the work they love with the realities of the future. Is it possible to share pieces of themselves through plexiglass barriers? How will they connect to people from 6 feet away? What is to become of the measures they had put into place to improve access prior to the pandemic (e.g., removal of huge service desks that separate the public from the staff)?

This notion of reconciling work is very complex. On one hand, these public servants shared what drew them to the work, often rooted in personal experiences with the arts and a desire to share their passion with others. One of the librarians told us that it was all about the books. She loved the tactile nature of her job, the feel, the smell, the visual pleasure she gets from holding a book in her hands; and the prospect of sharing that joy with others was what drew her to the work. She also shared that over the past few years she has seen a growing trend toward technology-based systems, primarily to increase access so that more people could experience the joy that comes from attaining new knowledge. While she understands and is quite proud of how libraries responded to the mandatory closures associated with the pandemic and how they are improving access through technology, she also must grapple with the fact that this is not the job she signed up for.

Conclusion

Despite the many challenges of 2020, public servants in the creative economy responded by elevating the value of the work through story, thereby connecting students, families, and adults to the arts, informational and educational resources, and most importantly to a sense of community. The stories we heard acknowledged the *challenges* and underscored how they continued their work from a distance. They acted with the *confidence* that—although there were no "right" answers or "one best way" during the unprecedented pandemic disruptions—the "wrong" path would be to no longer provide patrons and residents necessary services, cultural enrichment, and opportunities for education and virtual connection. In fact, the challenges of 2020 provided an opportunity to showcase the value, adaptability, and creativity of both the public servants and their institutions.

To do this work, the arts and cultural management field workers told stories that underscored how the ability to *think critically* was essential in designing and adapting systems and processes to continue to effectively and equitably provide their arts, cultural, and library services. They also took time to reflect on and *communicate* their public value. Ultimately, this process capitalized on an innate quality of all artists, their ability to lead with an observant stance toward their work. These public servants know that to be successful, they must be attuned to *observing* not just the creative world around them but also the shifting needs of their audiences and the broader needs of civil society. Figure 13.1 demonstrates this process creatively, starting with COVID-19 disruptions and ending with a new way forward. The arts and cultural management professionals come to their jobs as observant servants, and those skills helped them to respond to the pandemic in a way that explicitly acknowledged chal-

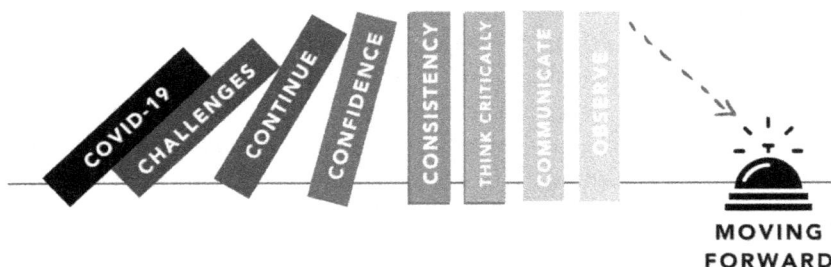

Figure 13.1. Moving Forward in Arts & Cultural Management. *Source*: Author-created.

lenges, continued to provide critical services, adjusted course effectively, and proceeded with confidence and critical thinking. They noticed a tremendous opportunity to be even better stewards of public funding and democratic institutions as they move forward in the post-pandemic world.

At their core, libraries, museums, and arts venues are civic institutions. Even when the public servants who keep these institutions running are working from home, behind the scenes, or not interacting daily with their patrons and constituents, they operate within a broader civic context. As Kranich (2020) notes, "With their legacy of civic activism, librarians can catalyze the shift from merely informing citizens to engaging them in the issues of their communities. As the nation's great experiment in democracy undergoes a momentous test, [these institutions] are poised to reunite their communities, recommit to democratic practices, and reclaim their essential role as cornerstones of democracy" (p. 121). These assertions apply not just to librarians, but also to public servants in museums and the arts, to those working in spaces and community hubs that elevate and expand knowledge, creativity, and inspiration. The stories captured here showcase and underscore the value that committed, creative, and observant public servants bring to these institutions, one "key to democracy," during challenging times and into the future.

References

Americans for the Arts. (2018). *Percentage of foreign visitors participating in arts & culture while visiting the U.S. 2006–2016*. https://www.americansforthearts. org/sites/default/files/2018ForeignVisitors.pdf

Bowley, G. (2021, January 15). Trump tried to end federal arts funding. Instead, it grew. *The New York Times.* https://www.nytimes.com/2021/01/15/arts/trump-arts-nea-funding.html

Fontana, A., & Frey, J. H. (1994). Interviewing: The art of science. In Y. L. Denzin (ed.), *Handbook of qualitative research* (pp. 361–376). Sage Publications.

Gerring, J. (2012). *Social science methodology: A unified framework* (2nd ed.). Cambridge University Press.

Kranich, N. (2020). Libraries and democracy revisited. *The Library Quarterly,* 90(2), 121–153.

Merriam, S. B., & Tisdell, E. J. (2016). *Qualitative research: A guide to design and implementation* (4th ed.). Jossey-Bass.

Meyer, D. Z., & Avery, L. M. (2008). Excel as a qualitative data analysis tool. *Field Methods, 21*(1). 91–112. https://doi.org/10.1177/1525822X08323985

National Assembly of State Arts Agencies. (2020). *Creative economy arts profiles: South Carolina.* National Endowment for the Arts and U.S. Bureau of Economic Analysis. https://nasaa-arts.org/nasaa_research/creative-economy-state-profiles/

National Endowment of the Arts (2020). *During economic highs and lows, the arts are key segment of U.S. economy.* https://www.arts.gov/about/news/2020/during-economic-highs-and-lows-arts-are-key-segment-us-economy

Reissman, C. K. (2008). *Narrative methods for human sciences.* Sage.

Roth, W. M. (2005). *Auto/biography and auto/ethnography: Praxis of research method.* Sense Publishers.

Saldaña, J. (2015). *The coding manual for qualitative researchers.* Sage.

Trahar, S. (Ed.). (2013). *Contextualising narrative inquiry: Developing methodological approaches for local contexts.* Routledge.

U.S. Department of Commerce, Bureau of Economic Analysis. (2020). *Arts and cultural production satellite account, U.S. and States 2017.* https://www.bea.gov/news/2020/arts-and-cultural-production-satellite-account-us-and-states-2017

Woronkowicz, J., Nichols, B., & Iyengar, S. (2012, November). *How the United States funds the arts.* National Endowment of the Arts. https://www.arts.gov/sites/default/files/how-the-us-funds-the-arts.pdf

14

Inconspicuously Indispensable for India

The Untold Stories of
Accredited Social Health Activists (ASHAs)

NANDHINI RANGARAJAN, AROON P. MANOHARAN,
AND BIANCA ORTIZ-WYTHE

> He who has health, has hope; and he who has hope, has everything.
>
> —Thomas Carlyle

Public administrators are *quietly* delivering a multitude of essential public services that are indispensable for the effective functioning of societies. One such group comprises community health workers (CHWs) who are an essential part of the public sector health care workforce across many nations. CHWs in India have shouldered critical health service responsibilities during the pandemic in relative anonymity without much recognition or support.

The National Association of Community Health Care Workers (2021) defines CHWs as "frontline public health workers who are trusted members of and/or have an unusually close understanding of the community served. This trusting relationship enables CHWs to serve as a liaison/link/intermediary between health/social services and the community to facilitate access to services and improve the quality and cultural competence of service delivery. CHWs also build individual and community capacity by increasing health knowledge and self-sufficiency through a range of activities such as outreach, community education, informal counseling, social support and advocacy."

CHWs have also played important roles in mitigating chronic diseases and aiding in better childbirth and wellness metrics (Balcazar et al., 2011). The emergence of CHWs has also been infusing a new paradigm in public health research, as collaborators and partners in intervention studies. CHWs have been included as partners in evaluative research (see, for example, Peacock et al., 2011) and have played crucial roles in the management of communicable and noncommunicable diseases (Jeet et al., 2017) and in the reduction of neonatal mortality (Gogia & Sachdev, 2010).

Community Health Workers in India

Although India has made considerable progress in life expectancy at birth and reducing infant mortality, a significant percentage of the population, particularly in rural areas, are at risk of preventable diseases, malnutrition, and pregnancy- and childbirth-related hurdles. Community health work in India has only recently received major momentum through the launch of certain important missions. The first program to address such community health issues in India was launched in 1977, followed by a second initiative in 2005, namely the National Rural Health Mission (NRHM). The flagship initiative of the mission is the Accredited Social Health Activist (ASHA) workers program.

The ASHA program was introduced at this crucial time to address public health issues through a comprehensive and inclusive approach to health care in rural areas, with particular emphasis on women and children (Jamil et al., 2017). A new group of community health workers called ASHAs—women, 24 to 45 years of age, literate, with good communication skills and leadership qualities, with at least an eighth-grade level education—were trained in critical health practices to enhance community health in rural India (Shrivastava & Srivastava, 2016). The selected workers received basic training for about a month on health topics, first-aid practices, and issues related to water, sanitation, nutrition, and other core knowledge and skills in a community health setting. A selection committee chooses one ASHA for every village with a population of 1,000 to facilitate the achievement of community health goals. The ASHA worker is a vital link between the community members and the health services, and the first point of contact for any health-related necessities.

Prior to 2005, it was the Auxiliary Nurse Midwives who were primarily responsible for public health. However, because of their commitment to natal care, there was less emphasis on public and community health. It was precisely for this reason that the ASHA program was established. "An ASHA is a woman selected by the community, resident in the community and who is trained, deployed, and supported to function in her own village to improve the health status of the people through securing their access to healthcare services" (Fatima et al., 2015, p. 2). ASHAs are the cornerstone of the NRHM, playing a critical role in connecting the health care system to rural populations where health care facilities are chronically understaffed because of well-documented physician preference to work in cities (Alcoba, 2009).

Akin to the National Rural Health Mission, the National Urban Health Mission (NUHM) was launched as a sub-mission of the National Health Mission in 2013. The main objective of the NUHM is to address the health care needs of the urban population, especially the urban poor. The mission of NUHM is to "cover all State capitals, district headquarters and cities/towns with a population of more than 50,000 people. It would primarily focus on slum dwellers and other marginalized groups like rickshaw pullers, street vendors, railway and bus station coolies, homeless people, street children, construction site workers" (https://nhm.gov.in). NUHM has adopted a cohesive strategy that strengthens health care service delivery in conjunction with existing programs "implemented by the Ministries of Urban Development, Housing & Urban Poverty Alleviation, Human Resource Development and Women & Child Development" (https://nhm.gov.in).

The ASHA program today is more than a million strong and is the largest CHW program in the world. Since the inception of the ASHA program, significant declines in infant mortality rate and the maternal mortality ratio have been observed (Mane & Khandekar, 2014). The ASHA workers are expected to undergo training and participate in capacity-building programs to ensure that they are equipped to meet the needs of the communities. They receive performance-based incentives for helping to promote immunization, aiding in the construction of sanitary facilities, and providing referral for reproductive and child health (RCH). As a health activist providing specific services, the ASHAs are also expected to promote public health awareness and mobilize the community for adoption of better health practices (Aruna, 2019). The social interactions that ASHA members have with the community have the potential to shape the community norms and behavior (Ved & Scott, 2020).

Chapter Purpose

The primary objective of this chapter is to profile the life and work of three ASHAs: Dilara, Sujana, and Momitha. Using a narrative approach,[1] this chapter provides insights into the unseen and unappreciated stories of these three women from Bengaluru, India. Through their stories, the primary motivations of these health workers to join the public service, the value they add to community health, the factors that facilitate and inhibit their work, and other specific insights about occupational safety are highlighted. Before a discussion of the life circumstances and work experiences of these women, this chapter presents a brief introduction to Bengaluru to provide the geographical, cultural, and economic contexts in which these women perform their duties. This chapter then presents a discussion of some important lessons learned from the experiences of these women and how they tie into findings from the literature. The potential of these ASHAs for a better community health care delivery system informed by their past and current experiences is presented.

Research Setting

Bengaluru, formerly known as Bangalore, is the capital of Karnataka state in southern India and is the third most populous city with an estimated 2021 population of approximately 12.7 million inhabitants (https://worldpopulationreview.com/world-cities; Reddy & Ramaswamy, 2020). The city has witnessed large-scale immigration of people from other parts of India during various phases of its history. The city's sizeable investment in the public sector and education initiated a first wave of immigration in the 1950s (https://www.britannica.com/place/Bangalore-India). In subsequent decades, economic growth in the city was spurred by manufacturing industries, and for the past three decades Bengaluru has had an influx of migrants from other parts of the country because of its newfound identity as the Silicon Valley of India.

Its investment in the information and communication technology industries has made it a much sought-after city. In addition to the economic, professional, and financial prospects provided by the city, it boasts of a cool climate for most of the year, which has always been a major factor in attracting new inhabitants. Despite the city's progressive urban profile, 21.5% of the city's population are in slums, and there are approximately 387 slums in the city (George et al., 2019). Slums with high population density are rife with sanitation and health issues. The city's municipal government, referred to in the local language as the Bruhat Bengaluru Mahanagara Palike (henceforth BBMP) has been working with the NUHM's state affiliates to address community health in general, particularly in such marginalized areas. ASHA workers play a prominent role in the city's urban health initiatives, and the stories of three women are presented below.

Profiles of ASHA Workers

Dilara[2]: ASHA Work as a Fallback, Flexible, and Fulfilling Option

"Every human has his/her own suffering."

Dilara was clad in a black *niqab* and a loose-fitting *abaya* as she made her way toward the coffee shop where she had agreed to meet the interviewer. Her nervousness was palpable despite her eyes being the only part of her body visible to the interviewer. Every response was interspersed with a worried check of the time as Dilara, a 32-year-old divorced young mother of a child with special needs, had little time to spare between caring for her young son and her duties as a CHW. Her journey as an ASHA worker began after her husband, who did not want to share the burdens and responsibilities of raising a special needs child, abandoned her rather abruptly. With only one year of college education to her credit, Dilara had to find a way to support herself and her son. Dilara is thankful that community health work was a fallback option that offered her the much-needed flexibility in work schedule and, although not adequate, a pay that allows her to live with some measure of dignity. ASHA workers typically get paid around 4000 rupees, which translates to approximately $58 every month. Dilara has been an ASHA worker in the cantonment station area of Bengaluru for 18 months, and her fluency in Urdu and Kannada has helped her communicate with her clients. She serves a predominantly Muslim community given her own religious identity and fluency in Urdu, a language spoken by many in her community. She was introduced to this line of work by her friend and was drawn to public service and motivated by the potential impact of her work on community health.

Every day when Dilara leaves for work in the morning, her son is cared for by a neighbor who watches him or puts him down to sleep until the lunch hour to enable Dilara to visit her community clients. She returns at lunch time to feed and play with him for a couple of hours and then returns to her work, entrusting her son once again with her neighbor. Her main responsibilities during the pandemic included creating general awareness of COVID-19; generating specific awareness of initial symptoms of the infection, such as high fever for more than 3 days and loss of taste and smell; and convincing her clients to take COVID-19 tests.

In addition to these responsibilities, she provides information about sanitation, women's health, and hygiene to the community and collects information from the community about vaccination, family history of illness, and nutrition intake. Data that she collects are tracked by the health division of BBMP (Bruhat Bangalore Mahanagara Palike), the city's municipal government. Dilara's biggest fear is falling sick and not being healthy enough to care for her son and other community members who depend on her. She collaborates with minority women organizations and minority health organizations as part of her duties.

Dilara did not feel safe sometimes during the pandemic, as people were anxious and scared of her. She recalled one instance when stones were thrown at her and another when she was chased away by dogs that were explicitly unleashed by clients who were reluctant to share health data with her. She would feel happy when the community she serves understands the purity of intention behind her services. Dilara, who was consumed by fear about how to raise her son on her own and who agonized about the abandonment of her husband, after working as an ASHA has learned that "every human has his/her own suffering." Despite the occasional humiliation she has faced from her clients and threats to her own safety because of the onset of the pandemic and the ensuing lack of protective equipment and safety protocols, Dilara was eager to emphasize that her experiences as an ASHA worker have put things in perspective for her.

Sujana: ASHA work as a Pathway to Dignity

"I miss my farming and cows, but humans are good, too."

Sujana, a 39-year-old married woman with twin boys, is originally from a town called Raichur in Karnataka. She has a high school education and fluency in Kannada and Telegu to her credit. Her family has an agricultural background, and she was married off to her husband, also a farmer and a widower, at the age of 28. She helped her husband and their family with areca nut and rice paddy farming for almost a decade. One of her favorite memories of her Raichur days is of preparing a special dessert for her twin boys, the main ingredients of which were the first yield of cow's milk in the morning and palm sugar. Sujana's contentment with life and marriage gradually morphed to unhappiness when she discovered her husband's affair with a family friend. She was crestfallen when her parents-in-law did not question the impropriety of this liaison. Unable to deflect the community's attention from her failing marriage, she and her twin boys moved to Bengaluru to stay with a female friend in an area close to Vannarpet and Vivek Nagar. After only a few months in Bengaluru, she heard about a call for ASHA workers and signed up for it to be distracted from her marital woes.

Sujana has about a year's worth of experience as an ASHA worker. She remarked that "I felt trapped and let down because of my husband's affair. I am happy that this corona [virus] helped me to find myself and stand up for my family and myself. I am liking this new life." During a typical workday, Sujana visits houses in Vannarpet and Vivek Nagar discussing the importance of wearing masks and sanitizing. She particularly emphasizes the importance of personal hygiene and engages in pandemic record keeping by documenting the name, age, address, body temperature, and destination and date of last travel in a notebook, which she then shares with her supervisor. She teaches her clients and their children about the importance of using toilets instead of open spaces, among many other tasks she performs. The community she serves is somewhat close to a set of army quarters. She believes that despite the struggles of other ASHA workers during the pandemic owing to client noncompliance, the proximity of her neighborhood to the army quarters has probably contributed to the relative safety of ASHA workers in her community.

Sujana's primary fear is that "people have stopped using masks and that is a great concern for the BBMP. They are asked to insist and provide masks to people who are unable to afford the purchase of them."

When asked about her remuneration for ASHA work, Sujana stated that "the income is not sufficient to take care of my children." She has begun working part-time at a sari shop helping organize boxes of new stock and fold saris tried on by customers. This side stint at the sari store helps her supplement her income to a certain extent. Sujana is grateful that "people are kind and have accepted me. They treat me as their family member. With all this experience, I will soon make a living and prove myself."

Her one-year experience as an ASHA worker has led her to the realization that "helping others can be a way of life." Sujana is appreciative of the work she does and acknowledges that "there are several workers whose stories are sadder than mine." However, because the salary is not adequate, she is unsure about recommending this line of work to others: "I don't know if I should recommend or not. But this is a decent form of living for me and my family."

Momitha: ASHA Work as a Potential Stepping-stone to a New Career

Momitha is a 39-year-old Nagamese woman who has settled in cosmo-politan Bengaluru. Although she exuded immense confidence and was well put-together for her interview and also willing to be photographed if need be, behind that façade of strength is a painful past from which she fled about 6 years ago. She relocated to Bengaluru in 2015 after leaving behind her life in Nagaland, a northeast Indian state where she lived with her four sisters and parents. Momitha remembers her childhood and adolescent years as rife with taunts for being one of five girls in a family with no male heir. Societal taunts aimed at her parents were then promptly redirected at Momitha and her siblings as well. She went into a state of depression after completion of her first year in college and quit higher education altogether despite ambitions of being a nurse. Momitha was quite self-aware of her free-spirited and independent nature and wanted to give herself a fresh start in life. The gender-related emotional taunts that were a constant in her life further reinforced the need to be free and emboldened her to leave.

Bengaluru's cosmopolitan vibe and its promise of economic prosper-ity and inclusion made it an attractive place to live. During her initial days in Bengaluru, she worked at a beauty salon for a rather paltry pay of 2500 rupees or roughly $35 a month. She chose to volunteer as an ASHA to gain some knowledge and practical experience needed to transition later to a full-time nursing career. Her work as an ASHA does not pay much either, but she notes that it "has helped me to get out of fear and feel dignified about myself, since I am helping others selflessly." She currently lives in the Ejipura area of Bengaluru with her husband, who is a cleaner at an Asian restaurant. Her husband, also a northeast Indian, sometimes wishes she would work in places far away from their residence, but, despite such seemingly negative thoughts about her work, he is supportive of her decisions and her dream of one day becoming a full-time nurse at a private or public hospital.

Momitha teaches the community about healthy eating, eating for immunity, self-hygiene, and vaccination schedules for infants; and checks in on pregnant women periodically. As required by her work, she collaborates with BBMP and Mahila organizations and the geriatric department of Vani Vilas Government hospital. Her responsibilities include collecting information about abandoned elders and those with illnesses or signs of malnutrition in community members and reporting unavailability of quality foods provided by the government. Momitha is intent on learning everything taught to her with the belief that all this would help her realize her dream of one day becoming a competent nurse. In response to questions about her safety during the pandemic, Momitha indicated that she received training about self-sanitizing and social distancing but felt unsafe when "people would intentionally sneeze or throw their masks at me to stop me from testing them for temperatures."

She wishes that people would respect the selfless work done by ASHA workers. She remarked that "people think low of ASHA workers as they are being selfless in helping others. It makes the public feel that something is wrong with us to be doing this for them with no big financial motives. That makes it harder for us to reach people with awareness programs. If women can handle that, this is a great place since we are best in the form of mother and a strict teacher in educating people about health and hygiene."

Lessons Learned

EMBRACING NUMEROUS ROLES

The stories of Dilara, Sujana, and Momitha reinforce some important observations about ASHA workers. Although ASHAs' primary contributions are tied to maternal and child health, they perform other far-reaching critical functions such as creating community awareness about health issues, facilitating community access to health care and facilities, and reporting birth, death, and disease outbreak statistics (Mane & Khandekar, 2014). ASHAs take on multiple roles as link workers, educators, service providers, and activists (Saprii et al., 2015, pp. 5–6) and derive fulfillment from serving the community and strengthening the public health system. Warier (2020) notes that during the pandemic, ASHAs have embraced numerous additional responsibilities without much increase in remuneration, protection, or recognition.

Empowerment, Meaning, and Fulfillment

Women report several positive benefits of becoming ASHAs. ASHA work empowers women by elevating them as role models and female leaders. Research studies show that becoming an ASHA enables women to gain knowledge, self-confidence, and social status by taking on an important role in their communities (Gopalan, Mohanty, & Das, 2012; Roalkvam, 2014; Scott & Shanker, 2010). Dilara, Sujana, and Momitha's stories show that they were able to escape the hardships of spousal abandonment, emotional abuse, and gender-related ridicule to find meaning and fulfillment in their role as ASHAs. Each of these women found solace in this line of work. While Dilara and Sujana are more focused on the short-term solace and benefits provided by this work, Momitha has focused on the long-term benefits she could derive from this type of work.

Gendered Challenges

Despite the benefits derived from their work, ASHAs continue to face significant gendered challenges. Research findings have extensively documented ASHA workers' dissatisfaction with their pay in relation to their workload and contribution and identified negative consequences linked to the limited renumeration structure (Gopalan, Mohanty, & Das, 2012; Pandey & Singh, 2016; Scott & Shanker; 2010; Srivastava et al., 2009). Limitations on their movement outside the home and heavy domestic responsibilities often restrict ASHAs' ability to perform their professional roles (Pala et al., 2011; Saprii et al., 2015), and ASHAs were discouraged from working and belittled by family members when their remuneration was delayed or when incentives were found to be extremely low (Bhatia,

2014). Dilara's story ties in with these specific findings from the literature, as most of her pay is probably spent on her son's treatment, and if her neighbor's generosity as her son's caretaker during the day ceases, she will not be able to perform her professional role effectively. Limited space for career progression is linked to low institutional recognition, demotivation, and curtailed opportunities for growth (Bhatia, 2014; Nambiar, Sheikh, & Verma, 2012; Roalkvam, 2014; Sharma, Webster, & Bhattacharyya, 2014). Momitha could potentially stay on as an ASHA and progress up the career ladder if such opportunities were available. But, given the lack of such opportunities, her desire to become a nursing professional will probably take her away from community health work.

ASHAs face sexual harassment by other health workers and community members linked to their mobility and public profile (Dasgupta, Velankar, Borah, & Nath, 2017). In 2016, an ASHA was sexually assaulted by community members and subsequently died, highlighting the extent of gender-based violence and security facing ASHAs (Ved et al., 2019). Dilara and Momitha's experiences with being ridiculed and taunted underscores the need for more government protection and action.

In response to these issues, government health policy is engaged in ongoing efforts to improve ASHA well-being through increasing ASHA economic security, developing career progression strategies, and addressing gender-based violence (National Health Mission 2013, 2017, 2018). These include providing support to ASHAs and their families in the form of life and accident insurance and pension, immersive learning and continued development of knowledge and skills, career progression opportunities, and an increase ASHA safety and comfort when escorting women to facilities. While these policy changes are developed at the national level with state-level consultation, actual implementation varies widely according to state priorities.

STRUCTURAL BARRIERS

Numerous structural barriers present challenges to the effectiveness and provision of care given by ASHAs. To date, the NHM has not established a maternity leave policy for ASHAs. One study has highlighted that because most ASHAs are of childbearing age (25–40), absenteeism due to pregnancy/maternal health impacts health service delivery in the area she works in (Sharma, Webster, & Bhattacharyya, 2014). One of the biggest concerns that has been consistently raised is the shortage of medical supplies and equipment available in their communities (Puett et al., 2013; Sharma, Webster, & Bhattacharyya, 2014). The lack of medical resources has been found to be an important factor in job dissatisfaction among ASHAs (Das & Dasgupta, 2015; Gopalan, Mohanty, & Das, 2012; Sharma, Webster, & Bhattacharyya, 2014).

In addition, economic barriers at the community level are another important factor. Research shows that families with limited resources to provide food or access transportation were less likely to adopt the advice given by their community ASHA (Puett et al., 2013). With the onset of the pandemic, there was widespread media coverage about the lack of personal protective equipment for ASHA workers. In addition, ASHA workers were subjected to abuse from clients. Dilara and Momitha's experiences show that they had to fend for themselves when stones were hurled or dogs were unleashed on them or when they were sneezed on. This shows a glaring structural barrier in employee protection and occupational safety.

CONCLUSION

ASHA workers are the backbone of primary health care in India, connecting millions of lives to health care access, resources, and education. Warrier (2020, p.1) observed that "at the very center of this public health system, stand over 900,000 women called as ASHA workers who are taking on the pandemic—unarmed, unseen, and unheard." They are an important example of the anonymous public servants who are quietly performing their duties for the community. The sheer number and magnitude of the ASHA workers in India make them a considerable workforce of silent public servants with wide societal impact. The main purpose of this chapter is to highlight the stories of three such women and through narrative inquiry learn from their experiences about the hardships they endure and the potential for systemic changes from their life and professional experiences.

The presence of ASHAs have had multiple positive impacts on the community and for the self-esteem and confidence of individual ASHAs themselves. The capability to provide critical functions, particularly during emergencies, has made them an indispensable resource for the administrative apparatus. As Chandra stated (2021), an important factor in addressing the pandemic in India was the extensive administrative outreach aided by the utilization of the ASHA workers. The specific role of ASHA workers in overcoming the "last mile connectivity" problem that hinders public service delivery in India needs to be highlighted and recognized.

This chapter identified key areas that require focus and support by state and national governments, and more importantly recognition for their valuable service. Their stories provided some important lessons about societal and structural barriers that must be addressed for their valuable work to receive the acknowledgment it deserves. Maintenance of their focus solely on community health work could be accomplished by raising their pay. Increasing salaries would help channel their focus exclusively on this work instead of finding additional means of sustenance. Mutually beneficial outcomes for the ASHAs and the communities they serve could be accomplished if their multidimensional roles were acknowledged, if pay was raised, if they were empowered further and provided meaningful work, if structural and systemic barriers such as lack of adequate medical/health supplies were addressed, and gendered challenges and threats to their safety were addressed.

This chapter also contributes to the understanding of the CHWs in the context of developing nations and COVID response in the global South. *Asha* is the Hindi word for *hope*, and the acronym ASHA for this cadre of CHWs could not be more appropriate, as these workers are the "brightest ray of hope" (Hariprasad & Mehrotra, 2016) in terms of improved health and wellness to innumerable rural and urban areas in India.

Notes

1. Qualitative data for this chapter were collected via an interview protocol provided to two field researchers in India who had contact with these women. The field researchers collected interview data in the local Kannada and Hindi/Urdu languages, retranslated them back to English, and sent them to the authors.

2. Names of all three ASHA workers profiled in this chapter have been changed to protect their identities.

References

American Public Health Association (2021, July 29). Support for community health workers to increase health access and to reduce health inequities.

Policy no. 20091. Washington, DC. https://www.apha.org/policies-and-advocacy/public-health-policy-statements/policy-database/2014/07/09/14/19/support-for-community-health-workers-to-increase-health-access-and-to-reduce-health-inequities

Alcoba, N. (2009). Hitting the road to alleviate India's rural doctor shortage. *Canadian Medical Association Journal, 180*(10), E34–E36.

Aruna, K. C. (2019). Health communication for social change: A case study on communication strategies of ASHA workers. *International Journal of Scientific Research and Review, 7*(5).

Balcazar, H., Lee Rosenthal, E., Nell Brownstein, J., Rush, C. H., Matos, S., & Hernandez, L. (2011). Community health workers can be a public health force for change in the United States: Three actions for a new paradigm. *American Journal of Public Health, 101*(12), 2199–2203.

Bhatia, K. (2014). Performance-based incentives of the ASHA scheme: Stakeholders' perspectives. *Economic and Political Weekly*, 145–151.

Bhutta, Z. A., Lassi, Z. S., Pariyo, G., & Huicho, L. (2010). Global experience of community health workers for delivery of health related millennium development goals: A systematic review, country case studies, and recommendations for integration into national health systems. *Global Health Workforce Alliance*.

Bullappa, A., & Kengnal, P. (2017). Assessment of quality of life of ASHA workers using WHOQoL-BREF questionnaire. *International Journal of Community Medicine and Public Health, 4*(6), 2060–2064.

Bhatia, K. (2014). Community health worker programs in India: A rights-based review. *Perspectives in Public Health, 134*(5), 276–282.

Chandra, S. (2021, March 26) What helped India's COVID situation? Our vast administrative reach. Over2shailaja Blog. https://over2shailaja.wordpress.com/2021/03/26/what-helped-indias-covid-situation-our-vast-administrative-reach/

Das, A., & Dasgupta, A. (2015). An exploratory analysis of knowledge and practice, job-related difficulties and dissatisfaction of ASHAs in rural India. *International Journal of Current Research and Review, 7*(10), 14–19.

Dasgupta, J., Velankar, J., Borah, P., & Nath, G. H. (2017). The safety of women health workers at the frontlines. *Indian Journal of Medical Ethics, 2*(3), 209–213.

George, C. E., Norman, G., Wadugodapitya, A., Rao, S. V., Nalige, S., Radhakrishnan, V., Behar, S., & de Witte, L. (2019). Health issues in a Bangalore slum: Findings from a household survey using a mobile screening toolkit in Devarajeevanahalli. *BMC Public Health, 19*(1). https://doi.org/10.1186/s12889-019-6756-7

Gogia, S., & Sachdev, H. S. (2010). Home visits by community health workers to prevent neonatal deaths in developing countries: a systematic review. *Bulletin of the World Health Organization, 88*, 658–666.

Gopalan, S. S., Mohanty, S., & Das, A. (2012). Assessing community health workers' performance motivation: a mixed-methods approach on India's Accredited Social Health Activists (ASHA) programme. *BMJ Open, 2*(5), e001557. http://doi: 10.1136/bmjopen-2012-001557

Fathima, F. N., Raju, M., Varadharajan, K. S., Krishnamurthy, A., Ananthkumar, S. R., & Mony, P. K. (2015). Assessment of 'accredited social health activists'—a national community health volunteer scheme in Karnataka State, India. *Journal of Health, Population, and Nutrition, 33*(1), 137–145.

Hariprasad, R., & Mehrotra, R. (2016). Role of accredited social health activists in cancer screening in India: Brightest "ray of hope." *Asian Pacific Journal of Cancer Prevention, 17*(7), 3659–3660.

Jamil, N., Vysak, A. S., Parihar, A., & Banerjee, S. (2017, January). Understanding the hope harbingers—ASHA, the women foot soldiers of India's National Rural Health Mission. In A. Chakrabarti and D. Chakrabarti (Eds.), *Research into design for communities: vol. 2. ICoRD 2017. Smart Innovations, Systems and Technology, vol.* 66 (pp. 199–208). Springer. https://doi-org.proxy-bc.researchport.umd.edu/10.1007/978-981-10-3521-0_17

Jeet, G., Thakur, J. S., Prinja, S., & Singh, M. (2017). Community health workers for non-communicable diseases prevention and control in developing countries: Evidence and implications. *PloS One, 12*(7), e0180640. https://doi.org/10.1371/journal.pone.0180640

India, M. (2013). Guidelines for community processes. *New Delhi: Ministry of Health and Family Welfare, Government of India.*

Mane Abhay, B., & Khandekar Sanjay, V. (2014). Strengthening primary health care through ASHA workers: A novel approach in India. *Primary Health Care, 4*(149). https://doi.org/10.4172/2167-1079.1000149

Marks, S. M. (2006). Global recognition of human rights for lesbian, gay, bisexual, and transgender people. *Health and Human Rights, 9*(1), 33–42.

Nambiar, D., Sheikh, K., & Verma, N. (2012). Scale-up of community action for health:

Lessons from a realistic evaluation of the Mitanin program in Chhattisgarh, India. *BMC Proceedings, 6*(5). https://doi.org/10.1186/1753-6561-6-S5-O26

National Association for Community Healthcare Workers July 2021. *What we do.* https://nachw.org/about/

National Health Mission. (2018, February). Meeting of the Mission Steering Group. New Delhi. http://nhm.gov.in/New_Updates_2018/Monitoring/MSG/5th-MSG-of-NHM-Minutes.pdf

National Health Mission. (2017, January). Meeting of the Mission Steering Group. New Delhi. http://nhm.gov.in/images/pdf/monitoring/mission-steering-group/Minutes_of_4th_MSG-of-NHM.pdf

National Rural Health Mission. Meeting people's health needs in rural areas. Framework for implementation (2005–2012). https://nhm.gov.in/WriteReadData/l892s/nrhm-framework-latest.pdf

Pala, S., Kumar, D., Jeyashree, K., & Singh, A. (2011). Preliminary evaluation of the ASHA scheme in Naraingarh block, Haryana. *The National Medical Journal of India, 24*(5), 315–316.

Pandey, J., & Singh, M. (2016). Donning the mask: Effects of emotional labour strategies on burnout and job satisfaction in community healthcare. *Health Policy and Planning, 31*(5), 551–562.

Peacock, N., Issel, L. M., Townsell, S. J., Chapple-McGruder, T., & Handler, A. (2011). An innovative method to involve community health workers as partners in evaluation research. *American Journal of Public Health, 101*(12), 2275–2280.

Puett, C., Sadler, K., Alderman, H., Coates, J., Fiedler, J. L., & Myatt, M. (2013). Cost-effectiveness of the community-based management of severe acute malnutrition by community health workers in southern Bangladesh. *Health Policy and Planning, 28*(4), 386–399.

Reddy, S. L., & Ramasamy, K. (2020). The significant challenges in Bangalore—An introspection. *Adalya Journal, 9*(4), 228–247.

Roalkvam, S. (2014). Health governance in India: Citizenship as situated practice. *Global Public Health, 9*(8), 910–926.

Rosenthal, E. L., de Heer, H., Rush, C. H., & Holderby, L. R. (2008). Focus on the future: A community health worker research agenda by and for the field. *Progress in Community Health Partnerships: Research, Education, and Action, 2*(3), 225–235.

Saprii, L., Richards, E., Kokho, P., & Theobald, S. (2015). Community health workers in rural India: Analysing the opportunities and challenges Accredited Social Health Activists (ASHAs) face in realising their multiple roles. *Human Resources for Health, 13*(1). https://doi.org/10.1186/s12960-015-0094-3

Scott, K., & Shanker, S. (2010). Tying their hands? Institutional obstacles to the success of the ASHA community health worker programme in rural north India. *AIDS Care, 22*(Suppl. 2), 1606–1612.

Scott, K., George, A. S., & Ved, R. R. (2019). Taking stock of 10 years of published research on the ASHA programme: Examining India's national community health worker programme from a health systems perspective. *Health Research Policy and Systems, 17*(1). https://doi.org/10.1186/s12961-019-0427-0

Sharma, R., Webster, P., & Bhattacharyya, S. (2014). Factors affecting the performance of community health workers in India: A multi-stakeholder perspective. *Global Health Action, 7*(1). https://doi.org/10.3402/gha.v7.25352

Shrivastava, A., & Srivastava, A. (2016). Measuring communication competence and effectiveness of ASHAs (accredited social health activist) in their leadership role at rural settings of Uttar Pradesh (India). *Leadership in Health Services, 29*(1), 69–81.

Smittenaar, P., Ramesh, B. M., Jain, M., Blanchard, J., Kemp, H., Engl, E., & Namasivayam, V. (2020). Bringing greater precision to interactions between community health workers and households to improve maternal and newborn health outcomes in India. *Global Health: Science and Practice*, 8(3), 358–371.

Srivastava, D. K., Prakash, S., Adhish, V., Nair, K. S., Gupta, S., & Nandan, D. (2009). A study of interface of ASHA with the community and the service providers in Eastern Uttar Pradesh. *Indian Journal of Public Health*, 53(3), 133–136.

World Health Organization. (1987). *The community health worker*. World Health Organization.

Ved, R., Scott, K., Gupta, G., Ummer, O., Singh, S., Srivastava, A., & George, A. S. (2019). How are gender inequalities facing India's one million ASHAs being addressed? Policy origins and adaptations for the world's largest all-female community health worker programme. *Human Resources for Health*, 17(1). https://doi.org/10.1186/s12960-018-0338-0

Ved, R., & Scott, K. (2020). Counseling is a relationship not just a skill: Reconceptualizing health behavior change communication by India's Accredited Social Health Activists, *Global Health Science and Practice*, 8(3), 332–334.

Warrier, A (2020). "The Women Warriors Fighting COVID-19 at the Frontline: ASHA Workers Left Without Hope," Working Papers id:13066, eSocialSciences, 1–6.

15

Multiple Mandates, Competing Goals, and the Challenges of Working in Combined Environmental Agencies in the United States

JoyAnna S. Hopper

In the early days of my interviews with environmental agency workers in the states, I tried to carefully comb through my interview notes to find indications that a worker was "disgruntled," or that their concerns about the agency's work were about personal disputes or a personal dislike for the type of work. I thought that it may be misleading to include these individuals as part of my analysis of environmental agencies' cultures and the challenges brought forward by competing goals and mandates. However, after many hours of interviews with workers, I found that almost all workers—from regional inspectors, to managers, to those on cleanup crews—expressed frustration with the internal battles they felt preoccupied their agencies' energy. Even if they enjoyed their work and felt that they were part of successful efforts to protect the environment and human health, they still described the experience of navigating disputes over which agency activities should be prioritized and publi- cized, how much leeway should be given to special interests and leering legislators, and how to work alongside other employees in the agency who appeared to "not speak the same language." Environmental agencies' multiple and competing mandates were causing confusion, animosity, and ineffectiveness.

These frustrations were expressed by employees working in environmental agencies where mandates had been intentionally combined. At the time of my interviews (2014–2019), 20 states in the United States had chosen to combine environmental regulation mandates with public health (PHEPs) or natural resource conservation (NREPs) mandates (see Figure 15.1). Employees often noted that at least some of the motivations behind these continued combinations made sense. Public health mandates are inseparable from the consideration of environment. Natural resource conservation is a central component of protecting the healthy ecosystems that underlie a fragile balance between humans and the natural world. It is not that these mandates are directly in competition with one another; however, they are also not directly aligned. As I discuss in my earlier work on the effects of combining natural resource conservation mandates with environmental enforcement, natural resource agencies tend to adopt an approach of negotiated compliance, which encourages direct partnerships and cooperation with industry as part of the regulatory process (Hopper, 2017; see also Hunter and Waterman, 1992; Shover et al., 1986). This is in direct opposition to environmental regulation's reliance on an enforced compliance approach, which values the process of command and control. Public health agencies are much more focused on providing services than in regulation, and they actively hire epidemiologists instead of the technical specialists (e.g., hydrologists and engineers) generally employed by environmental agencies (Hopper, 2020). Between competing visions of the purpose and place of regulation and the difference in employee background, agencies that combine environmental regulation with public health or natural resource conservation invite a considerable amount of conflict—conflict that I found impeded environmental agencies' regulatory functions (Hopper, 2017; 2019; 2020). Communities were potentially unprotected because of agencies' inability to manage goal competition and ambiguity.

What is notable about these findings is the degree to which they are generalizable. At both the state and federal levels (and globally), agency mandates are combined in efforts to promote efficiency and effectiveness and to garner more political control over unelected bureaucrats. Combinations are sometimes careless, but more often they are considered with serious intention. It is not easy or desirable to replicate the grueling and expensive reorganization process. Regardless of intention, however, these combinations result in a number of complications for the employees who

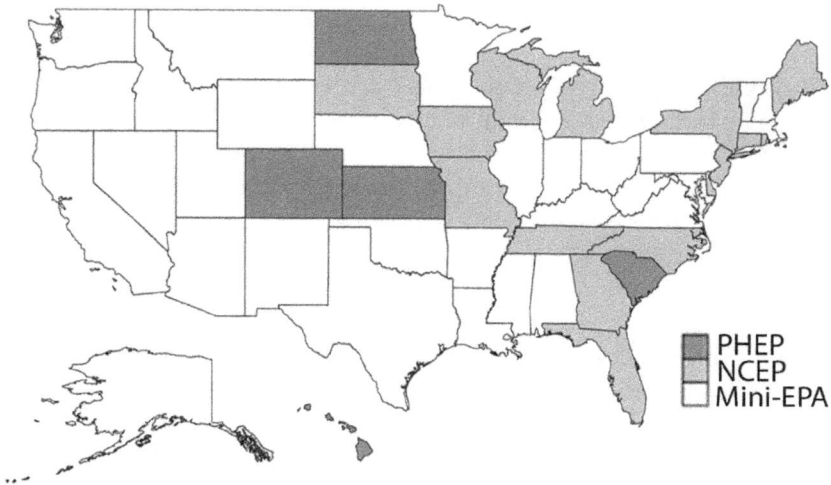

Figure 15.1. Combined Environmental Agencies by State. *Source*: Author-created.

manage them. They create communication problems between—sometimes warring—factions within the agency. They shift priorities so abruptly that employees focused on a secondary mandate become disillusioned, and the agency may face the consequences of increased employee turnover. And as was the case for the environmental agencies in my own research, these conflicts and shifts in prioritization may also lead to failure to adequately serve some of the agency's mandates.

In this chapter, I detail some of the implications of combined agency mandates for bureaucrats and the reforms that may help to combine agencies with greater understanding of implications. Interviews with combined environmental agency workers (CEAWs)—those employees working in environmental agencies that combine environmental enforcement with either public health or natural resource conservation mandates—reflect both the personal and institutional effects of combinations, effects that are often overlooked or misunderstood by elected officials and appointed agency heads. While neither I nor any of the agency workers I interviewed believe that we should reject the combination of mandates entirely, to understand how to do so successfully requires understanding the implications of those combinations from those who live with them.

Working in a Combined Environmental Agency

While CEAWs serve in a variety of agency roles (e.g., inspectors, legislative liaisons, public outreach specialists, epidemiologists, state park managers), the one factor that they all mention as crucial to their positions is coordination—coordination between state geographic areas, between office departments and divisions, with elected officials, with stakeholders, and with other CEAWs. The importance of coordination for these employees is emphasized by the variation in tasks and goals represented in their respective agencies. Combined environmental agencies may include several mandates, including environmental enforcement, state park management, resource conservation, medical marijuana management, health finance, food sanitation, and countless other tasks and responsibilities. There are a number of options for combined environmental agencies' focus, and, depending on agencies' understanding of their central and primary mandates, workers may feel more or less central to the agencies' day-to-day functions.

According to CEAWs, several factors determine the focus of combined environmental agencies. Specifically, employees noted that Environmental Protection Agency (EPA) funding and priorities, stakeholders' interests, and political priorities shaped agency goals and the nature of their daily work, and these interests and priorities do not always overlap. One worker noted that the EPA's funding "determine[s] what [we] focus on and spend money on." The employee stated that "if the focus nationally changes, then [the agency has] to change the focus." This can be problematic because a state's stakeholders (e.g., regulated entities, interest groups, etc.), who are also applying pressure to environmental agencies, may have goals that differ significantly from that of the EPA. An employee argued that "they (CEAWs) are in the trenches, and . . . are interacting with local industry. . . . We are much closer to the regulated facilities and the other local organizations and government . . . we have ongoing relations . . . we know the playing field, the players, and how to get something going." From this employee's perspective—a perspective mirrored by other CEAWs—the EPA is not always cognizant of the state pressures that may limit an agency's ability to focus on a particular program area or goal. As a CEAW stated, "sometimes we have to point out the differences [between our state and others] and how hard it might be to implement something in our state."

In particular, state-level industry stakeholders are often more concerned with issues of economic development. For example, one agency worker spoke about an algae issue in one of the state's most economically important recreational areas. The agency and stakeholders were greatly "concerned because of the economic impact" that continued algae issues at the recreational area could cause; however, the EPA was never able or willing to offer additional funding to address this problem. The employee noted that "hours and resources [had] to be taken out of other programs to compensate for that." In this situation, state stakeholders pressed the agency to divert resources to focus on a problem that EPA funding and support provided did not allow.

Additionally, CEAWs' focus is determined by the governors and legislatures that control their hiring, state-level funding, and the assignment of their top administrators. CEAWs varied on their assessment of support from elected officials—everything from "absolutely no support" to "considerable support" was mentioned. However, no CEAW denied the power elected officials wield over agency focus. One employee noted that they had to be "more privy to the concerns [of elected officials] and political involvement." They stated that they had to "respond to senator so-and-so with receiving complaints" and that depending on the agencies' actions, elected officials may be more or less supportive. Like industry stakeholders, elected officials, particularly in Republican-controlled states, may be more likely to prioritize economic development over environmental enforcement. This makes the jobs of regulators more difficult, as they are often asked to focus their attention away from their primary mandate of regulation. As a CEAW employed as a regulator mentioned, "attention [from elected officials] can be both positive and negative . . . we have to be careful where we spend money and that we have good priorities." From this employee's perspective, "good" priorities meant priorities that would be embraced or supported by state officials and/or stakeholders. While EPA funding is crucial, it may be "easier to do what the state wants to do," particularly if state employees can "avoid some [EPA funding] pressure by turning to local industries to help fund regulatory programs through fees." In this way, CEAWs may work closely with industry, allowing industry to have some input over regulation, if they are willing to help fund programs and cooperate. This more cooperative relationship with industry is noted by CEAWs as crucial to any state-level agency success in environmental protection.

While arguably all state environmental agency workers are affected by competing pressures (e.g., see Konisky, 2008), the competing pressures placed on CEAWs are emphasized by the combination of mandates in their agencies. In particular, combining mandates leads to ambiguous organizational goals, where the possibility exists for multiple interpretations (Chun & Rainey, 2005). This is especially the case when two mandates directly compete with one another, which is likely when agency combinations are undertaken to join related activities. For example, CEAWs working in PHEPs noted that "if things are going to affect public health, this makes things more of an emergency." More simply, environmental issues become priority for a PHEP *only* if the issue can be traced directly back to a public health issue. Otherwise, environmental issues are secondary to public health issues. In an agency where only environmental mandates exist, environment is—by default—the main priority of the agency. The same is also true for NREPs. As one NREP worker noted, "other programs, more popular, more voluntary programs, [the agency] emphasizes those—they try to downplay the negativity of enforcement" by focusing on things like state parks, trails, and conservation programs. Again, the combination of mandates allows for environmental enforcement to become secondary, thus making the work of environmental regulators more difficult than their counterparts serving in public health or conservation roles. These difficulties lead to challenges for CEAWs, whether they are working on the environmental side of the agency or more directly serving public health or natural resource conservation mandates.

What Do Mandate Combinations Mean for Environmental Bureaucrats?

We can categorize the challenges CEAWs face into three primary issues that affect their day-to-day work: communication problems, program effectiveness, and disillusionment and turnover. These challenges are notable for their effects on individual workers and in that they likely determine the efficacy of the agency as a whole.

Communication Problems between Divisions

"Logistically, combinations are challenging," a CEAW noted in a 2019 interview. One of the reasons combinations are so challenging for employees is that they introduce the need for a higher level of communication and knowledge to successfully coordinate across divisions (Bacharach & Aiken, 1977). The variation in employee backgrounds and values in combined environmental agencies is problematic, creating consistent conflict, as employees from different departments try to pursue common goals in light of their polar preferences and unique understanding of how problems should be solved.

In interviews with CEAWs,[1] workers noted that even though divisions are under the same agency and headed by a single appointee, as one stated, "there is a very distinct separation between [divisions] . . . the funding is completely different. Types of people are different. Really, for the most part, [the parts of the agency] are joined only in name." This division can create animosity between workers tasked with different mandates. For example, as I argued previously, PHEP employees serving environmental mandates noted that those on the public health side of the agency were concerned about regulation only if the activity in question related directly and immediately to public health (e.g., "if things are going to affect public health, this makes things more of an emergency").[2] One employee argued that they and their fellow environmental regulators "want *all* streams and water clean, even if people are not around . . . there will be health people and environmental people [working together] and to some extent we don't really speak the same language. Our missions go separate ways, and they may overlap, and they may not sometimes." Additionally, environmental regulators expressed frustration that they couldn't simply say "you aren't following the regulation, and you need to." Instead, "there is a different mind-set, where public health will work with you and no consequences."

There were frustrations for CEAWs serving public health mandates as well. One worker expressed that "there are just people in the environment side that feel like I work for the environment, and I don't have anything to do with health and vice versa." These assertions highlight one of the primary paradoxes of agency mandate combinations: Actions meant to connect programs and staff serving similar goals may serve only to remind them of their differences. CEAWs express that while the "concept [of the combination] is wonderful," the promised integration between environmental protection and other mandates often fails to come to fruition. Unfortunately, as one employee states, "there isn't a lot of that connectivity."

CEAWs emphasize the need for liaisons between divisions to help facilitate those connections. Unfortunately, most of the employees I spoke to could not identify successful efforts to translate and find common ground, with one noting that there are "no real liaisons working between [agency divisions]." This CEAW also noted that it was difficult to know who to bring in to handle a particular issue; there is no training to help employees identify when, say, an epidemiologist is the appropriate point person to handle a problem or whether the appropriate point person is an engineer. The CEAW argued that "[they] have to know when to bring in an epidemiologist" without formal assistance and that this kind of knowledge comes only through experience; it is "entirely on the job training." Knowing enough about another division to know when they would be helpful in collaborating to solve a problem is imperative in successfully combining mandates. However, employees acknowledged that they are siloed, even if they share committees/task forces and physical workspace. One CEAW stated that their two agency divisions "work separately almost entirely," even though they acknowledged that CEAWs, regardless of division, now work in the same workspace. Without consistent and meaningful focus on building bridges between divisions, divisions of the agency continue to work independently from one another—or, worse, against one another.

Divisional Effectiveness

While communication issues within agencies with multiple mandates likely affect those working within all divisions of the agency, other challenges are likely to have a disproportionate effect on certain parts of the agency. As I discuss previously, confusion over the goals of the agency is likely to occur when any kind of combination is implemented; however, when a politically/socially popular program is combined with a less popular program area, goal ambiguity allows for some mandates to receive less attention and support, along with fewer resources. In the case of combined environmental agencies, environmental regulation or enforcement programs may suffer from a combined structure because of the political and economic pressures placed on regulators to place less emphasis on the penalization of valuable local industries (Hopper, 2020). Day-to-day pressures and interactions for CEAWs lead to those enforcement decisions.

In discussions with CEAWs, it was obvious that regulatory programs—often on the environmental side of the agency—are more controversial than other programs (e.g., public health or natural resource conservation programs). One employee stated that "a lot less money comes to address environmental [issues]. A *lot less*." Another expressed that "the resources aren't there" and that "there certainly is an emphasis and greater support for more popular programs with the public." In comparison to recreational programs or programs focused on public health services, regulatory programs were noted to suffer from funding, fees, and staff that "[are] not sufficient." According to combined agency employees, the cause of this deprioritization of regulatory or enforcement programs is varied. In some cases, the employees pointed to an agency culture in which "there's not really a strong regulatory emphasis. It's not even spoken about. People just believe it's there; it's just natural there. The way people think it should be." Others noted that the regulatory division's reliance on permittees for funding, as opposed to the state tax dollars that may help to fund public health or natural resource efforts, meant that they had to "adjust their compliance strategy" to work more closely and cooperatively with industry and downplay enforcement. In general, almost all combined agency employees claimed that their agencies sought to "downplay the negativity of enforcement" and set themselves apart from the federal EPA.

In addition to agency culture and funding mechanisms, employees noted that elected officials also often support a shift of focus away from regulatory programs, even within other divisions of the agency. For example, as one employee succinctly stated, "politics has focused us away from things like health and worker safety and [regulating] the oil and gas industry." The concern from environmental employees, especially, was that this dynamic could be problematic because "upper management is going to emphasize things that are not regulatory in nature because [those things] are more popular—even when causing widespread pollution." Workers were not surprised when I told them that combined agency structures, such as theirs, produced less stringent enforcement—flexibility that could lead to worse pollution and poorer health outcomes (Hopper, 2017; Hopper, 2019; Hopper, 2020).

In general, CEAWs from across divisions admitted that while the integration promised by combining environmental mandates with public health or natural resource conservation mandates was possible—and even desirable—it did not match up with their experiences. As one CEAW noted, "if there was a focus that was strictly on [environmental] enforcement, the managers would know that was their sole job and they would do much more enforcement." As it is, enforcement is a "controversial area." Even CEAWs who thought that the mandates should continue to be combined noted that the combination caused some difficulties, especially for environmental divisions. One CEAW explained that they were "fortunate to be working within a voluntary program—not [a program] as controversial as the regulatory programs we have." When given the opportunity to prioritize some mandates over others—an opportunity that often presents itself when mandates are combined—environmental agencies routinely downplay enforcement and regulation in favor of more politically and socially palatable programs. And those on the environmental side of the agency feel that lack of support every day.

DISILLUSIONMENT AND TURNOVER

In my interviews with CEAWs, it was obvious that employees felt less valued and less supported than those in other divisions. In the beginning of the interviews, I always asked whether they felt their work was related to the agency's main goals and priorities, and one worker joked that "because they put the word 'environment' in the name [of the agency]" he supposed his work was related, but "pragmatically, [their work] is less prioritized." We laughed, but their point stood. Environmental programs were not a priority, and, therefore, neither were they. What do these challenges mean for the careers of combined agency workers? Unfortunately, for those working in a less prioritized division, it can mean separation or a transfer. In particular, employees noted that regulatory divisions were subject to much higher levels of turnover. In describing those who chose to leave the agency, one employee expressed, "why should I accept low pay and be stressed out all the time and every time I try to do my job there's pushback." Another agreed that "if you every day [have to] tell [clients] to do something they don't have the funding for or could lead to penalties or violations, it can definitely be really defeating." The work of regulation and enforcement is difficult and rarely rewarded in an agency where more popular programs absorb focus. And, as an employee noted, the lack of support is "demoralizing." "Most of the people that work for the agency believe in the mission and try to do a good job, but . . . they'd be happier if they were supported."

Unfortunately, it is not just a lack of support that plagues environmental workers in combined environmental agencies. At times, there are active efforts to obstruct their work. One environmental employee stated that they came into the work with high expectations and "wanted to conquer the world and save the environment," but even though they'd tried to do everything they could to "excel and make a difference," they had actively been "held back in [their] career" because managers were "more interested in protecting their positions and not rocking the boat." Upper managers were not interested in elevating individuals who valued regulation as a fundamental part of the agency. Additionally, attention paid to environmental divisions in combined agencies is rarely fruitful for divisions and workers because the attention often centers around controversy. An employee stated, "the attention is more of scrutiny, and criticism, rather than excitement." Ideally, employees wanted their most controversial decisions (e.g., a significant monetary penalty for a large industry) to be backed—or at least not undermined—by the agency as a whole. This kind of support would indicate that regulatory actions were legitimate and the employees making those decisions were in line with the agency's mission. "Knowing your work is in line with the common goal of the division—you have a purpose," an employee expressed.

Purpose and alignment with mission is an important determinant of employee retention in bureaucratic agencies (Bertelli, 2006; Kim & Fernandez, 2017). Bureaucrats working in divisions that are actively or indirectly starved of resources, in addition to receiving less recognition and support for their day-to-day work, are likely to be dissatisfied. The combination of mandates, regardless of which mandates are combined, forces prioritization to take place. Some bureaucrats will always end up in programs of lower priority. Here we are likely to see the disconnect from agency mission and frustration with circumstances that often leads to separation or transfer. And high levels of employee turnover are damaging and costly to bureaucratic agencies. High turnover levels lead to the loss of institutional knowledge, a rise in backlogged work, high costs for recruiting and training new employees, and a decrease in morale (Bertelli, 2006; Kim & Fernandez, 2017; see also Boushey & Glynn, 2012; Cho & Lewis, 2012; Kim, 2005; Selden & Moynihan, 2000). As one CEAW claimed, "the general public has no idea . . . they think there's an agency in the state protecting the environment and in some cases it could not be further from the truth." Additionally, CEAWs noted that the lack of support—financially, logistically, and interpersonally—led to problems hiring: "we can't bring new people in." Not only is turnover high, but hiring replacements is difficult, further weakening agencies' efforts.

How Generalizable Are CEAWs' Experiences?

While the experiences of CEAWs are undoubtedly shaped by the nature of the mandates they serve—environmental protection, public health, and/or natural resource conservation—the difficulties they encounter because of combined mandates are likely shared by other government employees juggling multiple—and often competing—mandates. For example, the creation of the Department of Homeland Security (DHS) involved the combination of 22 bureaucratic agencies into a single department. According to Cohen et al. (2006), this combination of mandates forced agencies to transfer resources from their legacy mandates to new homeland security goals and priorities and allowed for elected officials to downplay parts of DHS that continued to focus on their legacy mandates. In particular, the Federal Emergency Management Agency's difficulties in dealing with the fallout from Hurricane Katrina are thought to be related to the hollowing out of the agency's identity and—more literally—of the agency's resources and staff (Cohen et al. 2006). Similarly, the downfall of the U.S. Minerals Management Service (MMS)—an agency charged with both revenue collection from offshore drilling and the regulation of offshore drilling—is thought to be an artifact of the combination of regulatory and nonregulatory mandates.

Carrigan (2017) notes that the combination may have allowed MMS to focus more heavily on revenue collection and the use of energy resources than regulation, as regulation was a less rewarding mandate. The lack of focus, resources, autonomy, and support for agency mandates in both DHS and MMS is similar to what CEAWs (specifically those serving environmental mandates) experience within combined environmental agencies.

Additionally, even when mandates are not in direct competition with one another, we should expect that one mandate will be elevated at the expense of another (Chun & Rainey, 2005; Perry et al., 1999). As with workers in any organization, when given multiple goals and tasks to choose from, bureaucrats must decide how to allocate their time and efforts. Incentives to pursue goals or perform specific tasks differ. Therefore, time and efforts are unlikely to ever be distributed equally (Dewatripont et al., 2000). Researchers have found that regardless of the mandates combined, the agency becomes splintered, with some who identify strongly with one mandate while others identify strongly with another (e.g., Hopper, 2020). These differences in identification and priorities create discord in the agency that may ultimately undermine the goals of streamlining and efficiency that are central to justifications for combination. Additionally, the discord created by these competing "camps" within an agency is likely to make the agency more susceptible to pressures from elected officials and special interests. When bureaucrats are uncertain what their goals are, it is much easier for an outsider to push an agenda.

What Does Responsible Mandate Combination Look Like?

The truth about mandate combination is that it is not going anywhere. Agency reorganizations that involve the streamlining of common mandates and goals is still a popular means of adjusting to new needs or political realities. Although CEAWs expressed both personal and institutional concerns related to the combination of environmental protection and other mandates, they noted that combination, itself, was not necessarily a problem. In fact, most of the CEAWs I interviewed were reluctant to give up on the combination because they clearly saw the advantage of working closely alongside those who shared similar goals. Employees saw the potential for more effective and efficient work. It was simply potential that had yet to be realized.

To protect the bureaucrats who handle the day-to-day difficulties of policy implementation, mandate combinations must be carried out with intention and with recognition of the many challenges that combinations may introduce. In particular, three factors may help to make mandate combinations more successful for employees and agencies: (1) input on organizational decisions; (2) installment of liaisons between divisions; and (3) active protection of less popular programming.

As part of my interviews with CEAWs, I asked them what conversations or debates they encountered related to the combination of agency mandates. More simply, I wanted to know if they were aware of or part of debates over the continued combination of environmental protection with other mandates. It was clear from my conversations with these employees that while they may have heard isolated complaints or observed debates happening in state legislatures or among upper management, they were not actively invited or involved in those conversations. One employee noted about the most recent change in structure to the agency that they were "not sure what they did—way above my paygrade.

I think I just got an e-mail." Another employee stated that they weren't "sure any people at the top know what we do. It sure seems that way. Pretty much stays the same, regardless of who is at the top." More simply, these employees felt they were subject to the whims of elected officials and top administrators, and it was up to them to deal with the consequences of decisions made without their input. Without the input of employees during the reorganization process or regular evaluations of that reorganization process, top administrators and elected officials are not able to anticipate potential conflicts or areas of confusion. The employees I spoke with usually had their own ideas about how a combination of mandates could be successful; however, they had rarely—if ever—been asked for that kind of input.

In addition to helping top administrators and elected officials reorganize in a way that fits employees' wants and needs, employee empowerment through inclusion in decision-making processes will likely also improve employee performance (Paarlberg & Lavigna, 2010). Increased "autonomy in the workplace enhances employees' intrinsic motivations by allowing employees to internalize organizational regulations and integrate rules with their own values" (Paarlberg & Lavigna, 2010, p. 715; see also Park & Rainey, 2008). Considering employees' thoughts during decision-making encourages workers to find creative solutions to problems, energizes workers, and increases their perception of self-efficacy (see Conger & Konungo, 1988). All these effects are related to improved employee morale, retention, and performance.

Had top administrators and elected officials made efforts to include their employees in conversations about reorganization, they would have realized how important it is to install liaisons between agency divisions. Many of the problems that exist for combined agency employees originate in communication problems or a lack of goal clarity. By intentionally installing liaisons to help facilitate communication and cooperation between divisions, agencies can purposefully identify areas in which employees are struggling to work toward a common goal. Liaisons can help form partnerships between divisions that may not be obvious to siloed employees, they can help employees understand divisional hierarchies, and they can actively align divisional activities and ideas to a shared mission or set of goals. For combined agency employees—especially those involved in less popular programming—there is often a disconnect between the agency's mission and their day-to-day work. Liaisons can clarify and elevate a common mission or set of goals between divisions that will connect all employees' work to a higher purpose. Paarlberg and Lavigna (2010) describe how efforts to connect each employees' daily tasks with the agency's goals improves employee satisfaction and performance: "Establishing clear goals requires managers to explain not only what employees should do, but also why they should do it. This includes how their actions contribute to organizational goals and connect to the larger mission of the organization, thus reinforcing employees' public service motivations" (p. 713; see also Wright, 2007; Paarlberg & Perry, 2007). Liaisons between divisions are uniquely and appropriately situated to take on this task, as they are identified as a knowledge source of the commonalities between divisions.

In addition to the installment of liaisons, agencies should also make efforts to protect the resources of less popular programming and the autonomy of the employees serving those mandates. Regulatory divisions, for example, are likely to suffer from scarce resources and may be encouraged to limit regulatory efforts for the sake of cooperation with stakeholders (e.g., the CEAW that noted they were told to "adjust their compliance strategy" to work more cooperatively with industry). Employees expected to serve in more confrontational positions should be compensated accordingly, and the agency should actively protect the resources available to these divisions, which may be more subject to political attacks.

Additionally, efforts should be made to ensure that managers are able to serve their respective mandates adequately. If managers' efforts are consistently undermined by agency heads or managers from other divisions, expertise and knowledge no longer drive the implementation of policy; political interests do. Active protection means that combined agencies must acknowledge that goal and task prioritization is a reality and that they must ensure that each part of the agency receives the support they need to do their job. Unfortunately, this asks for agencies to elevate and protect the parts of the agency that they often seek to hide in fear of public or political retaliation. However, the protection of these divisions allows for effective and efficient policy implementation. And the support for employees in this division will improve morale, connection to the organization, retention, and performance.

Of course, much of what I suggest here is premised on an important assumption: Elected officials and top administrators want combined agencies to effectively implement policy. However, elected officials and administrators may actively choose to introduce complexity into an organization to paralyze the organization or certain divisions. In this case, poor organizational or divisional performance is the goal, and reforms are not carried out in good faith. Reorganizations offer elected officials the opportunity to quietly dismantle or starve programs of resources. While reorganizations are difficult and often controversial, the implications for employees and programs are less direct than a bill that shutters an existing program or drastically cuts its budget. Reorganizations, even after they are completed, reorient programming and funding and can be manipulated to serve political interests. Therefore, in addition to the reforms I note thus far, elected officials and upper managers must be skeptical of the motivations behind agency combinations.

The challenges CEAWs face are like those faced by employees in other agencies serving multiple mandates. However, public servants also share a resiliency to these challenges that I find striking. While the CEAWs I interviewed faced an expanding backlog of tasks amid political and personal controversies, they were consistently invested and interested in their respective agencies' future. They continuously sought out ways to align their work with agency goals and to advocate on the behalf of their colleagues' work. While many of them were not certain that their agencies clearly saw a place for them in their agency's mission, CEAWs always saw a place for the agency's mission within their own work. They—like most public officials—are true public servants, looking to improve their organizations from within to serve those of us on the outside. In understanding their struggles and the reforms or best practices that may help them to serve more effectively, we can uplift policy decisions that protect public servants and the important programs they design and implement.

Notes

1. Between 2014 and 2019, I performed interviews with workers from combined environmental agencies across a variety of states, including states that vary in their political control, region, and environmental issues. I am unable to disclose the specific states to protect the anonymity of the interviewed employees.

2. I use the term "sides" intentionally, as this is how bureaucrats referenced the various agency divisions/departments in interviews. This language insinuates conflict, reflecting some of the latent feelings of frustration that bureaucrats face when trying to work with and alongside those they think hold different priorities.

References

Bacharach, S. B., & Aiken, M. (1977). Communication in administrative bureaucracies. *The Academy of Management Journal, 20*(3), 365–377. https://doi.org/10.2307/255411

Bertelli, A. M. (2006). Determinants of bureaucratic turnover intention: Evidence from the Department of the Treasury. *Journal of Public Administration and Theory, 17,* 235–258. https://doi.org/10.1093/jopart/mul003

Boushey, H., & Glynn, S. J. (2012). *There are significant business costs to replacing employees*. Center for American Progress.

Carrigan, C. (2017). *Structured to fail?: Regulatory performance under competing mandates*. Cambridge University Press.

Cho, Y. J., & Lewis, G. B. (2012). Turnover intention and turnover behavior: Implications for retaining federal employees. *Review of Public Personnel Administration, 32,* 4–23. https://doi.org/10.1177/0734371X11408701

Chun, Y. H., & Rainey, H. G. (2005). Goal ambiguity in U.S. federal agencies. *Journal of Public Administration Research and Theory, 15*(1), 1–30. https://doi.org/10.1093/jopart/mui001

Cohen, D. K., Cuellar M., & Weingast B. (2005). Crisis bureaucracy: Homeland security and the political design of legal mandates. *Stanford Law Review, 59*(3), 673–760. https://www.jstor.org/stable/40040307

Conger, J. A., & Kanungo, R. (1988). The empowerment process: Integrating theory and practice. *Academy of Management Review, 13*(3), 471–482. https://doi.org/10.2307/258093

Denhardt, R. B. (2011). Theories of public organization (6th ed.). Wadsworth.

Dewatripont, M., Jewitt, I., & Tirole, J. (2000). Multitask agency problems: Focus and task clustering. *European Economic Review, 44*(4–6), 869–877. https://doi.org/10.1016/S0014-2921(00)00059-3

Hopper, J. S. (2017). The regulation of combination: The implications of combining natural resource conservation and environmental protection. *State Politics and Policy Quarterly, 17*(1), 105–124. https://doi.org/10.1177/1532440016674235

Hopper, J. S. (2019). Having it all?: The implications of public health and environmental protection partnerships in the American states. *Environmental Policy and Governance, 29*(1), 35–45. https://doi.org/10.1002/eet.1838

Hopper, J. S. (2020). *Environmental agencies in the United States: The enduring power of organizational design and state politics*. Rowman and Littlefield: Lexington Books.

Hunter, S., & Waterman, R. (1992). Determining an agency's regulatory style: How does the EPA water office enforce the law? *Western Political Quarterly, 45*(2), 403–417. https://doi.org/10.2307/448718

Kim, S. (2005). Factors affecting state government information technology employee turnover intentions. *American Review of Public Administration*, 35, 137–156. https://doi.org/10.1177/0275074004273150

Kim, S. Y., & Fernandez, S. (2017). Employee empowerment and turnover intention in the U.S. federal bureaucracy. *American Review of Public Administration*, 47(1), 4–22. https://doi.org/10.1177/0275074015583712

Lewis, D. (2004). *Presidents and the politics of agency design*. Stanford University Press.

Norton, B. G. (2005). *Sustainability: A philosophy of adaptive ecosystem management*. The University of Chicago Press.

Paarlberg, L. E., & Lavigna, B. (2010). Transformational leadership and public service motivation: Driving individual and organizational performance. *Public Administration Review*, 70(5), 710–718. http://www.jstor.org/stable/40802368

Paarlberg, L. E., & Perry, J. L. (2007). Values management: Aligning individual values and organizational goals. *American Review of Public Administration*, 37(4), 387–408. https://doi.org/10.1177/02750740062972

Park, S. M., & Rainey, H. G. (2008). Leadership and public service motivation in U.S. federal agencies. *International Public Management Journal*, 11(1), 109–142. https://doi.org/10.1080/10967490801887954

Perry, J. L., Thompson, A. M., Tschirhart, M., Mesch, D., & Lee, G. (1999). Inside a Swiss army knife: An assessment of AmeriCorps. *Journal of Public Administration Research and Theory*, 9, 225–250. https://doi.org/10.1093/oxfordjournals.jpart.a024409

Selden, S. C., & Moynihan, D. P. (2000). A model of voluntary turnover in state government. *Review of Public Personnel Administration*, 20, 63–74. https://doi.org/10.1177/0734371X0002000206

Shover, N., Clelland, D. A., & Lynxwiler, J. (1986). *Enforcement or negotiation: Constructing a regulatory bureaucracy*. State University of New York Press.

Wilson, J. Q. (1989). *Bureaucracy: What government agencies do and why they do it*. Basic Books.

Wright, B. E. (2007). Public service and motivation: Does mission matter? *Public Administration Review*, 67(1), 54–64.

Conclusion

A Path Forward for the Field

STACI M. ZAVATTARO, JESSICA E. SOWA,
ALEXANDER C. HENDERSON, AND LAUREN HAMILTON EDWARDS

Through the stories shared in this book, we hope we have achieved the goal we set out in the introduction: to expand our knowledge of the breadth and depth of public service through stories about lived experiences. In this volume, public servants were highlighted for the roles they play in decision-making, policy making and shaping, community building, and service delivery. These public servants are dedicated to their cause and public service, often experiencing emotional stress and challenges as they do their best with often scarce resources. Readers saw both the highs and lows of public service under strain and should be left with an appreciation for what these public servants give, day after day. We know that we as the editors were deeply inspired and moved by these stories. In addition, sharing stories of these lived experiences is a way to not only connect with public servants but also expand a research agenda, one that can bring the myriad of jobs and actions involved in public administration to the forefront of the public administration knowledge base and build a more inclusive dialogue in the field.

Authors in this volume brought to life what McDonough (2006) describes as the habitus of public service. The realm—or habitus—of public service is littered with complexities and sometimes competing ideals such as efficiency versus effectiveness, or government (one-way) versus governance (collaborative). These tensions sometimes add additional stress to people trying to deliver a public good or service within ever-increasing resource constraints. Borrowing from Bourdieu's theory of practice, McDonough (2006) explains how public servants create and re-create their social world and space of influence for the public good. The power of the state—of the people implementing public policies—can be wielded for good or weaponized, depending upon the rules of the game (McDonough, 2006). Stories throughout this volume saw that tension, the life-and-death decisions, the challenges of living in a complex world of public service delivery. And these stories showed how public servants overall try to work for the good of those they serve, even when there are costs.

Given this, we conclude by offering some ideas for the future, based on the stories shared here.

Street-level Bureaucracy Expanded

One clear theme to emerge was the role street-level bureaucrats play in decision-making outside the traditionally studied frontline occupations such as police officers, teachers, counselors, and social workers (Maynard-Moody & Musheno, 2003). Street-level bureaucrats are everywhere, some visible but underrecognized, some clearly ignored and/or actively disparaged by the public and other stakeholders—and we need to explore the wide variety of agencies and professions that fall within this category of public servants to capture the full scope of their impact on the public. Prottas (1978) notes that in large agencies, the street-level bureaucrats carry out governing functions, making them ideal for studying how government works or does not. Chapters in our book highlighted how those less-visible public servants do this through ways including but not limited to scientific research on weather, climate scientists, photographers who document our world for public policy, air traffic controllers, librarians, arts personnel, and public defenders who protect the constitutional rights of those least fortunate. Some questions/themes we offer for future study include:

- How many voices of the "other" are we missing from the public administration knowledge base (with the "other" being those who work in hidden public service work or dirty work and those who are served by these public servants)?

- How do hidden/less visible public servants carry out their functions as street-level bureaucrats?

- How does this lack of visibility affect these street-level bureaucrats' understandings of their role as public servants?

- How can and do these public servants affect the citizen-state encounter?

- What tacit and explicit knowledge can hidden/less visible public servants share to guide theory building in the field?

- How would mapping the full landscape of public servants shape the knowledge base of the field of public administration and the career opportunities of our students?

- At a time when government is increasingly criticized and even cast as the villain in many narratives, can showing the full scope of the good that public servants do improve how people see the role of government?

Connection to Community Building

Public servants are deeply embedded in their community, a community that they seek to shape, but are equally shaped by in their work. Chapters in the book highlighted the role public servants can play in building community through bringing health services into the community and helping communities deal with emergencies in multiple ways, including the work of ASL interpreters during times of emergency. Public administrators help people get access to affordable housing, education, and other services that lead to a connection to one's community. One area that does not often get sufficient attention in public administration is the role of arts, libraries, and cultural institutions as community hubs, gathering places, and anchors for communities.

Efficiency reforms in government often see these institutions as extras or nice-to-haves, but museums serve as places to educate people perhaps not exposed to art, culture, accessibility, and education (Brenton & Bouckaert, 2021). Libraries are gathering places where people have access to computers, books, movies, and each other to connect and bridge community members together. Cultural institutions, though, such as museums, libraries, and arts nonprofits, naturally have a political component worth studying (Gray, 2011). Chapters herein open more research for studies on internal management and structure, the role of cultural institutions in community building, and the effects of citizen-state encounters in these institutions on the public/users.

Arts and cultural institutions have prominent roles in community health. For instance, the Rockefeller Foundation spearheaded the Arts and Culture Indicators in Community Building Project from 1996 to 2006, focusing on creating arts-related indicators for community health and well-being (Jackson, 1998). Some problems arose, however, including no standard measures and exclusion of inner-city communities from measurement development (Jackson, 1998). Despite potential challenges, cultural organizations have the potential to connect people with their places in meaningful, hopeful ways (Barge, 2003). Some questions/themes that emerged from these chapters are:

- What are the public institutions (and public servants within them) most critical for building strong communities? How does this depend on how we conceptualize and operationalize a strong community?

- What other realms of the public sector are unexpected opportunities for building stronger communities?

- For health services, what is the best way to bring services to the community to accomplish public purposes? How do public servants working in communities negotiate between the citizen and the state?

- In the area of managing emergencies, who are some of the public servants we may not currently be studying? What public servants—government, nonprofit, or volunteer—may be missing from the public administration knowledge base?

- For cultural institutions, which are underexplored in the public administration knowledge base, how can public administration scholarship better address the roles cultural institutions play in community building? What might be unique about these institutions?

- If cultural institutions are often on the chopping block in times of financial struggles, how can research provide evidence of their value to communities and make the case for investment in these institutions?

- What public-private partnerships might offer best practices for integrating nonprofit cultural institutions with governing institutions?

Policy Implementation Needs Depth

Stories throughout the book demonstrated the myriad ways in which public servants implement public policies through using their discretion when facing resource limitations (Lipsky, 1980). While there is significant research on how street-level bureaucrats and unseen public servants use their discretion to create rules, we draw attention here to additional research needed to push the field beyond only looking at frontline public servants. Fouassier, for instance, detailed how his and his colleagues' roles in the tax assessor's office affect the ability of other city officials to deliver much-needed services. This interdependence—where the work of many public servants is dependent on others in the system for success—could use renewed attention to make sure that relationships are maintained and systems do not break down. Holmes, in another example, details how a photographer can shape public policy and public narratives by choosing what to focus on—quite literally. The question of visual narratives and documenting government and policy in everyday life is one that has not been sufficiently explored in public administration.

Based on these observations, we offer the following questions for additional research:

- What is the role of underexamined public servants in policy implementation? For those not readily visible on the front lines, what is their influence on policy implementation? What are the implications of their influence?

- What does it mean for theory development in public administration to focus on a narrow concept of government service related to implementation?

- In what ways do public servants influence the public narratives about societal issues and the proverbial policy agenda?

- How we do we better define and discuss the realms of influence of public servants that span wider than their immediate organization? How can we understand governments and governance as collaborative systems that require attention to interdependence, cooperation, and coordination for success?

The Continuing Importance of Emotional Labor in Public Service

One of the most meaningful streams of research in public administration over the past twenty years has recognized the importance of emotions in public service work and the emotive component of public service (Guy, Newman, & Mastracci, 2008). As many of the stories presented in this text demonstrate, public service involves interpersonal interactions, where public servants engage with citizens, often when they may be at the lowest and/or most stressful moment of their lives. In addition, public servants such as emergency managers, air traffic controllers, and public defenders must handle enormous stress and often life or death decisions, decisions that require maintaining control over their emotions when performing their duties.

Emotional labor is public service work that moves beyond the cognitive components of a job and requires complex management of emotions, both on the part of the public servant themselves and in relation to the clients with whom they are interacting (Guy, Newman, & Mastracci, 2008). The study of emotional labor continues to expand the public administration knowledge base, but there remain more questions to explore about how public servants of all kinds experience emotions in the workplace and how emotions factor into their jobs (Guy, Mastracci, & Yang, 2019; Humphrey, 2021; Mastracci & Adams, 2019). Making emotions visible and encouraging recognition of this critical component of public service work will expand the field and improve government service.

Based on these observations, we offer the following questions for additional research:

- What are public service positions that may require significant emotional labor that have not yet been brought into the public administration literature? How does emotional labor work in those positions? Does it depend on the nature and depth of public encounters with citizens?

- What is the impact of compassion fatigue on public servants working in environments that require more emotional labor? How do public servants deal with compassion fatigue or even burnout in these situations? Are there tools that organizations can use to ease the impact of high-stress positions on public servants?

- How do we better train future public servants to prepare them for public encounters with empathy and compassion?

- What outcomes result from public servants who engage with citizens with empathy and compassion?

Classroom Implementation: Using Stories and Cases

In the introduction, we shared our hopes for this volume: expanding the public sector realm beyond a set expectation. We also noted the book would be an excellent addition to classrooms, everything from introductory public administration and management courses to even doctoral seminars focused on interpretive methods. Street-level public and nonprofit roles are useful here in that they embody some of the most important characteristics and attributes of public service where discretion, rules, decision-making, relationships, resources, and situations are central to the work being done; indeed, it's challenging to find a core public administration or policy topic that could not be studied extensively in frontline services. Some of the ways our book could be used within the classroom include:

- Supplement in an introductory master of public administration (MPA) or nonprofit management course.

- In a social justice class focusing on issues such as homelessness, election access, and community activism.

- In an ethics class or a course focused on the complexity of decision-making.

- In PhD-level courses on qualitative analysis or interpretive methodology as examples of writing up interviews or conducting narrative analysis.

The Importance of Public Service Stories

We began this text with a call for recognizing the importance of narratives for capturing the complexity of public service work and highlighting the often unsung but dedicated work of public servants. With the chapters in this text, the voices of those public servants are heard, and important lessons are drawn to help us research, train, and appreciate public servants in government and nonprofit settings across the world. At a time when government is increasingly questioned and misinformation abounds, shining a light on the true service of those working for the public good is even more important than ever. We hope that other scholars take up the stories in this text and continue building narratives on public service work.

Staci: *This book was really fun to create, to edit, to read. I had the idea back in 2020 and reached out to my friends and colleagues asking them to be part of this journey. Since then, the world has changed in demonstrable ways. As we write this conclusion in summer 2022, the world is still gripped by another wave of the COVID-19 pandemic. A former world leader in Japan was assassinated on the campaign trail. The U.S. Supreme Court took away a woman's right to choose. Trust in public institutions continues to erode. All four of us have talked about: well, now what? Reading the research in these pages, realizing the depth of the field we have chosen to work in and study brings to life the good that government can do—that government must do.*

We hope readers had several "a-ha" moments like we did. We would encourage people to continue the conversation with us, to share stories of their experiences in and with public service. We know there are stories of struggle and challenge, especially when it comes to social justice and equity, yet we know there are also bright spots. As we write this, the January 6 Committee is meeting to investigate the riots at the U.S. Capitol in 2021. We see public servants coming forward to tell their tales, to fight for American democracy. There are countless examples of this same bravery around the world, and we do everyone service by shining a bright light on public servants doing the right thing each and every day. We feel incredibly fortunate to see these current and future public servants in our classroom and remain inspired by them.

We hope you feel that inspiration reading these stories and contribute to the dialogue on the power of public service.

References

Barge, J. K. (2003). Hope, communication, and community building. *Southern Communication Journal*, 69(1), 63–81. https://doi.org/10.1080/10417940309373279

Brenton, S., & Bouckaert, G. (2021). Managing public museums appropriately and consequentially: The distinctiveness and diversity of leading organizations. *Public Administration Review, 81*(4), 715–727. https://doi.org/10.1111/puar.13323

Guy, M. E., Mastracci, S. H., & Yang, S-B., eds. (2019). *The Palgrave Handbook of Global Perspectives on Emotional Labor in Public Service*. Palgrave Macmillian.

Guy, M. E., Newman, M. A, & Mastracci, S. H. (2008). *Emotional Labor: Putting the Service Back in Public Service*. M. E. Sharpe.

Gray, C. (2011). Museums, galleries, politics, and management. *Public Policy and Administration*, 26(1), 45–61. https://doi.org/10.1177/0952076710365436

Humphrey, N. M. (2021). Emotional labor and professionalism: Finding balance at the local level. *State and Local Government Review, 53*(3), 260–270. https://doi.org/10.1177/0160323X211048847

Jackson, M. (1998). Arts and culture indicators in community building: Project update. *The Journal of Arts Management, Law, and Society, 28*(3), 201–205. https://doi.org/10.1080/10632929809599554

Mastracci, S., & Adams, I. (2019). Is emotional labor easier in collectivist or individualist cultures? An East–West comparison. *Public Personnel Management, 48*(3), 325–344. https://doi.org/10.1177/009102601881456

McDonough, P. (2006). Habitus and the practice of public service. *Work, Employment and Society, 20*(4), 629–647. https://doi.org/10.1177/0950017006069805

Prottas, J. M. (1978). The power of the street-level bureaucrat in public service bureaucracies. *Urban Affairs Quarterly, 13*(3), 285–312. https://doi.org/10.1177/107808747801300302

Contributor Biographies

Sameen A. Mohsin Ali, PhD, is a lecturer in international development at the University of Birmingham. She was previously an assistant professor of political science at the Lahore University of Management Sciences.

Sarah Berry works for Capacity Interactive, a digital marketing consulting firm for the arts and cultural sector. She received a Master's in Public Administration and a Graduate Certificate in Arts and Cultural Management at the College of Charleston in 2021.

Amanda D. Clark, PhD, is an assistant teaching professor with the Department of Public Policy and Administration in the Steven J. Green School of International and Public Affairs at Florida International University. Prior to her work in higher education, Dr. Clark worked in the international trade industry as a licensed customs broker. She also recently served at the Palm Beach County Supervisor of Elections Office in 2020, where she ran early voting. Dr. Clark's research focuses on social movements, election administration, and the U.S. policy process. Her recent work has focused on social equity in local public administration, including examining how austerity policies impacted U.S. COVID-19 policy. She is also researching the impact of the 2020 election on local election officials, the vast majority of whom are women. Dr. Clark and her co-authors will examine how the perception of administrative burden and emotional labor among election workers has changed because of the implicit and explicit violence of the 2020 campaign.

Adam Croft is a PhD candidate at the University of Colorado at Denver's School of Public Affairs. He studies the human elements of public service delivery with a focus on emotional labor, upward management, and social equity. He serves as the editorial assistant for the *Journal of Social Equity and Public Administration*.

Stephanie Dolamore, D.P.A., is an Assistant Professor of Public Administration at Gallaudet University and the Director of Policy Initiatives for the Maryland Developmental Disability Council. She teaches using American Sign Language and English in the bilingual Master of Public Administration program for D/deaf, hard of hearing, and hearing students. Her research explores the intersection of social equity, disability justice, and organizational culture in the public sector. Pronouns: she/her.

Lauren Hamilton Edwards, PhD, is an associate professor at the University of Maryland, Baltimore County. Her work is rooted in pursuit of helping government and nonprofit organizations work better; meaning more efficient, more effective, and, more equitable for public employees and the citizens we serve. Her current research focuses on the various strategies employed by government to reach their goals, make workplaces more inclusive, and manage resources.

Michael Fouassier, DPA, is Senior Director of Property and Tax Map Operations at the New York City Department of Finance. Michael has been working in the field of municipal tax policy and administration since 2006. At the beginning of his career, while attending graduate school, Michael worked as a market analyst at the New York State Office of Real Property Tax Services in Albany, NY. Coordinating with villages, towns, and counties, he conducted sales ratio analyses to set residential assessment ratios and equalization rates. In 2011 Michael accepted a position at the NYC Department of Finance and has since worked in several supervisory and managerial roles. Most recently Michael has been serving in operations and is responsible for many of the core functions of the property valuation and mapping division. Outside of his professional duties at the Department of Finance, Michael recently earned his doctorate from West Chester University and currently serves as an adjunct lecturer at the John Jay College of Criminal Justice in New York City. The focus of his research is tax policy and administration, equity, and public-sector transparency to improve the understanding stakeholders have of property taxation in New York.

Alexander C. Henderson, PhD, is an associate professor in the Department of Public and Nonprofit Administration at Marist College. His current research focuses on frontline policy implementation in public and nonprofit organizations, rules and discretionary decision-making, personnel management, and collaboration and interorganizational relationships. He is a research fellow of the Center for Organization Research and Design (CORD) at Arizona State University; an academic fellow of the Local Government Workplace Initiative (LGWI) at the University of North Carolina at Chapel Hill; and previously served as a chief administrative officer, operational officer, director, and volunteer with several nonprofit organizations in the Philadelphia area.

Maja Husar Holmes, PhD, is an associate professor with the Department of Public Administration at West Virginia University. Her research examines emerging opportunities for cultivating inclusion and diversity through leadership and governance in the public sector and higher education context.

JoyAnna Hopper, PhD, is an assistant professor at the University of Scranton, where she teaches courses in American politics and public policy. Her research focuses on environmental agencies in the states and how organizational factors affect enforcement decisions.

Gabriela Lotta, PhD, is a Professor of Public Administration at Fundação Getulio Vargas (FGV). She was a visiting professor at Oxford in 2021, at Universidad del Chile (2022), at PUC Peru (2021) and at Aalborg in 2019. At FGV, she coordinates the Bureaucracy Studies Center (NEB). She is a professor at the National School of Public Administration, ENAP, a researcher at the Center for Metropolitan Studies (CEM), and a researcher in Brazil.Lab from Princeton University. She works mainly in the areas of bureaucracy and policy implementation. Lotta received her B.Sc. in public administration and Ph.D. in Political Science at the University of São Paulo. She is currently developing research about street-level bureaucrats and inequalities and about bureaucratic resistance when facing democratic backsliding. In 2021 was nominated as one of the 100 most influential academics in the world in the governmental area by the Apolitical.

Moiz Abdul Majid is a graduate from the Lahore University of Management Sciences in Lahore, Pakistan.

Aroon P. Manoharan, PhD, is associate professor in the Department of Public Service and Healthcare Administration, Suffolk University, and executive director of the National Center for Public Performance (NCPP) at the Sawyer Business School. The primary focus of his research and teaching is to determine strategies that improve the performance of public and nonprofit organizations. His research interests include e-government, performance management, strategic planning, public communication, administrative capacity, comparative public administration, and pedagogy. His recent books include *E-Government and Information Technology Management: Concepts and Best Practices* and *E-Government and Websites: A Public Solutions Handbook*. He served as the editor of the *Occasional Paper Series* of the ASPA Section on International and Comparative Administration (SICA). He received his PhD from the School of Public Affairs and Administration (SPAA) at Rutgers University-Newark, MPA from Kansas State University, and BE from PSG College of Technology, India.

Sean McCandless, PhD, is an assistant professor and the director of the doctorate in public administration program at the University of Illinois Springfield. His research centers on how accountability for social equity is achieved in public service institutions. His research appears in several journals and edited books. With Mary E. Guy, he is co-editor of the book *Achieving Social Equity: From Problems to Solutions* (Melvin & Leigh). With Meghna Sabharwal and Shilpa Viswanath, he is co-editor of the forthcoming *Handbook of Diversity, Equity, and Inclusion in Public Administration* (Elgar Publishing). With Staci Zavattaro, Brandi Blessett, and Esteban Santis, he is co-editor of Routledge's new social equity book series. Sean is an avowed aviation nerd.

Judith Millesen, PhD, is a professor and MPA director at the College of Charleston. Her research makes a link between theory and practice and is focused on nonprofit administration and capacity building with special interests in board governance and community philanthropy.

Juliana Rocha Miranda is a researcher at the Bureaucracy Studies Center (NEB) and junior researcher at the Center for Metropolitan Studies (CEM). Juliana has a master's degree in public administration and government from Fundação Getulio Vargas (FGV, Brazil) and a BSc in law school from the University of São Paulo (USP).

Bianca Ortiz-Wythe is a PhD candidate in the Public Policy doctoral program at the University of Massachusetts Boston. Her primary research interests focus on immigration and deportation policy, gender and migration, mixed-status families, and economic inequality. Currently, she is writing her dissertation which examines the impact of Alternative to Detention programs on asylum seekers from Guatemala.

Kyle R. Overly, DPA, MS, CEM, is an accomplished emergency management practitioner and educator. He has held many roles throughout his career including serving as the director of Disaster Risk Reduction with the Maryland Department of Emergency Management. In addition, he has traveled internationally, providing emergency management services and speaking. With more than 10 years of experience, he has responded to major disasters including Hurricane Irene, Hurricane Sandy, the Baltimore City civil unrest, Ellicott City flash flooding (2016 and 2018), and the COVID-19 global pandemic. He is also an educator with more than 10 years of teaching experience, primarily at the University of Maryland Global Campus. He holds a doctor of public administration degree from West Chester University and a master of science degree in fire and emergency management administration from Oklahoma State University. He is a graduate of the National Emergency Management Executive Academy and the Executive Leaders Program at the Center for Homeland Defense & Security–Naval Postgraduate School. Finally, he is a certified emergency manager.

Dutch Reutter is the director of communications at the Charleston Library Society in Charleston, South Carolina. He has firsthand experience working with nonprofits within the arts and cultural sectors.

Nandhini Rangarajan, PhD, is associate professor of political science at Texas State University. Her research interests are in public management, human resources, and public affairs education. Her articles have appeared in prominent journals such as the *Review of Public Personnel Administration*, *Public Productivity and Management Review*, *Quality and Quantity*, and the *Journal of Public Affairs Education*. Her co-authored book, *A Playbook for Research Methods: Integrating Conceptual Frameworks* *and Project Management*, provides useful tools for graduate students to manage the research process.

Alicia Schatteman, PhD, is the current director of the Center for Non-profit and NGO Studies and an associate professor of nonprofit management in the Department of Public Administration at Northern Illinois University. She received her PhD in public administration from Rutgers University-Newark and a master's degree in communications management from Syracuse University. She consults and conducts research in nonprofit strategic planning, financial management, and performance measurement. Before completing her PhD, she worked for 10 years in the public and nonprofit sectors, including 4 years as an executive director.

Jessica E. Sowa, PhD, is a professor in the Joseph R. Biden, Jr. School of Public Policy & Administration at the University of Delaware. Her research focuses on public and nonprofit management, with an emphasis on the management of human resources (HRM) in public and nonprofit organizations, organizational effectiveness, and collaboration. Current projects include a textbook on public and nonprofit human resource management, research on public leadership, executive succession in nonprofit organizations, volunteer management in fire departments, and HRM in local government. She serves on the editorial board of a number of journals in public administration and public human resource management. She is the editor-in-chief of the *Review of Public Personnel Administration and co-editor-in-chief of Perspectives on Public Management and Governance*.

Kelly A. Stevens, PhD, is an assistant professor in the School of Public Administration at the University of Central Florida and a member of the Resilient, Intelligent, and Sustainable Energy Systems (RISES) Center. Her research focuses on energy and environmental policy, air quality, and science and technology policy. She has a master's degree in meteorology and public administration from Florida State University, and a PhD in public administration from the Maxwell School at Syracuse University.

Maren Trochmann, PhD, (she/her) is a Supervisory Housing Program Specialist with the federal government. She has previously taught courses on ethics and human resources management in MPA Programs. Her research interests include social equity, public personnel administration, and the nexus between public administration theory and practice.

Geoffrey Whitebread, PhD, is an assistant professor in the School of Civic Leadership, Business, and Social Change at Gallaudet University. He teaches in American Sign Language and English for the bilingual master of public administration program for D/deaf, hard of hearing, and hearing students. His research uses a variety of methodological tools to advance the understanding of social equity in the public sector as well as the intersectionality framework.

Staci M. Zavattaro, PhD, (she/her) is professor of public administration at the University of Central Florida. She serves as editor-in-chief of *Administrative Theory & Praxis*. Her latest research focuses on death management in the public sector.

Index

www.ingramcontent.com/pod-product-compliance
Lightning Source LLC
Chambersburg PA
CBHW031409270326
41929CB00010BA/1387